WALKING ON WATER

Andy Martin lectures in French at Cambridge University and has written on sport and travel for *The Times* and the *Independent on Sunday*. He is the author of two works of literary criticism, *The Knowledge of Ignorance* and *The Mask of the Prophet: the Extraordinary Fictions of Jules Verne*.

WALKING ON WATER

Andy Martin

Photographs by John Callahan

Minerva

A Minerva Paperback
WALKING ON WATER

First published in Great Britain 1991
by John Murray (Publishers) Ltd
This Minerva edition published 1992
by Mandarin Paperbacks
Michelin House, 81 Fulham Road, London SW3 6RB

Minerva is an imprint of the Octopus Publishing Group,
a division of Reed International Books Ltd

Copyright © Andy Martin 1991
The author has asserted his moral rights

All photographs except No. 14
copyright © John Callahan 1991

A CIP catalogue record for this title
is available from the British Library
ISBN 0 7493 9914 7

Printed and bound in Great Britain
by Cox and Wyman Ltd, Reading, Berks

For Heather, my shaper

Acknowledgements

I AM grateful to *The Times* for permission to quote the article on pp.115–16, to McIntosh and Otis Inc. for permission to quote from Duke Kahanamoku's *World of Surfing*, to Dolle Latronic for material from *The Boyfriends* (unpublished *mss.*), to Michael Willis for *Manifesto of the Surfing Masses*, and to Betty Depolito for her letter describing the Quiksilver in Memory of Eddie Aikau. This book is dependent on information and conversation issuing from a large number of generous sources, including the following: Terry Ahue, Bernie Baker, Steve Barilotti, Debbie Beecham and Louis, Sidney E. Berger, Carlos Blackburn, Peter Bothwell, Ken Bradshaw, John Callahan, Aaron Chang, Peter Colbert, Richie Collins, Ace Cool, Mark Cunningham, Ted Deerhurst, Darrick Doerner, Mark Foo, Johnny Boy Gomes, Ricky Grigg, Hailama, Paul Holmes, Al Hunt, Dave and Shelaine Jerrome and their friend Cathy, James Jones, Don and Lisa King, Barton Lynch, Roger Mansfield, Dan Merkel, Martin Potter, Randy Rarick, Paul Sargeant, Betinna Schneider, Jack Shipley, Greg Taylor of Quiksilver, Bodo and Liese Van der Leeden, Carwyn Williams, Milton Willis, and Yvon. I am also indebted to *Surfing*, *Surfer*, *Groundswell*, and the staff of the Bishop Museum and library. Thanks are due to Tom Clarke, Sports Editor of *The Times*, Simon O'Hagan, Sports Editor of *The Independent on Sunday*, Alex Hamilton, Travel Editor of *The Guardian*, and Michèle Young of André Deutsch for encouraging me to go to the North Shore, and to Kay Ward of HM & Gannaway and Continental Airlines for getting me there. Lindy Boyes in Honolulu and Lyn Pearce in London, both of the Hawaiian Visitors Bureau, pointed me in the right direction. Jeanne Park and the Turtle Bay Hilton gave me the best hotel room I've ever stayed in. D'Amicos made me some great pizzas.

Carol Hogan of Ocean Promotion granted my wish for Christmas pudding.

Finally, Sara Menguc at Murray Pollinger and Caroline Knox at John Murray have been indispensable in transforming typescript into book.

In the beginning, God created the heaven and the earth. And the earth was without form, and void; and darkness was upon the face of the deep. And the Spirit of God moved upon the face of the waters.

The Book of Genesis

Hence in a season of calm weather
Though inland far we be,
Our souls have sight of that immortal sea
Which brought us hither,
Can in a moment travel thither,
And see the children sport upon the shore,
And hear the mighty waters rolling evermore.

Wordsworth, 'Intimations of Immortality'

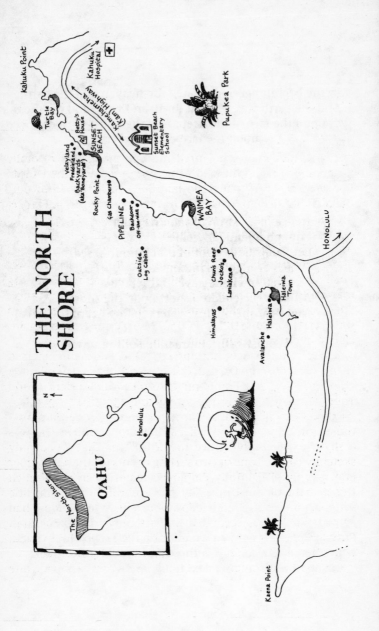

1

IT WAS Callahan who lured me out there. 'It's a totally happening place', he said. 'The biggest party in the world.' For years my personal credo had been 'surf Hawaii or die'. Callahan mulled this over after he had seen me surf in France: 'In your case, it will probably be surf Hawaii *and* die.'

I first met Callahan in Lacanau, just west of Bordeaux. I was on a surfing honeymoon, hugging the Atlantic coast of France from Brittany to Biarritz, looking for the perfect wave. I had a map. I found it while leafing through a French surfing magazine. The map pinpointed *'208 spots pour surfer'* in France, Spain and Portugal and awarded an accolade of three stars to some forty or so 'SUPERSPOTS'. My planned itinerary included every single superspot on the map.

It was pure chance that our arrival in Lacanau coincided with the start of the Quiksilver Lacanau Pro, one of the three grand prix events in France on the professional surfers' World Tour. I hurried to the press tent and identified myself as 'Surfing Correspondent to *The Times*' and my long-time Australian girlfriend, now my wife, as the photographer. This was a slight exaggeration, since the truth was that I had only sketchily covered one or two surfing events for the newspaper and was more gainfully employed lecturing in the French Department of the University of Cambridge. Still, the title sounded impressive and fellow journalists in London had agreed that it was second in impact only to *'Playboy* Staff Photographer'. It worked wonders on the French PR woman, who offered us a room in a three-star hotel for the week.

Callahan was standing next to me. He was wearing a white

baseball cap back to front, a tee-shirt emblazoned with the name of the magazine he worked for, *Surfing* (which he pronounced *SurfING*, to distinguish it from its rival, *SurfER*), and blue striped baggy shorts. He sounded a touch sceptical; his lazy voice always sounded sceptical. 'So *The Times* is interested in surfing now, huh?'

'Has been for a while', I said firmly. 'I suppose you missed my report on the British championships in Thurso?'

'Are you the dude who wrote that piece on Thurso for *SurfING*? I never even knew Scotland had waves.'

'Best tubes in Britain – maybe even Europe.'

'Did you catch any?'

'You should have been there.' The only thing I had caught in Thurso was the worst cold of my life.

Callahan was a photographer and a writer on the side. But like all surfing journalists, he was first and foremost a surfer. He was twenty-seven years old, the son of an American Air Force pilot who had been posted to Pearl Harbor and never left. He had graduated in fine arts at UCLA, but was eventually drawn back to Hawaii.

I ran into him a lot in the following days. Lacanau is a quiet little town that for a week in August goes berserk during the Quiksilver Lacanau Pro. Pilgrims and groupies flocked in from every corner of the globe. With marquees mushrooming, flags fluttering from a hundred flagpoles, and surfers brandishing boards like lances, it had the flavour of some medieval jousting tournament.

Callahan didn't think much of the waves in Lacanau. 'You call this surf?' he jeered. 'In Hawaii you get bigger waves than this in your bath.' Hawaii boasted the biggest waves on the planet. This made Hawaiians disdainful of European surf – disdainful of Europe. They were like conquerors of Everest being asked to scale Primrose Hill.

Callahan was staying with another Hawaiian photographer, Don King. I already knew Don King. I had a calendar of his surfing photographs on my wall back in Cambridge. He was the consummate 'waterman' and master of the water shot, taking close-up portraits of homicidal waves. The first water shot I ever saw I thought must have been published posthumously. The board was obviously about to slice the photographer's head clean off and a billion tons of water were poised to obliterate the remains. It had been taken by Don King. When I was introduced to him, it felt like meeting a ghost or an angel. Callahan spoke reverently of his ability to get ten cover shots off a twelve-frame roll. He was loose-limbed and buoyant and did everything in slow motion, moving on land as he moved through water, carried along by invisible currents. He was never excited or agitated or wasteful of energy; he remained perpetually calm. He wore an Hawaiian 'reverse-shirt', designed to be worn inside out, presenting only muted tones to the world. Understatement was his characteristic rhetorical mode.

The high point of the Quiksilver contest came when I nearly won the Women's Event. I knew the form: I paddled out well up the beach from the competition zone. Having been worked over by one or two foaming six-footers I heard a booming announcement over the PA – *Will the surfer in the blue wetsuit on the white board get out of the water because he is interfering with the competitors*. I looked up to see four strapping women steaming towards me: I was the surfer in the blue wetsuit; that white board was mine. A furtive rip had swept me into the collective gaze of a hundred thousand spectators. A score of yard-long telephoto lenses swivelled to track my every move.

Resisting the temptation to pull off some eye-catching radical manoeuvres and get a centrefold in *Surfing*, I cruised in on my belly only to be turned upside down by a punchy six-inch wave two feet from the beach. I got the biggest round of applause of the day. A kid with glasses asked for my autograph.

I stripped off my wetsuit and raced back to the press tent like a murderer in search of an alibi. 'Did I miss anything?' I asked nonchalantly. 'Biggest laugh of the day', said Callahan. 'Some crazy kook got in among the women.'

'Bloody tourist!' I said, joining in the abuse.

That night we had dinner together. 'Was that you out there

this afternoon, making a fool of yourself?' he asked. I fumbled with a denial and he said, nodding, 'Funniest thing I ever saw.' He paused. 'How much will you give me for the shots? They're worth $500 to the magazine.'

We haggled and eventually settled for the price of dinner and a lift down the coast. That was how I came to leave town with an Hawaiian photographer on board.

Having put their heads into the mouths of the man-eating waves of Waimea Bay, Hawaiians have an air of transcendent wisdom and tranquillity. I was anxious about getting my board stolen, an old, heavy, beaten-up sort of board, a barge with a fin on it. 'Don't worry,' drawled Callahan, 'nobody's going to steal *that* board.' A week later it disappeared in Biarritz.

I should have had no illusions about Callahan's infallibility. His girlfriend back home was apprehensive about him coming to France: 'Isn't that where all the topless women are?' He wrote her a postcard that said 'Don't worry, there's no nudity here', meanwhile sketching out an article that owed much to Rousseau's theory of the noble savage and taking plenty of shots of women in the state of nature.

Callahan and I surfed together in Hossegor. I loaned him my board. He picked off a string of four-footers, a model of casual equilibrium. He surfed as he spoke, in long, languid lines, with a hint of mockery. I took over and got mowed down by columns of churning whitewater. When I came in he was snoozing in the late afternoon sun.

'What happened to you, Andy? I thought I saw you doing some great things out there and then I realized it was some other guy.'

All three of us shared a room in Hossegor. Heather thought this was an odd way of spending a honeymoon, so she was glad when at last we drove off on our own again. I was sorry to say goodbye to Callahan, though: I felt some of his Hawaiian grace might rub off on me if I stuck around him long enough. But all he left behind was a pair of white underpants, a navy blue skateboarding vest, and some old socks in the back of the car.

The Arena Surfmasters in Biarritz was won by the same man who had won the Quiksilver Lacanau Pro. His name was Martin Potter, he was now streets ahead of his closest rivals in the race for surfing's world championship, he was rumoured to have earned over a million dollars in prizes and endorsements since the start of the season, and, incredibly, he was British. He was also my passport to Hawaii.

2

*M*ARTIN POTTER'S nationality was a matter of some controversy on the circuit. He was English, he was South African, he was Australian; he was all of those; he was none of them. I didn't care that other British surfers complained bitterly that he never surfed in Britain. I wouldn't have cared if he surfed the canals of Mars so long as he carried a British passport. That was all I needed to clinch the deal that would get me to Hawaii.

Most world-beating wave-riders come from California, Australia, Hawaii. Martin Potter's career began inauspiciously on the bleak shores of Blyth, Northumberland, twenty-four years ago. His family emigrated to South Africa before he had done more than dip his toe in the North Sea. He first learned to surf in Durban's Bay of Plenty. Then one day, when he was only twelve years old, some strange men carrying scaffolding and flagpoles showed up on his home beach. They asked him if he wanted to compete in the junior division. He didn't have anything better to do so he caught a few waves and wound up surfing everyone else off the beach. Wooed by sponsors and enticed by the prospect of stardom, he turned pro at fifteen, bought his mother a house in Newquay, packed his wetsuit and wax, and set out on his travels.

He was a prodigy. With two second places in his rookie year, Pottz (as he became known to the surfing *cognoscenti*)

5

was soon the youngest ever to win a professional contest. He was rated the hottest free-style surfer on the Tour, but continued to yo-yo up and down the seeded Top 16. In 1989 Australian coach Derek Hynd decreed that Martin Potter would never win the world championship. As if on cue, Pottz took off on an unparalleled winning streak that propelled him into the Corona Triple Crown in Hawaii over two thousand points ahead of the competition.

That was what I told Simon O'Hagan, then deputy sports editor at *The Times*. His brother was a surfer and he had a soft spot for surfing. He asked for a big preview of the Triple Crown and reports on each of the three contests: the Hard Rock Café World Cup, the Marui Pipeline Masters, and the Billabong Pro. All I had to do was get out there and find someone else to foot the bill.

I talked the travel editor at *The Times* into accepting a piece on the wild side of Hawaii. 'On the North Shore,' I told her, 'you know when the surf's up because the pictures fall off the walls.' Then I phoned Continental Airlines. They offered me a free ticket in exchange for a mention in the travel article and anything else I wrote. It turned out they couldn't actually get me back again – they were booked solid in January – so I might be marooned there forever. It was a risk I was prepared to take.

It was late November. The Hard Rock Café World Cup opened on 1 December. I was ready to leave.

But was I? I was going to Hawaii on the pretext of reporting on the Triple Crown. But my secret motive was the compulsion to pit myself against one of the most powerful forces in nature – everything else was just marmalade.

The trouble was, I was one of nature's least powerful forces: in the Charles Atlas ad, I would have had sand kicked in my eye. I was a 'before' man wandering prematurely onto the 'after' beach. I launched myself on a crash fitness course. Over the next week or so, in between lectures, I tortured my muscles with weights at the university gym, spluttered several times round Midsummer Common, and flailed up and down the municipal baths. My mind urged me to devote myself to the pure exertion of the body; but my body was telling me I'd better stick to the life of the mind. I couldn't even manage a couple of lengths of the pool without getting out of breath. Hawaii would be terminal: I might just as well jump out of the plane without a parachute.

Or so I thought in my more pessimistic moments. And others seemed on the whole to agree. I wondered whether I would be able to cope with twenty-footers. 'Twenty-footers?' queried Heather. 'I've seen you get into trouble on two-footers. Promise me you won't do anything crazy.' I promised but I knew our ideas of what counted as crazy were poles apart.

Albert, my barber, who usually told me tales of his exploits as a Desert Rat in the Second World War, didn't fancy my chances much either. The last time I'd come back from a trip he rattled me with his casual judgement, 'The bloom's gone. And once that bloom is gone, you'll never get it back.' I often asked him afterwards if there was any sign of the bloom returning, but the most he would concede was that 'it was definitely looking better'.

Now he had a new and still more apocalyptic warning. 'Watch out for the salt,' he muttered darkly while trimming my neck, 'it'll ruin your hair.' He remembered a bloke who had gone to the South of France. 'Lovely head of hair he had, like a gorilla he was. Went right down his back – you didn't know where to stop cutting. And when he came back, well – I won't say he didn't need a comb no more, but it was a pretty thin covering. That salt water will do it for you every time.'

Valeria, an Italian friend, suspecting that surfing was a cover for sex, did a fair imitation of a hula girl in a grass skirt and waggled her finger sternly at me as if summoning up some incurable venereal nemesis.

One way or another I was doomed: if the waves didn't get me, the women would. The best I could hope for was to come back bald.

Shortly before I was due to leave, a letter arrived from Callahan putting my mind at rest over at least one of these alternative calamities. He said there had already been one twenty-five-foot plus swell in November and everyone was talking about this being a *big* year. He concluded with yet another warning: 'Bring a date with you. There are no girls here, none, they're all taken.'

My old friend from King's College, Diego Gambetta, was going to Leningrad for Christmas and was unsympathetic to what he saw as a merely adolescent urge.

'You should be heading East, not West,' he said at High Table, 'seeing the dying days of communism, not decadent late capitalism.'

'Surfing transcends mere politics', I said.

'Everything is politics.'

'Surfing is everything.'

He carefully weighed up this view and then issued his considered verdict. 'Prick.'

3

WHEN CAPTAIN James Cook discovered the Sandwich Islands in 1778 on the third and last of his voyages of discovery, he was mistaken for a god. As it happened, his arrival in Hawaii coincided with the culmination of the three-month festival of dancing and sports known as the *Makahiki*. It was January, the climax of the season of rough seas and high surf, when warfare was forbidden and men and women left their work in the fields to swim and play in the ocean. Lono was one of the three great rulers of the Hawaiian pantheon, the god of peace and light, but he was also the patron saint of the *Makahiki*. His alias meant 'dwelling in the water' and his symbol was a staff bearing a banner of *tapa* resembling the square sail of a ship. It was prophesied that he would come again, bearing gifts. The high priests, first on Kauai, then on the Big Island, assumed Cook was Lono. The god of surfing, aboard his great canoe, had returned.

This might account for the extreme friendliness of the Hawaiians, who swam and paddled out to greet him, and in particular of the women, who offered themselves to the sailors under the impression that they would be copulating with deities. There was an Hawaiian tradition that the queen of Kauai had given one of her daughters to Lono. Captain Cook tried in vain to stop his men associating with the promiscuous natives, in order to prevent the spread of 'the Venereal'. Indifferent to his orders, the gonococci and spirochaetes swarmed ashore, the vanguard in the migration of pathogenic micro-organisms.

I knew Cook came from Yorkshire originally, but someone had told me that his family were now based or buried in Cambridge. So I couldn't help thinking of myself as a latter-day Cook, setting out to explore the Pacific. On the bright December morning I left Cambridge, Christ's Pieces looked as if it had just been taken out of the freezer: the trees were crusted with frost and the brittle grass crunched underfoot. Gatwick was embalmed in fog. Stranded in the departure lounge, I overheard fragments of conversation:

'My entire weekend has been ruined, of course.'

'With a few small revisions, you should get it published without too much difficulty.'

'I'm not much of a Lacanian myself.'

I had been to Hawaii once before. But that was in summer. I was on a globetrotting lecture tour of Australia, the United States and Central America. Bali was my first stop and my downfall. Looking down from the temple of Pura Luhur at Ulu Watu on the southern tip of the island, wearing a sarong, with a frangipani flower behind my ear, I beheld surfing for the first time. I was dazzled, blinded, transfixed. As if I'd been staring for too long at the sun, the image would be forever branded on my retina. Henceforth, wherever I looked all I saw was surf. The American writer Jack London, when he discovered surfing in Hawaii in 1907, felt he had found something worth worshipping. The prose in which he records his experience is exultant:

And suddenly, out there where a big smoker lifts skywards, rising like a sea-god from out of the welter of spume and churning white, on the giddy, toppling, overhanging and downfalling, precarious crest appears the dark head of a man. Swiftly he rises through the rushing white. His black shoulders, his chest, his loins, his limbs – all is abruptly projected on one's vision. Where but the moment before was only the wide desolation and the invincible roar, is now a man, erect, full-statured, not struggling frantically in that wild movement, not buried and crushed and buffeted by those mighty monsters, but standing above them all, calm and superb, poised on the giddy summit, his feet buried in the churning foam, the salt smoke rising to his knees, and all the rest of him in the free air and flashing sunlight, and he is flying through the air, flying forward, flying fast as the surge on which he stands.

London sought to master this mystic art on the shores of Waikiki. His inconclusive initiations in *The Cruise of the Snark* are rounded off with the ringing declaration: 'Upon one thing I am resolved: the *Snark* shall not sail from Honolulu until I, too, wing my heels with the swiftness of the sea, and become a sunburned, skin-peeling Mercury.' I read on hungrily, but there was no further talk of surfing. I never found out whether he succeeded in realizing his ambition.

I was just as determined as Jack London. The quest that had begun in Bali continued in Australia. I still gave a few distracted lectures on Napoleon and Jules Verne, but all I could think about was waves, big waves, crashing endlessly on the shore.

I changed my Sydney to New York flight to incorporate a stopover. I was due to give a paper at Columbia University, which left me only twenty-four hours to surf Hawaii. I was no fool: I had read the magazines in Australia. I knew that Hawaii was a constellation of cooled magma, ejected through a crack in the earth's mantle opened up by the slow and inexorable grinding of the great Pacific plate. I knew that, unprotected by a continental shelf, the North Shore on the island of Oahu was visited by the most glorious and terrible waves in the world. What I didn't know was that it wasn't until winter that the Pacific storm track whips up a succession of huge swells that sweep over 1,500 miles of open ocean before smashing into the jagged lava and limestone of the coast and throwing up the surfer's equivalent of Everest and K-2. In summer the North Shore was a paddling pool for toddlers.

Captain Cook perpetually complained of the 'great surfs' off the Hawaiian shores that prevented him finding safe harbour. 'I have nowhere within the Tropics met with so high a sea as we have had since we have been about these islands', he wrote; 'it has never been once down, though it frequently shifts three or four points, or more.'

From several thousand feet up over Oahu, I thought I could make out great surfs besieging the diamond-shaped island on all sides. No sooner had I landed in Honolulu than I bought a map, rented a car, and headed north on the H-2 Highway. I toured the legendary sites of Waimea Bay, Pipeline, and Sunset Beach, names which had as much resonance in my mind as those of Troy, Hastings, and Waterloo for a student of warfare. At every major battlefield on the northern front I stopped, got out, and scoured the ocean. There was golden sand, there were palm trees, fronds wafting in the sultry breeze; but of waves there was not a sign.

At one corner of Sunset Beach I tracked down a small, narrow peak and paddled out on a second-hand board I'd picked up in Sydney. The wave had its work cut out to reach three feet and even so I was scared out of my wits. Knowing what I knew, I was convinced some all-devouring thirty-footer would be on my heels the minute I turned my back. I scanned the horizon anxiously, ready to hightail it for the beach if I so much as spotted a shadow out there. I paddled back in looking over my shoulder.

Still quaking with imaginary terror, I drove back into Honolulu to find that at Waikiki – the subject of scorn and derision among surfing magazines – clean four- to five-footers were breaking all along the shore. I bought myself an hour's tuition from a beachboy by the name of Mike.

He took me out on a board that must have been all of twelve feet long and two feet wide. It was like riding a small aircraft carrier. When a nursery wave perambulated by he would point me in the right direction and all I had to do as I was cradled towards the beach was clamber triumphantly to my feet, wobble and fall off. I had surfed Hawaii, I had even, in a sense, surfed Sunset Beach. But that day the North Shore wasn't really trying; it was just the second eleven, or maybe the third team. I knew I would have to go back.

US immigration officials are paid to be sceptical, but you get the feeling they'd be like that for nothing. 'What are you doing in the United States, sir?' asked one of them at Denver, all the while chewing gum and exercising his Zapata moustache.

'I'm covering some surfing contests in Hawaii for *The Times*.'

His eyes narrowed in disbelief. 'You're reporting on surfing for *The Times* of *London*?'

'That's right.'

'Go and see that man at the window.' He put a quizzical sign on my entry form.

'What are you doing in the US, sir?' I repeated my tale to the older man at the window, who with his small round glasses and deep lenses could easily see through my transparent masquerade. Even I found the story threadbare and ridiculous. Obviously, the game was up.

'Do you have any accreditation from your newspaper?' I showed him my card. It read:

Andy Martin
SURFING CORRESPONDENT TO *THE TIMES*

I'd had it made up as a joke.

It was clear that there was an irresolvable contradiction between 'surfing' and '*The Times*'. *The Times* was cool, Nordic, solid, black and white, prosperous, decorous, sober, middle-aged, authoritative; surfing was hot, exotic, wild, crazy, subversive, intoxicated, drugged-out-of-its-mind. It was pure oxymoron, a conjunction of opposites.

Inexplicably, they let me through.

I had twelve hours to kill in Denver. The Museum of History, amid its wagons, reconstructed battles with Indians, stuffed buffalo and mining machinery, was staging an exhibition of the history of skiing in the Rockies. Imported by immigrant Scandinavians, skiing was at first purely functional: it was just a faster way of getting from A to B in the snow. Skis were originally called Norwegian snowshoes. Prospectors used them to trek to mines and deliver supplies. John A. ('Snowshoe') Thomson carried the mail over the Sierra Nevada in midwinter. There were even military skiers: 'the 10th Mountain Division'.

People sometimes mix up surfing and skiing. Surfing is just skiing on water, skiing is surfing on snow, they think. But the difference is crucial. There are no military surfers (the American GIs who surfed in Vietnam were simply soldiers who happened to go surfing). Surfing is resolutely non-functional. It doesn't get you anywhere. It is futile. But still, beneath the brilliant winter sun the chilly snow-capped Rockies that surrounded Denver seemed to anticipate the foam-tipped mountains of the North Shore.

4

IT WAS a moonless night as I drove out of Honolulu, through the pineapple plantations and banana groves, past the observatory on top of the mountain, and along the Kamehameha Highway, the coast road. Again I couldn't see the waves. But I could hear them: a distant whisper that was almost drowned out by the air conditioning. The air conditioning was all that was audible in my room at the Y-shaped Turtle Bay Hilton, cunningly designed so that every room overlooks the frothing sea. Until, that is, I threw open the doors. It was like being deaf and then miraculously hearing for the first time. My ears were filled with an immense roaring and pounding and hammering and hissing as the might of the ocean unleashed its fury on this tiny volcanic rock of an island that had got in its way.

It was only in the morning that I could see the clean, well-cut corduroy lines stretching right across the Bay. The waves were overhead, perhaps six to seven feet, and there were two surfers already slashing across them. We are indebted for the earliest written description of surfing (as practised at Kealakekua Bay) to Lieutenant James King, who completed the journal of the Third Voyage after Cook was killed in Hawaii:

The surf, which breaks on the coast around the bay, extends to the distance of about 150 yards from the shore, within which space the surges of the sea, accumulating from the shallowness of the water, are dashed against the beach with prodigious violence. Whenever, from stormy weather or any extraordinary swell at sea, the impetuosity of the surf is increased to its utmost height, the islanders choose this time for their amusement.

Twenty or thirty of the natives, taking each a long narrow board, rounded at the ends, set out together from the shore. The first wave they plunge under, and suffering it to roll over them, rise again beyond it, and make the best of their way by swimming out to sea. The second wave is encountered in the same manner as the first; the great difficulty consisting in seizing the proper moment of diving underneath it, which, if missed, the person is caught by the surf and driven back again with great violence, and all his dexterity is then required to prevent himself being dashed against the rocks.

As soon as they have gained, by these repeated efforts, the smooth water beyond the surf, they lay themselves at length on their boards and prepare for their return. As the surf consists of a number of waves, of which every third is remarked to be always much larger than the others and to flow higher on the shore . . . their first object is to place themselves on the summit of the largest surge, by which they are driven along with amazing rapidity toward the shore. The boldness and address, with which I saw them perform these difficult and dangerous manoeuvres, was altogether astonishing, and is scarcely to be credited.

The first person I met at Sunset Beach was Randy Rarick, contest director of the Triple Crown, a tall, fair-haired Californian with a lop-sided smile who now lived permanently on the North Shore. 'This is a real mellow place,' he told me, 'I know you're going to have a great time here. Just give it a couple of days and you'll be slotted right into the groove.'

I gazed out over the sea. The early stages of the Hard Rock Café World Cup were already underway, and out on the peak, almost half a mile away, you could see tiny figures dancing on top of what looked like harmless five-footers. I was impatient to get wet. I saw Derek Hynd, coach of the Rip Curl team, taking notes. 'Looks like a piece of cake', I said. 'I think I'll go out.'

I had seen a video called *North Shore* in which a young rookie surfer from a wave pool in Arizona comes to Hawaii and, after a few initial hiccups and some words of wisdom from a grizzled veteran, triumphs in the Triple Crown. I envisaged a similar scenario for myself.

Hynd seized me by the arm and bellowed, 'ARE YOU KIDDING? We're talking real power out there. This is twice as heavy as anything in Europe, even when it's no bigger. You've got to build up to Sunset.'

I wandered over to the orange lifeguard tower. 'You should have been here yesterday', said Joe, a big-boned *hombre* with a sooty tan whose teeth flashed like a torch in a coal-hole. I'd heard this before. Wherever you went it always seemed as if you should have been there yesterday. 'It was like putting gladiators in the pit. It was kind of out-of-control, breaking all over the place – but just try to stop surfers going out in it.'

Sunset Beach is just a beach with a few palm trees and a lot of sand, but on the surfing map it outranks Paris and Rome. It is the most consistent of the North Shore breaks, hoovering up swells and spraying rollers all round its cluster of peaks. There are two main reefs, West Point and Kammies, fanning right-handers and lefts either side of a channel where the water flows back out again and surfers get an assisted paddle-out. It can be big and clean – up to around fifteen feet or so – and it can be messy. Joe and his friend Victor competed with each other to recollect the goriest, most gruesome fate that overweight tourists had met with at Sunset.

'So where could someone pretty mediocre get started around here?' I asked.

The question provoked a withering outburst. 'There's *no-where* for anyone mediocre to go out! It's dangerous *everywhere* on the North Shore!' The exclamation marks were deafening.

Maybe I was rushing. It could be Randy Rarick was right and I needed a couple of days to slot into the groove. I decided I had better get various practical matters straightened out before settling down to the serious business of surfing.

I ran into Callahan back at the press trailer. He was carrying a lens the size of a bazooka under his arm. He looked me up and down. I was wearing a threadbare cotton jacket and a pair of jeans. He took me on one side, as if to spare me embarrassment. 'On the North Shore,' he confided, 'you've got to learn to slob out. You should stop shaving and grow a raspy little beard.' He fixed his gaze on my clothes. 'You can't wear your suit to the beach.'

He zipped open his shoulder bag and hauled out a tangerine vest with a *Surfing* logo on it. 'Here, wear this', he said. 'It'll help us identify the body.'

5

I WENT into Honolulu to swap my rental car for another one from a company that had a special deal going with the Triple Crown organizers. The name of the new car was 'Sprint'. As I was driving back north up the H-1 it coughed, spluttered, and died. I coasted over to the hard shoulder, cursing. I was in a concrete wilderness, a no-man's land between city and country.

I gathered up my gear, locked up the car, and jammed out my thumb at the passing traffic. It was like rubbing a magic lamp. Almost instantly, a dazzling Californian blonde materialized. Her name was Chris. She was sympathetic to my plight, she told me, having broken down in the same spot herself some months before. 'It's a bad place to break down in all right. I'll drop you at the Yum Yum Tree. You can phone from there.'

She told me she'd been back to the mainland a couple of times, but couldn't take it. 'Hawaii is a sweeter, easier-going sort of place. It doesn't matter so much what kind of car you drive.'

'Just so long as it doesn't break down on you', I said.

The Yum Yum Tree in Mililani was a clean, well-upholstered café, a few miles up the road, where eager waitresses vied with each other to feed me large slices of macadamia cream pie. When I heard Bing Crosby crooning in Hawaiian to the twang of a ukulele I thought for a moment I must have died and gone to heaven. On reflection, it reminded me more exactly of Charles Fourier's nineteenth-century earthly utopia of the phalanstery, where all your desires are carefully monitored and if you ever get into trouble there are the 'Philanthropic Associations' – bands of erotic girl guides – to help out.

That evening, I had dinner with Jeanne Park – who had fixed me a free room at the Turtle Bay – in the plush, candle-lit restaurant of the hotel. She was an attractive divorcee in her late thirties with a dark river of hair rippling about her shoulders. She complained that there was a dearth of males in Hawaii and estimated the ratio of men to women at about one to five. Callahan had told me virtually the opposite, that there was one girl for every ten men on the North Shore.

'Are you sure?' I asked.

'Believe me, I've done some serious research on this', she said.

The wine waiter advised against a Californian Chardonnay — 'too emphatic' — and served us a subtle Sauvignon instead.

Jeanne told me all the big names came to the hotel: golfers, movie-stars, captains of industry.

'Any surfers?' I asked.

Jeanne didn't know.

'I wonder if I can help you, sir.' It was the wine waiter, who shimmered Jeeves-like at my elbow. 'I'm a surfer.' His long stringy form seemed to bow almost imperceptibly at the waist.

His name was Dave Jerrome. He turned out to be from Long Island, like Jeanne, and had once dated her younger sister. So he was an East Coast surfer in his origins — a tough and sometimes forgotten breed — who'd won a few competitions out there and done his fair share of winter surfing.

'I used to get the old ice-cream head', he said. 'I even got hypothermia a few times. Once you've been in an hour or so you don't notice the temperature any more. Then you get out and they have to take you to hospital.'

He'd been drawn to California and then, in the westward drift that affects all surfers, he'd come to the North Shore. And there he'd stayed. He didn't clock on at the Hilton till four in the afternoon so that left him plenty of time in the water.

I'd heard a rumour that about eighty per cent of the hotel staff were surfers. 'They all are', he said. 'The Turtle Bay Hilton is the best thing that ever happened to surfers on the North Shore. It keeps them alive and doesn't stop them surfing.'

I told him I was interested in doing some surfing myself while I was in Hawaii. He invited me to go out with him. Where did he think we should go? What about Sunset? No less a connoisseur of fine waves than of wines, he advised against.

'I would recommend Jocko's. A mellow break, I think you'll find, sir.'

6

'*I* DIDN'T expect to hear from you so soon', Dave said.

It was the morning after our conversation at the Turtle Bay. At 7 a.m. Randy Rarick had surveyed the surf, decided it wasn't up to scratch and called off the Hard Rock for the day. Sunset still looked pretty big to me.

I warned Dave I didn't have a lot of experience on the North Shore. 'I'm not ready for Pipeline yet.'

'No problem, Jocko's is a mellow wave. You won't have any trouble with that. Do you have a board?'

I didn't.

'That's okay. You can borrow one of mine. Meet me in the lot of Foodland in fifteen minutes.'

Foodland was the only supermarket for miles around, south of Sunset between Pipeline and Waimea Bay. It was reputed to be the most expensive store in the United States and was the social hub of the North Shore. Dave arrived and introduced me to his wife, Shelaine. I followed them a few miles down the road, beyond Waimea, heading towards Haleiwa. They pulled up outside a house right on the beach which was owned by a friend of theirs, Cathy. I changed in her bathroom. There were some signs pinned up on the walls: 'Let God be your Guide' and 'Jesus lives'.

I remembered that Jack London had been disabled by sunburn on his first day out at Waikiki, so I took my time slapping on the waterproof sunblock. I could tell Dave – who didn't have to bother with such elementary precautions – was getting impatient.

'Come on, Andy, let's get out there and shred up those waves.' He had that faraway look in his eye that surfers get when the surf is up and they're ready to move.

We left the two women in the house and carried our boards out onto the beach.

'Can't you feel that old adrenalin running faster through your veins?' he asked.

I looked out at the ocean. 'More a sort of fear', I said.

Dave laughed. He thought I was joking. 'That's Jocko's out there', he pointed. 'A nice little intermediate wave. That shouldn't give you too much trouble.'

About two hundred yards out beyond a rocky point a left-hander was breaking. It looked not much smaller than Sunset to me: all of six feet. I could see cascades of whitewater plummeting down in the distance.

'What foot are you?'

'Natural.'

'You'll have to surf this one backside then.'

I surfed with my left foot forwards. That meant on a left-hander – breaking from right to left as you faced the beach – I would always be looking over my left shoulder to see what the wave was doing. The thought passed through my mind that this might be pushing it a bit for my first outing.

Dave must have read my thoughts because he said: 'That's Chun's Reef over there', indicating another break on the right. 'That's a mellower wave. See how you get on with Jocko's first. That's pretty mellow too. We can always move over to Chun's later.'

I liked the sound of that mellower wave. But I was loath to dissent. 'I might stay out on the shoulder for a while, just to get the feel of things.'

'That's fine. No one ever learnt anything sitting on the beach.'

We waxed down the boards. Mine was 7 ft 6 in long but a little narrow in the tail: balance would be critical. Dave gave it an extra coating. 'You can never have too much wax.'

I followed Dave into the water. The water was always warm in Hawaii, but it was still a little colder than I remembered it. This time it was winter.

'Stay with me and you can't go wrong.'

I'd heard this somewhere before. Dave was not my first guru. When I announced in Perth that I wanted to learn to surf, people clustered round and shook my hand and clapped me on the shoulder as if I were taking out Australian citizenship. I was promptly apprenticed to a champion surfer. In retrospect I realize that this was like expecting a Grand Master to teach me the rudiments of chess. He had forgotten what it was like to be a beginner.

Peter Bothwell was not the blond-haired muscleman I had anticipated. He was a couple of inches shorter than me, dark-haired, quietly spoken, with a bushy moustache. He might have passed for a long-distance runner. The boards strapped to the top of a Toyota, we ransacked the coast for the perfect wave. At last Peter declared himself satisfied with Triggs. Triggs was a compact bay sandwiched between rocky points which littered the two ends of the beach with jagged chunks of stone. 'No worries', Peter reassured me. 'You just steer between them, see?'

He had brought along a spare wetsuit for me. It was a couple of sizes too small. It was so tight my arms and legs poked out at odd angles. 'No worries. You'll soon loosen up in the water. Just follow me,' said Peter, 'and you can't go wrong.'

'Keep with me,' said Dave, 'and I'll guide you through the channel.'

Some channels are smooth as silk: the rip takes you out as though you were on a conveyor belt and drops you off right behind the line-up. But there are others where heavy waves fight you all the way. This channel was one of the latter. I was stiff and unaccustomed to the board and I soon fell behind. Dave waited patiently for me to catch up.

'You can hang on to my leash if you like.'

I reached out an arm, then pulled it back in. 'I'm fine', I gasped.

'One more push and we're through.' I gave a mighty heave. I felt like I'd just spent twenty-four hours in a labour ward. 'Okay, you can relax now. We're out the back.'

Just then, the biggest wave I'd ever seen burst out of nowhere and lurched drooling towards us. 'Oh-oh,' laughed Dave, 'you're going to have to dive under that one.'

I hurled myself off the board and dug down, silently praying the wave didn't extend too deep. I felt it roll over the top of me and swam back up, keeping an eye open for its brother.

'Damn sneaker wave', said Dave.

The North Shore specialized in 'sneaker sets'. These were waves that were bigger than the run-of-the-mill waves on any given day and broke beyond the normal line-up. You had to be constantly on the alert if you didn't want to get cleaned up.

'Now look, you see that tall palm tree?' Dave pointed back to the beach. 'If you stay this side of it you can't go wrong. Once you get on the other side, though, you're right in the impact zone. So watch out.'

Dave glided away and disappeared into a wave. Just twenty yards distant, blue pyramids were rising up out of the calm ocean and folding over. A handful of surfers warily circled the drop. The waves were the size of skyscrapers, of cathedrals, of palaces. It was like watching a whole architecture being thrown up and pulled apart again, in a matter of seconds. The idea of trying to stand up on my board didn't even occur to me. It would have been like trying to surf Niagara.

I knew that the wave was only, as Jack London put it, 'a communicated agitation'. At school I had learned that water remains stationary while the shape of the wave moves through it like a ghost. As I watched unimaginable tons of water unloading themselves in front of me, I tried to convince myself that it was all an illusion and that there was nothing to fear from these spectral undulations. But the waves at Jocko's were the least stationary-looking bodies of water I had ever come across. I speculated wildly about what that agitation would do if it should communicate itself to me.

I was still in a trance when Dave came stroking back. 'Wow, what a wave that was', he chirruped.

'It looks kind of meaty to me', I said.

'Yeah, it's bigger than I thought. This is a full-on intermediate all right.' He looked at me with compassion. 'Maybe you should try Chun's Reef to begin with. That's definitely mellow. Do you want me to come with you?'

'No, you carry on here. I'll be all right.'

There was a rip coming out of Chun's towards Jocko's. After a twenty-minute marathon I made it to within ten or twenty yards of a group of surfers sitting meditatively on their boards. Suddenly they were flat on their stomachs sprinting for the horizon. I knew what that meant. Desperately I windmilled my arms through the water. A mountain loomed up ahead. I raced towards it to get the soft side of its breaking point. I glided up its endless face, crashed through its crest, and sailed down the far side, with the same sense of relief as a reprieved man. There was still a faint hope I might get out of here alive.

I couldn't find any mellow waves. I was worn out and my face was burning up. I'd forgotten to put any sunblock on it. I looked back at the beach. It seemed a long way off. A wave that failed to register on my radar stole up behind me and hoisted me onto its shoulders. It was too late to duck out. I scooped up two skiploads of ocean with a single butterfly stroke and levered myself onto my arms.

There is something magical about the take-off. The initiate invokes the mysterious open-sesame to the wave, locking on to the vanishing point – like a subatomic particle in an accelerator that expires in an instant – between the breaking and the broken, the green and the white. As in a conjuring trick, the eye hardly has time to grasp what it sees. You need slow motion film to catch the arch of the back, the whipping of the trunk, the follow-through of the legs, all that sudden and radical rearrangement of the parts of the body. One second the surfer is prone on his board. The next, with a single, smooth, swift movement, he is on his feet, legs akimbo, arms carving the air, swooping down the face of the wave.

In my case, however, this little miracle failed to occur. Before I could get to my feet, the wave had smashed down behind me. It was like a bomb going off. The blast crushed me against the board and shot me at the beach like a piece of shrapnel.

7

*S*HELAINE AND Cathy were sunbathing. They both had on white scooped one-pieces. Oddly, they didn't have any tan. 'How'd it go?'

I collapsed in a heap and they gave me some cream and I smothered myself with it and wrapped my head in a towel. 'Maybe that's enough for my first time out. I don't want to overdo it.'

As I was sitting there, still shell-shocked and learning to breathe again, Cathy told me that she went to Bible class. 'Do you read the Bible, Andy?' she wanted to know.

'One of my favourite books', I said.

'But do you believe in the Truth?'

'There are many truths.'

'No,' she said firmly, 'there's only One Truth: God's Truth.' She told me that she and her husband and Shelaine and Dave were all born-again Christians.

'What is a born-again Christian?'

'Someone who was living in darkness but then sees the light.'

I felt I wasn't quite ready for this. I'd just come within a whisker of eternity. I was, narrowly, a survivor. It was like landing in Normandy, liberating Paris and then being harangued by Jean-Paul Sartre.

'I think women should be subordinate to men, don't you?'

Shelaine wasn't so sure about this choice of vocabulary. 'I wouldn't say "subordinate", exactly.'

'What other word is there?'

'Hang on', I said. I couldn't believe what I was hearing. 'So if men walk all over you and kick you in the teeth, you don't mind?'

'Men have pre-eminence over women. They are our masters.'

Cathy turned her sunglasses on me and gave me what I think was a look that didn't brook dissent.

'Whatever you say.' I hadn't liberated Paris after all. I'd been arrested by the Gestapo instead.

'Do you believe in God?'

I said I thought it was a fine idea.

'God is a reality, Andy, not an idea.'

'I thought for a while out there I was about to discover whether there is a God. I was praying anyway, just in case.'

Cathy didn't really approve of this kind of levity. 'You shouldn't use the name of God in vain.'

We talked about how the Bible was really *Bibles, ta biblia*, the books. Cathy said God spoke with one voice, but from different perspectives. He used various people who seemed to Him to be good at expressing themselves and inspired them to write. 'Andy, you're a writer. You see, if God were to come down here right now, to this beach, and choose someone to speak for Him, He'd choose you, not us.'

I thought this was probably the greatest compliment anyone had ever paid me.

Dave came in looking as if he'd just hit the jackpot. 'I'm stoked', he said. He smiled when he heard what we'd been talking about. Cathy said I hadn't seen the light yet. 'Believe me, Andy,' said Dave, 'you just have to invite Jesus into your heart and let Him dwell there. Then you will know. *Gignōskō*, that's the Greek word, I *know* Jesus.'

Dave slid back into the waves. I watched him for a while through binoculars, then I lost him. Cathy said: 'You can only suffer without God. You have to take the first step towards Him. But then He will take care of you for eternity. He took care of you today.'

I said I was glad Dave was there to keep an eye on me, too.

'Here comes Dave again', said Shelaine. 'That's quick. I wonder if anything's wrong?'

Dave wasn't exactly staggering, but he wasn't quite so bouncy this time. Blood was streaming from his nose and lip. 'I got nailed', he said. 'A sneaker set. I dived under the first two, but the third one got me. The board flattened itself against my face.' Shelaine tended his wounds and spooned on some soothing lotion. 'This is my worst injury in ten years.'

He was very tranquil about the whole thing. He rubbed his nose. 'I've learned something there. On the North Shore you're always learning.'

8

'*I*'*VE BEEN* hosed by the ASP.'

I'd met Ted Deerhurst in France back in the summer. He competed in each of the three ASP (Association of Surfing Professionals) contests. He surfed his heart out and was trounced in all his heats. He was an Englishman with a Californian accent, a hero of perseverance and never-say-die spirit. Aged thirty, he had spent over ten years on the Tour and was still struggling to get out of the qualifying rounds and into the main event. Ted was often referred to as 'Lord Ted' – his correct title was Viscount Deerhurst. But he hated his nickname because he felt it made him seem like a playboy instead of a serious surfer. He was the most serious surfer on the circuit.

'"Lord Ted – he doesn't need a break – he's rich". What do they know! I'm the only guy around here who has to earn his living.'

Ted was the son of the Earl of Coventry. His full name was Edward George William Omar Coventry. The motto of the family was *Candide et constanter:* Candidly and constantly. Brought up in England, Ted learned to surf in California when he was fifteen and never really thought about doing anything else. He had been largely self-supporting, and financed himself by a string of menial jobs – waiter, salesman, petrol pump attendant.

'I've got to make it in the next three or four months or I'm dead. I've got to make some dough here. Know anyone who wants a viscountcy?' He gave a bitter laugh. We were standing outside the ASP trailer on Sunset Beach. 'They've got to let me have a shot.'

I followed him back to Randy Rarick's house, where he had left his car. He and Randy Rarick were old friends. He shaped his boards in Randy's shaping room. But Randy had turned him down for an entry in the Hard Rock Café World Cup. He hadn't earned enough points over the year to qualify for a place by right, so he was counting on a wild card. But the ASP were favouring the young Brazilians and Japanese. Ted felt he was being discriminated against on the grounds of age, nationality, and title.

He wanted to perform in Hawaii for the same reason everyone did: Hawaii was the ultimate test. In a way it was the only one that counted. Hawaii was where you either made it or you didn't. If you didn't make it in Hawaii, you just hadn't made it. Hawaii carried maximum kudos, not to mention points for the world title, and money.

But he had other reasons, too. Ted had set up a charity in the States enabling handicapped and underprivileged youngsters to be introduced to surfing. The name of the charity was Excalibur. It was based in California in a town called Cambrialot. Its logo was a sword. Ted had gone to Sheffield to have a sword made up that was supposed to duplicate the magical sword once possessed by King Arthur. He was hoping Prince Charles (a former president of the British Surfing Association) would present it at an awards ceremony. 'It's a natural for the future king of England.' The motto of Excalibur was: SHARING THE SPIRIT OF SURFING.

Excalibur was a charity with commercial aspirations. Ted was planning to market boards and beachwear with the Excalibur label. But he desperately needed to attain some measure of sporting credibility to lift his profile and give the venture the boost it needed to take off. 'It's so hard to

27

break through into the big time. Quiksilver, Gotcha, Billabong, they've cornered everything. There's no room for the little guys any more.' Quiksilver had a publicity budget of $2 million. It cost $5,000 for a one-page ad in a magazine. If Ted didn't win – or at least show – Excalibur was doomed. Martin Potter had also set up a company, Pottz Australia, and was planning to launch it by winning the world title. Ted felt more than ever that he couldn't afford to give up. Most surfers want to win just for their own personal glory; Ted wanted to win for all those handicapped and underprivileged children, too.

He knew he was good enough. Back in the winter of 1978, he reached the semi-finals of the Smirnoff contest at big Sunset Beach. He was only defeated by the reigning world champion, who went on to win the contest. It was the equivalent of John Lloyd or Buster Mottram getting into the semi-finals at Wimbledon and being knocked out by Bjorn Borg. In those distant days, there was no *Times* man on the spot to broadcast word of his achievement to the world. He phoned up several newspapers in England to tell them the glad tidings. No one would accept reverse charges. One sports editor had asked to be kept informed, but he was on holiday when Ted phoned. The news of his near-victory sank without trace. It was the biggest day of his life, the best-ever result for an Englishman in Hawaii, and no one took any notice. His moment of triumph was soured with the bitterness of neglect.

Ted was bound to see me as coming to Hawaii over ten years too late. 'And now Pottz is winning the world title, I can't even claim to be the best Englishman on the circuit any more.'

Ted has never managed to repeat his historic result, in Hawaii or anywhere else. Every year he returns, hoping to pull off a miracle. Last year, he was only allowed to compete in one of the contests, and then only as a last-minute substitute. He was knocked out in the first round.

'If they'd just let me have my shot.'

Despite the rough treatment he'd received, Ted was still a fervent proponent of pro surfing. 'This place used to be cowboy land, a hippy heaven. Pro surfers made their money dealing dope. It wasn't even good business. They'd buy a bag of dope and then the guys who'd sold it to them would come right over and steal it back again. But all that was a long time ago. That era is gone. In the last ten years civilization has come.'

'What did you have in mind?'

He had to think about that for a while. 'Well, there's D'Amicos.'

I didn't know D'Amicos. But I didn't like to ask where it was. I had the impression it would be like asking where to find the Tate Gallery or the New York Museum of Modern Art. It turned out to be a friendly pizza and pasta bar half a mile up from Sunset Beach.

Ted showed me the boards he'd been shaping. He had a whole quiver, half a dozen ranging from a 7 ft 4 in thruster through to a big-wave elephant gun eleven feet long. They were all white, with the Excalibur logo at one end, while down the middle ran a blue triangular streak with prongs coming out of it. The triangle was a sword. The whole board, I realized, could be seen as a sword shaped out of polyurethane foam. When Ted Deerhurst paddled out, he saw himself not as Lord Ted but as King Arthur, a knight in armour, riding a white charger, the sword of Excalibur in his right hand. He didn't just want to win a surfing contest, he was looking for the Holy Grail.

9

I SAT through the early rounds of the Hard Rock Café World Cup in a kind of daze. I had just had my whole story kicked out from under me.

My story was that Martin Potter, the Great White Hope of the British People, would – although favourably placed in the race for the world title – have to tough it out in Hawaii to win the championship. The Triple Crown was critical: Hawaii would make or break him. The first day I turned up at the press trailer Peter Colbert, Pottz's exuberant and self-confident partner, formerly his coach and business manager, took me on one side and demonstrated to me, with arithmetical precision, that Pottz had already won. 'He could sit on his arse for the entire month and still no one could catch him', was the way he summed it up.

I was sceptical. After a clutch of victories on the ASP circuit, Pottz was something over 2,000 points ahead of the field. In all, the Triple Crown was worth 5,000. Surely, then, he could be overtaken. Not so, said Colbert. Because the world championship was decided on an aggregate of sixteen contests, and given that nearly everyone had already surfed sixteen or more, that meant that even if you scored zero, your existing points wouldn't be affected; and conversely, even if you scored the maximum, you would only be replacing your lowest score by your highest. For as much as you added on x number of points for winning, you would still have to subtract the y you previously had. 'Pottz is the champion, even before coming to Hawaii, make that your story', he said.

I didn't want to make it my story. I was here to report on Pottz *winning* the title, not on him *having won* it. One story compelled me to be in Hawaii, the other meant I might just as well have stayed at home. The Colbert line not only deprived me of a *raison d'être*, it also implied there was no suspense left in the Triple Crown. With the winner of the world championship a foregone conclusion, the whole thing was an anti-climax, at best a forlorn epilogue to the real drama.

My salvation came in the unlikely figure of Al Hunt, the ebullient 18-stone voice of the ASP, a full-time mathematical genius and an ex-rugby player. He was reputed to have every significant surfing statistic at his fingertips. He was He Who Knew All, he was the Brain. He was Moses. He dissented from Colbert's judgement. Having consulted his computer, he handed down an official announcement: Martin Potter had to get into the final of the Hard Rock to be formally declared world champion. He didn't have to win it, only compete in it. In other words, he had to win through every round up to and including the semi-final. If he failed, then the matter was still open.

The event had begun in relatively modest six- to eight-feet waves on Monday, 4 December. The hundred-odd trialists were gradually whittled down to the thirty-two who would qualify for the main event. In round one they were further reduced to the sixteen who would compete directly against the hallowed élite of the Top 16 in round two.

To get into the Top 16 is the ambition of every surfer on the circuit. Not only do you harvest more laurels, glory, and money, but you are seeded directly into the later rounds of every contest. This makes life a lot easier. Conversely, if you aren't in the Top 16, you have to struggle; the lower down the rankings you are, the harder you have to struggle. If you were Martin Potter, you would only have to surf four times to win the Hard Rock; if you were a lowly trialist, it would be twice that. And so much could go wrong in your heats: the waves could be too big or they could be too small; you could have a bad wipeout, bust your leash, bust your board, lose your rhythm, lose your concentration. You could even lose your life. And in twenty minutes or half an hour it was all over. You were finished, out. It was so easy to lose. Getting into the Top 16 was a way of minimizing your chances of losing.

Randy had called things off on Tuesday. It wasn't big enough, he said. From my perspective out at Jocko's, it had looked plenty big. I mentioned I'd been out.

'What time did you go?'

'Half ten, eleven.'

'Jesus, that's when the ocean boiled over! You're lucky to be here.'

I'd paddled out just in time to catch the swell of the week. But there were bigger waves still on the way. On Wednesday, 6 December, a north-west swell erupted, producing triple overhead sets peaking at fifteen to eighteen feet. The City of Honolulu Lifeguard Department declared all beaches along the North Shore officially closed. That might act as a deterrent to tourists and anyone with common sense, but it was like a red rag to surfers. Randy Rarick decided to surf off all the remaining rounds that same day, with the final to be completed by the end of the afternoon.

Ideal conditions at Sunset occur when there are north and west swells simultaneously: they meet and clash to produce towering peaks, with the north swell sustaining the inside bowl to give a longer ride. That morning, old timers were calling it 'epic' or 'classic' Sunset. The waves were heavy and chunky and frequently tubular. But as the day wore on the swell swung round and the water became increasingly unpredictable and harder to work. The rescue helicopter hovered overhead. Bernie Baker, Randy's adjutant, said it was like a slalom held in a blizzard.

Australian Dave Macaulay, running second to Potter on the ASP computer, went out early. 'He's the Invisible Man', said Randy. 'You won't see him here. He's a small-wave rider. He hasn't got what it takes to surf the North Shore.'

I asked what it took.

'You've got to have the desire. Macaulay hasn't got the desire. You've got to want to be a big-wave rider.'

'I've got the desire', I said. 'I don't know if I've got the guts.'

'Yeah, you've got to have the guts. But you need talent, too – that's the third factor. Look at Ted. Now, he's got the desire and he's got the guts: he just doesn't have the talent.'

Peter Colbert, nervously pacing the crowded spectators' stand and glaring at the uncooperative waves, looked as though his boy was about to be pulped by a heavyweight mauler rather than run away with the world title. But Potter came painlessly through his first four-man heat (the four-man format is preferred to man-on-man in Hawaii because the waves are so big and it takes so long to get into position that having only two men in the water is a waste of waves). Before coming to Hawaii Pottz had talked about pulling off his characteristically radical manoeuvres on big North Shore waves. The aerial floater which had become his trademark in France – shooting up the green unbroken face of the wave, taking off, and landing on the breaking section – was no longer on the agenda. But the high off-the-lips, acutely angled cutbacks, and wide slashing arcs, singled him out. He won his second round heat and the quarter final.

Hawaiians have an edge in Hawaii. The simple explanation is that experience helps in tackling the biggest waves in the world. But there is a widespread belief that Hawaiians are somehow superior beings in surfing terms. Hawaiians are to surfing what Brazilians are to football. There is something about their bodies or their minds or the combination of the two that cuts them out to be surfers. They have an age-old bond with the ocean, a partnership that carries exclusive privileges. 'None but the natives ever master the art of surf-bathing thoroughly', wrote Mark Twain, after briefly trying, and failing, to master it himself.

That is the idea. And events seemed to be bearing it out. The Hawaiians dominated the trials. There were still five of them in the last sixteen. Derek Ho, a poor boy who had made good and had surfed these shores all his twenty-year-old life, was (along with Dave Macaulay) one of the two remaining challengers for the world title. He was winning his heats at the Hard Rock with as much ease as Potter. By the semi-finals, there were only two other Hawaiians left in contention: Marty Thomas, who in 1988 had jumped from 44 to 12 on the ASP computer, and Hans Hedemann, a veteran thirty-year-old, once of the Top 16, who had slumped to a lowly thirty-something in the world rankings. He was a rich boy who didn't have the same incentive to chase the $20,000 first prize and the Geo four-track as Ho, but in front of his home crowd, he wanted to win as much as anyone.

The semi-final was Potter's chance to put an end to debate. But he had been surfing in the last of the quarters, which meant that there was only the first semi-final between his last effort and the next. After paddling in through the heavy seas, he and Marty Thomas had almost no time to recover before having to paddle back out to do it all over again. Pottz totted up the requisite four rides, but without the same fire and drive he had shown earlier. All he needed was to come second out of four and go through to the final. But he was scored third behind Hans Hedemann and Australian Gary Elkerton, who had won the Triple Crown in a previous incarnation when he was known – on account of his formidable build – as 'Kong' (a nickname he had since repudiated and which Callahan had warned me no one in their right mind would use any more). Pottz's fall at the last hurdle left the issue tantalizingly unsettled.

While the would-be world champion was being patched up by Peter Colbert, the other two candidates who lined up for the Hard Rock Café World Cup final were Richard Schmidt of California, another senior citizen among surfers who had come all the way through from the pre-trials, and the young Michael 'Munga' Barry of Australia. Derek Ho had been blown out along with Pottz, so he still couldn't cut back the Englishman's lead.

The four-man finalists' parade gave the surfers a chance to get their breath back before the climax of the contest. But it was essentially a public relations exercise. Photographers could take shots of potential winners while fans clustered round for a close-up of the heroes usually hidden behind curtains of foam. The grandstand, architecturally, was a purpose-built castle of wood and scaffolding, decked in banners, with sponsors' flags flying from its ramparts and the judges' inscrutable binoculars jutting out like cannon. But spiritually it was a mosque, from whose heights fanatical announcers, like muezzin, summoned the flock to worship. Loudspeakers piped out a mixture of Beach Boys and UB40 to the masses sprawling on the sand. Most of the time it was a kind of high-volume, continuous-play Tower of Babel, but now it had lapsed into respectful silence.

Elkerton was ashen as he mounted the platform. He had just survived the worst wipeout I'd ever seen. At the end of his semi he'd gone for the lip, mistimed it, parted company with his board, somersaulted backwards down the face of the wave, then been punched into the seabed by a fifteen-foot liquid piledriver. It was a long time before he was seen again, looking slightly two-dimensional. Right now, he hated Sunset

Beach. 'I nearly drowned out there!' was all he had to say. The languishing Munga Barry admitted he was looking forward to getting it over.

Big, bruising Sunset reminded me of the double-sidedness of surfing. You want to destroy the wave; the wave wants to destroy you. You are simultaneously propelled by the wave and pursued by it. The best position is the worst: the greatest power is closest to the curl. Apotheosis and annihilation are separated by the narrowest of margins.

It was a one-man final. Hans Hedemann, who had looked fresh and unflustered on the platform, continued to surf as solidly and serenely as he had all day, while his opponents faded away in the raging whitewater. Elkerton was given second, and had the additional compensation of winning the Wipeout of the Day Award. The prize was a free massage from Healing Hands of Haleiwa.

Ted Deerhurst phoned in thrice-daily reports on the contest to a radio station back on the mainland. At the end of the Hard Rock I overheard his sign-off line: '$20,000 plus a brand new car – not bad for a day at the beach!'

I caught up with Randy at his house. 'Ted's pretty fed up,' I said, 'feels he's not being given a shot.'

'Ted?' he snorted, squeezing an orange, 'I've given him so many shots and he's always failed. I've known him for fifteen years and the truth is he just doesn't have what it takes. Don't get me wrong. He's a great guy. But it doesn't come easy to him. He sees little kids come up and go right past him. I can't believe his perseverance. He's worked and worked and it's never got him anywhere.'

'What about '78?'

''78? Oh yeah, he did great that year. He beat some really hot surfers. But we're 1989 now. His star has definitely waned . . . ' He sketched out a falling arc with his arm and whistled.

10

RANDY WENT off to shower and we agreed to meet later at the 'Surf Night' that was being held at Sunset Beach Elementary School.

The school was on the far side of the highway, on the hill that rose up as you moved inland. It was a key landmark. If you wanted to find Pipeline, you drove away from Sunset towards Haleiwa, went past the school, and then it was on your right. Strictly speaking, it should have been called 'Pipeline Primary'. A couple of hundred yards away the most dangerous wave in the world was exploding: it was, like having a junior school in the shadow of Vesuvius.

I used to fantasize about my school being swallowed up in some major natural disaster, preferably while I wasn't in it. When it was foggy I liked to imagine it had disappeared, uprooted by a passing typhoon perhaps and deposited in the North Sea. Once my brother and I tried to put a match to it. If I'd been at Sunset Beach Elementary, my dreams would have stood a good chance of coming true. I felt that Pipeline only had to get big and angry, and the school wouldn't even be there any more. It seemed a fragile construction, like a Japanese house built in the expectation that an earthquake was bound to destroy it sooner or later. A dozen or so cabins huddled around a playground, some basketball courts, a little grass and a parking lot.

On the other hand, if I'd been at Sunset Beach Elementary, I wouldn't have wanted to see it wiped from the face of the earth. It wasn't like school so much as a beach with desks.

Surf Night was an annual event timed to coincide with the professional contests. The school was humming with manic excitement. Barton Lynch, the reigning world champion from

Manly, New South Wales, had been shanghaied by a gang of idolatrous six-year-olds and was signing autographs.

The main hall, a metal hut, was hung with the sort of Christmas decorations I used to love when I was five: gummed paper rings looped across the rafters, brightly painted paper stockings, cut-out pink pigs, Santas with cotton wool beards. But there were a few things I didn't have much early experience of at Gobions Infants – garlands of coconut shells, baroque edifices of used soda cans, period surfboards suspended from the ceiling like chandeliers. The floor was thickly carpeted with children, all races, sitting with knees hunched up and vibrating with anticipation. It was like an infantile ashram.

At one end of the hall, a trestle table groaned with brownies, popcorn, chocolate cake, pineapple juice, and cheap tee-shirts. A man named Skill, who had long blond hair under a blue baseball cap, a big belly, square glasses and a flowing beard which was not false, acted as compère and cheerleader. He sang out the results of a couple of raffles and distributed a boogie board and a bathing costume.

Randy Rarick donated a framed poster of the Triple Crown and a cheque for $1,000 to the school. Martin Potter donated a signed poster. The cheque got the biggest cheer. The ASP contributed a lot of money to community groups. This was mainly an exercise in diplomacy designed to head off any tensions over the month-long invasion by the pro surfing circus. But in the case of Sunset Beach Elementary, it was an investment in human potential.

'This school is important to us', said Randy. 'This is where all the future stars are going to come from.' He thanked the youngsters for their help during the contest. Diminutive armies ran around picking up litter at the end of each day. The beach was clean in minutes. It was the phalanstery again. One of Fourier's inspired ideas had been to use children as refuse collectors. He called these groups 'Little Hordes'. He reasoned that since kids basically liked getting dirty anyway, instead of always cleaning them up you should give vent to their natural tendencies and turn their disposition into a job. Surfing was full of Little Hordes.

All children were, I suspected, surfers at heart. Certainly all these children were. They didn't just talk waves. They ate, slept, and dreamed waves. They drank in sea water at the breast. Maybe surfing re-enacted that irresponsible period spent floating around the amniotic fluid.

The main event of the evening was the movie, *Gone Surfing*. I was standing next to Carlos Blackburn, the editor of *Groundswell*, a new surfing magazine on the island. He would say: 'That's Waimea', or 'That's on the West Side', and so on. The waves were all peas in a pod to me, but he could pick out every single pea and give it a name, on the basis of mysterious identification marks invisible to an outsider.

The children were in a state of barely controlled rapture. I asked one youngster, who looked to me nine or ten, if he was a surfer. 'Sure, my name is Occy', he said. 'I'm a big star already.' 'Occy' was the nickname of Mark Occhilupo, a popular Australian with a reputation for hell-raising.

'No he isn't', his friend said. 'He just thinks he is.'

'Yeah, I was just putting you on', 'Occy' admitted. 'My name isn't really Occy.'

One little girl told me, 'I surf every day. I love it when it's big. But my parents don't like me to go out when it's really big.'

Jack Johnson, an older, freckle-faced boy, had just won a junior contest. Was he aiming to be future world champ? 'Oh, no', he said modestly. 'Yes, he is', chorused two girls, each of whom claimed to be his girlfriend. Jack laughed.

The adults at the Surf Night were as emotional as their offspring. Deborah Fowler, who was selling tee-shirts, had been a pro back in the seventies but had given it up because she was a 'soul surfer' at heart.

'You won't see the best surfers in the world at these contests', Deborah said. 'They're not competing. Competition is not what surfing's all about.'

She admitted, though, that when she saw the women in action last year she had been tempted to go out and show them how it should be done. 'But then I thought, no, on these principles I stand and I'm not going to move.' Some weeks later, I saw her succumb to temptation: she didn't catch a wave and came last in her heat. Soul surfers aren't really cut out for contests. I was a soul surfer myself. I had pretty much ruled out my chances of winning the Triple Crown.

Claudia, a Brazilian bodyboarder, was there too. She worked in the Bay View Bar at the Turtle Bay Hilton. Three years before she had run away from Brazil, where her father wanted her to study as a doctor. 'I came for the waves. Thirty-foot Waimea: what more can you ask for?'

Claudia had been accosted by an evangelical eighteen-year-old who was trying to convert her. Claudia told her it was pointless really since she already believed in God. 'Yes,' said the girl, 'but have you invited Jesus into your heart?' Eventually Claudia introduced me to Mark Foo, who I knew was famous for riding big Waimea. Foo asked me what I was doing here and I told him. 'You know,' he said, 'most Hawaiians would rather win the Triple Crown than the world championship. The world championship is nothing. The Triple Crown is everything.' In the Potter camp, this would have been regarded as heresy. But the natives of the North Shore *were* heretics. They were living out what the rest of mankind scarcely dared dream of doing.

As we walked away, Claudia turned and fixed me with her gaze. 'You can't just turn up on the North Shore and say, I like the look of that, I think I'll give it a try. You have to be ready!' I had the feeling she was trying to tell me something.

Maybe I'd started too late. Surfing was like playing the violin: you had to start young. The pupils of Sunset Beach Elementary School spoke surfing as their mother tongue. It would always be a foreign language to me. Secretly, years before I'd set foot on the hallowed ground of Ulu Watu, I'd seen myself as a surfer, but having been born in Forest Gate my early contact with beaches was limited. If East London has a fault, it is that it lacks waves. Occasional excursions to Southend or Camber Sands hardly counted. I saw wavelets, ripples, wrinkles in a tired sea; I imagined titanic monsters rising up out of the deep, swamping ships, swallowing cities, erasing continents. It was as if the Wave were a Platonic Form I'd been acquainted with before birth. I was like Socrates fixated on Truth and Beauty and finding only falsehood and imperfection.

In my most recurrent dream a freak tidal wave swept up the Thames and engulfed London, drowning everyone, burying everything. Only I survived; as the awesome, redeeming wave loomed over me, I would leap onto a passing door or tree-trunk, rise effortlessly up the face to the crest and ride triumphantly to safety — while parents, brothers, friends, teachers, all disappeared without trace. By the time the tide had passed and London had turned into a lake, I was all alone and paddling contentedly over the horizon.

11

MY SHORT lease on charity at the Turtle Bay Hilton was running out. Ted told me where I could find a room for the month. He'd had a look at it himself but then found one that was cheaper and better. 'It's not too bad though. It's at Fat Eric's place.'

The Kam Highway ran parallel to the ocean the full length of the North Shore: it was the route to all the thirty-odd breaks, strung out along the road like colleges on the River Cam. Serious students of the surf lived on the beach side of the road. Fat Eric lived on the hill side. He amply justified his name. He was fat. Very fat. He weighed in, I guessed, at around twenty stone. He was a great balloon of a man who might go off bang at any moment. The room he was offering was pokey but clean. The bed was soft and spongey. I told him I liked a hard bed.

'You have back trouble?' he said. 'Take a look at this.' He

span round, lifted up his shirt, and signalled a neat slit in his back. 'You're looking at $80,000 of spinal surgery right there. Now you could roll a tank over me and I wouldn't even notice.'

We agreed he'd hold the room till I called him that evening. As Ted and I were leaving he said, 'I've been to Europe. I've sailed to Australia on the QE2. Do you know the QE2?'

I called him back at nine. 'Eric, I want to go ahead on that room.'

'Sorry, can't help you out. Room's gone.'

'But I thought you said you'd hold it till this evening.'

'Yeah, but only till eight.'

'You didn't say anything about eight.'

'No, you did. You said you'd phone by eight.'

'I don't remember saying anything about eight.'

'So when you didn't ring by eight, I let someone else have it.'

'Thanks a lot', I said. The simple record of those words cannot convey the venom I put into them. And I wasn't too sure they conveyed it to Fat Eric, either. A man who wouldn't notice a tank rolling over him wouldn't be too put out by my verbal pinpricks.

Fat Eric had done me a favour. To have lived on the hill side of the highway would have blown away whatever shreds of credibility remained to me. It was Banzai Betty who came to my rescue. Her real name was Betty Depolito; she got the Banzai from Banzai Pipeline. I was in the press trailer when she came up to me and said she'd heard I was looking for a room.

Betty's house was not only on the beach side of the road, it looked right out on the Pacific Ocean. Specifically, it overlooked Backyards, so named because it was in Betty's backyard – a break more spine-chillingly known as 'Boneyards', on account of its shallow reef. It was a few hundred yards to the north of Sunset. From the living room you could see the crowd of surfers swarming round Sunset Point. There was an old cane chair permanently drawn up to the window. It was a clapboard house, painted yellow, with lots of light and space.

The room Betty showed me had a bed, a desk, a cupboard, and a polite Japanese girl who was a surfer and photographer, but the girl was due to move out the next day.

Betty was working as assistant producer for an Hawaiian television company, interviewing pro surfers on the beach. She had once won the women's world title and was the only woman on the North Shore to go out in big Waimea. She was also starting to write magazine articles. 'I'm not too good at it, though. I'm a better surfer than writer', she said.

'I'm a better writer than surfer – in fact I'm a better anything than surfer', I said. 'Maybe we can do a deal.'

I'd been fortunate. I'd heard hard luck stories of people sleeping out on the beach. I imagined it was always difficult to find accommodation on the North Shore. But it depended a lot on who you were. And especially, according to Callahan, what sex you were.

I had met Kristin in France in the summer. She lived in California, but followed the circuit with all the fervour of a disciple. She was nineteen years old, had freckles, glossy hair, and good teeth. Callahan and I once made a date with her and her French friend Sabine. They didn't turn up. Neither did we, so it was a sort of stand-off. Kristin had phoned me at the Turtle Bay and warned me she was arriving with another French friend, also called Sabine. She seemed to have a soft spot for Sabines.

Kristin was counting on a Brazilian by the name of Bocão to put her up. But I had spoken to Bocão. He was in an apartment for two currently occupied by ten. And he had his wife with him. Kristin didn't even know he was married. 'No way I'm having those girls to stay with me.' I'd asked a few other Brazilians. They all seemed to be staying at Bocão's place.

I knew Kristin and Sabine didn't want to pay for anything. I imagined them ending up on the beach.

'Are you kidding?' said Callahan. 'Listen, there are so few women here and so many horny surfer dudes, they'll have no trouble finding a place to stay. 'Course, it won't be free.

They may not have to pay any money, but they'll pay all right. Especially if it's Brazilians.'

I agreed that, one way or another, the two girls would probably find a place in the end. But they were arriving at 4.30 that afternoon. How would they find a place for tonight?

'You just tour them around. Someone'll take 'em.'

I picked up Kristin and Sabine at the airport. Sabine was nineteen, had freckles, glossy hair, and good teeth. It was like having Kristin in stereo. They were both very excited as we cruised up the Kam Highway.

'I can't believe it', said Sabine, who was a bodyboarder from Biarritz living in California. 'The North Shore! This is the place I've dreamed about. Finding a room? Who cares? We'll sleep on the beach if we have to.'

I thought they would have to. They knew a few surfers, so we drove to D'Amicos to see if any of them were there. They weren't, but Occy said we should try a condo in the district known as Log Cabins, a mile up the road, past the school, past Pipeline, on the ocean side of the highway.

We drove up there and the girls got out of the car. It was dark. A couple of guys were standing around a telephone booth. Sabine embraced one of them. Kristin started speaking to the other. Five or six more emerged from the house and soon the two girls were completely engulfed. They surfaced briefly to collect their gear from the car and said good-night. I watched them disappear into one of the condos, saw them silhouetted against the light, and then the door closed behind them.

Less than half an hour had elapsed since their arrival on the North Shore. 'What did I tell you?' said Callahan. 'They'll be eaten alive by those guys. You may never see them again. Women are in short supply here. You won't get another chance like that.'

I had an arrangement to meet them the following night at D'Amicos. They didn't show up.

12

I WAS counting on Callahan to initiate me into the secret arts of surfing. Just about the first question I asked him when I arrived was: 'What do I have to do to be a good surfer?'

'Get yourself a good board', was his answer.

'Is that all?' I said.

Since I held Callahan partly responsible for the theft of my old popout in Biarritz, I had been hoping he might loan me one in return. 'Are you kidding?' he said. 'To a klutz like you? I can't just throw boards away, you know. What am I? Santa Claus? Find your own board.'

You couldn't just walk into a shop and expect to find the board of your life. It's easy to make mistakes. I bought my first board in a shop in Sydney's Coogee Beach. The bronzed owner dug out a battered seven-foot turquoise and green single-fin, looked me straight in the eye, and told me it was 'a good basic beginner's board'. I was a beginner, so this was the board for me. I don't think I ever managed to stand up on that slippery, slimy see-saw. Like Sisyphus and his stone, I carted it grimly from Australia to Hawaii to New York and finally back to Cambridge. I showed it to Tim Heyland of Tiki surfboards in Devon. 'That's not a beginner's board!' he laughed. 'That's a swallow-tail radical intermediate.' It was designed for beefy big-wave riders, not for Thameside tyros like me.

I like to think I was not taken for a ride in Coogee Beach, but rather that Australians have a lower scale for measuring degrees of difficulty, like centigrade instead of Fahrenheit. Our radical intermediate was their basic beginner.

I was more experienced now, but even so the choice would

not be easy. Surfboard technology had come a long way since the days when Hawaiian nobles rode the waves on hollowed-out trees. Then you carved your *olo* from the *koa* or the *wili wili* tree and blessed it with ritual prayers and a red fish called the *Kumu*. The *ali'i* (royalty) rode the biggest boards. High Chief Abner Paki, who died in 1855, rode a board sixteen feet long, with a thickness of six and a half inches, and weighing 160 pounds. It took two men to lug it to the water's edge and in a heavy swell it would have to be towed out. But once beyond the break, such a board could catch the biggest waves and give the longest rides. Commoners made do with the *alaia*, fashioned out of breadfruit and banana trees, thinner, lighter, and a paltry six feet. In the early twentieth century, the solid twelve-foot plank of redwood favoured by Duke Kahanamoku gave way to the hollow board invented by Californian Tom Blake. The square tail became V-shaped and acquired a fin. The introduction of balsa wood and, later, fibreglass reduced the weight still further; the sixties malibu was progressively abbreviated and the number of fins multiplied.

The North Shore was the leading edge of surfboard engineering and every shaper claimed to possess the secret of the perfect board. In the shaping chamber, the polyurethane blank is sculpted, planed, sanded, painted, and finally embalmed in gleaming fibreglass and resin. It can be a work of art and a masterpiece of precision aquadynamics, or it can be a useless lump of foam. It all depends on the shaper. Roger Mansfield, a former British champion, once confided to me: 'Your shaper is the most important person in your life.' The shaper takes a slab of inert matter and endows it with life. The shaper is artist, scientist, psychic, magician. The shaper is a shaman. His creations – his creatures – are more than mere wave-riding vehicles, they are energy conductors, status symbols, pagan idols. So I wasn't just looking for a board, I was looking for a way to heaven – or hell.

The etymology of the verb *shape* links it with the Old English *shop*, to recite or sing tales. Each of the many shapers I met on the North Shore had his own tale to tell. One, named

Danny, of Race Surfboards, followed me into church, stood by me for the whole of the service, then abducted me as I was walking out and coerced me into making a close inspection of the X-fin. The X-fin was a revolutionary new invention with numerous magical properties: it gave you more stability, propulsion, control, manoeuvrability. With its eight power pockets or 'cynergic vortices' grappling you to the wave with hoops of steel, it was wellnigh impossible to spin out. I wanted one, all right. All I was missing was a board to fit it to.

Milton Willis of Willis Brothers was more reticent. He didn't want to give too much away. 'For a long while people have been talking about *laminar* flow. *(Had they?)* But what we've discovered is that water flows in little ripples: in every direction, not just one. We call it *ripular flow.*' To exploit ripular flow for the first time in history, the Willis Brothers had devised the Phazer bottom, a pattern of a dozen hemispherical scoops on the underside of the board. 'There are twelve vacuums built into the board, minimizing friction, optimizing speed. It's an air-lubricated-hydro-concave system.'

I thought all my worries would be over if only I could fit an X-fin to a Phazer bottom. But Race Surfboards and the Willis Brothers heaped scorn on each other's innovations.

'An air-lubricated system? It must be hot air.'

'The X-fin? You might as well hang an anchor on the back of your board.'

There was no permanent board in my life on the North Shore, but I had a series of dangerous liaisons. Betty took pity on me. 'I'll loan you my Corona.'

I hadn't heard of Corona boards before. But if they came from the North Shore, they must be good. Betty had it hidden away behind a stack of other boards. It needed to be hidden. It wasn't particularly big: only 6 ft 10 in, but nice and wide for stability. And it was light enough to duck dive. What picked this board out from the crowd was that it was the colour of ketchup – except for the deck, which flaunted a six-foot long hyper-realistic image of a bottle of foaming Corona beer. It couldn't have been any louder if it had had a siren.

Betty had won it in a competition sponsored by Corona. 'Neat, huh? I sold it to a friend for $100 but she had to give it back to me. Said it kept her awake at nights. You can have it for the same price.'

I asked her if I could test it out before committing myself.

I decided to go out on my own this time, so as not to put anyone else at risk. The waves at Haleiwa were a gentle four to five feet. I bought a leash and some yellow 'Sex Wax'. I buttered my board thickly with wax and strapped on the leash.

It was an easy paddle-out through the channel in front of the lifeguard centre. Thus it was a relatively fresh and confident surfer who stroked for his first wave that afternoon. But somehow, at the crucial moment, I lost control and was tumbled. As I span around underwater like an old sock in a Hotpoint, I felt the leash give way.

One of the worst things that can happen to you in big surf is to lose your board. I'd learned that the hard way at Bondi Beach. When my second-hand ankle strap snapped beneath a bone-crushing wave and left me stranded in the impact zone a long way from shore, I could hear siren voices inviting me to surrender myself to the Great Oneness. Relax, they said, as every passing wave rocked me deeper into oblivion, why struggle? I fluttered a drowning arm at the Herculean lifeguards on the sand, but they were too busy performing their exercises to notice.

So I had a distinct sense of *déjà vu* when, having spluttered to the surface, a sinister shadow approached over my shoulder. I dived for the bottom as a rumbling fleet of juggernauts sought to flatten me into the ocean floor.

I laboured towards the beach, where a five-year-old kid had rescued my board. There seemed to be a lot of five-year-olds in the water. They melted into the waves and darted effortlessly among them. They probably came from Sunset Beach Elementary, but they looked like high school bullies to me. Try as I might to avoid them, I bumped into several before the afternoon was out. As I made my way meekly past knots of

47

small surfers on the beach, I heard whispered conversations break out behind me.

'There goes the jerk with the red board.'

'Yeah, the one with the dumb picture of a bottle of beer on it.'

It was a kind of fame, but not exactly what I had in mind. I realized that what I needed, until I got the hang of this business, was a board that would make me invisible.

My second board came from Ted Deerhurst. It was an early Excalibur, dating from Ted's abstract expressionist period. It had a spaghetti of technicolour lines snaking around the sword. I knew from the start it was the wrong board for me: it was a high-performance job, long and slim and narrow in the tail, whereas I needed something plumper, stubbier and more forgiving. But at least it didn't have a bottle of beer on it.

I took it out at Freddieland. Callahan had told me to try this break. 'It's a piece of cake', he said. It was only a stroll along the beach from Betty's house, the Sunset side of Velzyland. I knew Velzyland was named after Dale Velzy, who'd made a film there called *Slippery When Wet*; Freddieland, I supposed, was named after Freddie, but no one seemed too sure who Freddie was. I'd taken the leash off the Corona and transferred it to the Excalibur. Losing the Corona was my fault. I hadn't strapped the leash on tight enough. This time I was making no mistakes. I tied about ten knots and tugged on the leash relentlessly. It was rock solid. I was safe.

The sea was choppy, but I managed to make my way through to the line-up. While you're waiting for the right wave, surfing protocol requires you to sit up on your board. Anything else is uncool. I sat up on the Excalibur. But you have to know a board well to be able to balance on it in the water. I hadn't had long enough to get to know Ted's board, because I just toppled right over and became entangled in the leash.

If there is one thing I hate more than losing my leash, it is being gagged and bound by it. Old-timers refused to have anything to do with leashes. They were a new-fangled fad cooked up to featherbed wimps who didn't have the strength to swim back in for their boards, and they were a menace if you wiped out in big surf because they would likely wrench your leg off. Old-timers knew a thing or two.

I knew what it was like to be stitched up by a leash. As a novice in Australia I'd followed Peter Bothwell's instructions at Triggs to the letter. 'Here comes one', he cried. Suddenly I could feel the wave at my back, jacking up my tail. Out of the corner of my eye I saw Peter already astride his board. I remembered his first lesson: leap to your feet. It had seemed easy enough on the beach. But the beach had been more or less level. What Peter had neglected to tell me was that the board, by this stage, would have its stern in the air. With my feet almost vertically above me, I found it impossible to leap onto them.

The wave broke behind me and I was catapulted forwards. All too quickly rocks blossomed up ahead. I remembered another of Peter's tips: steer round them. Unfortunately, he'd neglected to tell me how. I drove straight into the rocks and the wave passed over the top of me and kept on going.

It was time to get back on the board. But while the board was on one side of the rocks, I was on the other. As I fought to unhitch the cord from an intervening crag, the next wave crashed over me and I went under again. Vainly contending with mighty Nature, I formulated the following inexorable law: that the interval between any two waves is always less than the time it takes to recover from being battered about by the last one. I'd never quite understood before what was meant by the phrase 'dashed on the rocks'. With whatever was left of my brains, I began to have an inkling.

My predicament at Freddieland was a minor one by comparison. It would be a matter of moments to disentangle the leash from around my leg. Or it would have been had it not been for a large wave that hove into view. I saw it coming, all right. But that didn't help. Instead of calmly reaching down and coolly disengaging my ankle from what had suddenly become a ball and chain, I twisted and turned in the water like a corkscrew and only succeeded in redoubling my imprisonment.

It was a perfect wave, not too steep, around five foot, and I felt a pang of regret as it dumped several hundred tons of water on my head.

Callahan was incredulous as I enumerated the wounds garnered on the reef at Freddieland: a gashed foot, a bruised head, and a strained muscle in my left arm. 'Parents take their babies out at Freddieland. It's the safest break on the North Shore.'

The word 'break' was beginning to take on some sinister connotations. Ted's board hadn't emerged unscathed, either. When I handed it back to him he noticed that one of the fins was dangling. It wasn't worth repairing. 'I'm going to make a bonfire and burn it', he said, tossing it aside. 'I never much liked that board. It was jinxed. How did you get on with it, anyhow?'

'Fine', I said. 'Thanks.'

'That was an apprentice work really. I'm a much better shaper now. Come back next year and I'll shape you a new one. It'll be even better than the last.'

13

OFFICIALLY, THE North Shore was known as District 3. For the Hawaiian Lifeguard Service, the South was 1, the East 2, and the West 4. The man who put names to everything for me was Bodo van der Leeden, Lieutenant of Lifeguards. I met him early one morning in the Haleiwa Lifeguarding Sub-station. He was at least 6 ft 3 in and his jutting nose looked as if it had been broken and remoulded a few times. Winter was his busiest period. It was like the Post Office at Christmas: they were having to take on extra staff to cope with the rush.

Bodo took me in his pick-up truck on a tour of the entire length of the designated patrol area of District 3, which stretched from Kaena Point in the south to Kahuku Point in the north. As we drove along, he identified the breaks. It was like listening to a speaking *A to Z*. 'That's Avalanche', he said pointing across Haleiwa harbour. It was an outer reef break with a 100-foot deep trench beside it. A mile or so up the road was another mountaineer's wave: Himalayas. Not far from Himalayas was a place I thought might be more my size: Piddley's.

In between was Jocko's. Did I know why it was called Jocko's? Bodo wondered. I had loosely imagined something to do with hunky males, but he explained that it was Jock Sutherland's wave. 'He made it his. Used to live at that house over there on the point. I was there the day he broke his leg.'

'Somebody told me it's a mellow sort of wave.'

He laughed. 'Only someone on the North Shore would say that. Jocko's can be big and nasty when it wants to be.'

Names had proliferated as surfers had spread out from the main breaks. And like explorers colonizing distant lands, they tended to call these new peaks after themselves. The original Hawaiian name of Waimea Bay (meaning 'reddish water') had been left untouched, though. 'That's sacred ground', said Bodo. 'It'd be like changing the name of Jerusalem.' After Captain Cook was killed at Kealakekua Bay, his two ships *Discovery* and *Resolution* put in to Waimea for water.

Past Waimea was Acid Drop. It got its name from a bunch of surfers who used to hang out there in the sixties. It was a nice wave, so when they went down the drop they said *Hey, man, this is like dropping acid*. The hippies had left their mark at Marijuana's and Uppers, too. Next door to Acid Drop was the less alluringly named Gas Chambers (still marginally preferable, perhaps, to Sewage Pipe Break in Thurso). 'It's the kind of wave where sometimes you pull in and you think you're never going to pull out again.' It was easy to figure out Rocky Point, Bodo's old home break: it was adjacent to a point with a lot of rocks jumbled round it. The rocks were cushioned with sand in the summer, but now the heavy swells had blasted the upholstery away to expose the jagged reef.

'See that out there?'

Bodo focused on infinity. I couldn't see anything.

'That one's called Revelations. It's an outside reef. Gets so big you think it's Armageddon.'

Further on he pointed out Phantoms. 'Plenty of ghosts there, all right.'

We drove to the most northerly break on the North Shore, past Turtle Bay, just to the east of Kahuku Point. 'Not many people know about Seventh Hole Break', he said. We were on a golf course by this stage, so he didn't have to explain that one. 'Seventh Hole usually is mellow. The swell has to wrap around the point to make it work.' All I could see was the monstrous cauliflowers of coral sprouting out of the water. 'Yeah, they're interesting. They can gouge tubular chunks out of your feet. Never really heals.'

Bodo took me to a spot most North Shore surfers eventually wound up at. Kahuku Hospital specialized in surfing injuries. 'You should go there some time. They'd give you some great stories.'

I said I'd probably make it to the hospital sooner or later. I hoped I wouldn't be one of the stories.

Most of the buildings along the North Shore looked new. This was because they were always being pulled down and put up again. 'Every time there's a *tsunami*, it washes the houses away. Destroyed about fifty in '69.'

Tsunamis (from the Japanese *tsu*, harbour, and *nami*, sea) were the tidal waves generated by underwater subsidences, volcanoes and earthquakes. I loved hearing about tidal waves. Probably the biggest wave ever recorded was in 1883, provoked by the volcanic eruption of Krakatoa in Indonesia. In the explosion, a 700-foot-high land mass was converted into five cubic miles of flying lava and ash and a 900-foot-deep crater. The greatest of the succession of resulting tsunamis was reliably estimated at 135 feet. Altogether they killed over 36,000 people in nearby coastal towns. Coral blocks weighing as much as 600 tons were flung ashore. The steamer *Berouw*, anchored off Sumatra, was carried two and a half kilometres inland; all twenty-eight aboard were killed; it was never refloated. Tsunamis can travel at 500 m.p.h.; within twenty-four hours the reverberations, on a reduced scale, were hitting Europe. In England Tennyson wrote of 'waves that echo round the world'.

In 1960 the city of Hilo on the Big Island of Hawaii was washed away by a series of seismic waves after a violent undersea earthquake off Chile. Hilo has since been rebuilt on higher ground. Its former site is now a recreational area called 'Tsunami Park'. There was a legend which told of a tsunami hitting the Big Island and sweeping an entire village out to sea. While others floundered amid the seething chaos, one man, named Holua, wrenched a beam off the roof of his house, clambered aboard, and stroked into the path of the next great wave. He mastered the 100-foot monster and rode it into the safety of the beach. This fable, which some said was historical truth, coincided so exactly with my own childhood fantasy of surfing the flooded Thames that I wondered if I myself, in a previous incarnation, had been Holua, or if the myth of deluge and redemption was simply an archetype of the collective unconscious.

In Jung's *Introduction to the Religious and Psychological Problems of Alchemy* I found another dream like mine: 'By the sea shore. The sea breaks into the land, flooding everything. Then the dreamer is sitting on a lonely island.' In Jung's analysis, the sea stands for the unconscious bursting into the *terra firma* of consciousness like a flood: 'Such invasions have something uncanny about them: they bring about a momentous alteration of the personality and produce something similar to the illusions and hallucinations that beset lonely wanderers in the desert, seafarers, and saints.' I realized that a man on a board on a wave is nothing other than a small island. Surfing amounted to a deliberate provocation of the forces of the unconscious.

Holua and I were descendants of Noah – or his Hawaiian counterpart, Nu'u, living out a fast-forward remake of the Flood. Our boards were one-man condensations of the Ark.

Holua, in making the wave, became one of the chosen; I, in coming to grief, was marked down as just another sinner, damned by moral laxity. Surfing incorporated both a positive and a negative potential. In another work, *Symbols of Transformation*, Jung makes it clear that the immersion of the conscious mind in the *prima materia* of the unconscious can lead either to visions of a world beyond, or to madness. The subtitle of that work is *An Analysis of the Prelude to a Case of Schizophrenia*.

The North Shore had its fair share of tsunamis and floods. 'We usually get plenty of warning these days', Bodo said. 'Everyone moves to higher ground. The few who stay behind start waxing down their boards.' When the true believer hears of a hurricane destroying towns and drowning hundreds of people, he gets a gleam in his eye and prays that the storm is heading his way. Every surfer wishes he'd been around when Krakatoa went off.

Bodo was a surfer, too. His career was a refracted image of Martin Potter's. He had been born in Germany, but was brought up in Durban and learned to surf in the Bay of Plenty just as Potter had. The North Shore had beckoned him over fifteen years ago.

Being a lifeguard taught you added respect for the ocean. Bodo liked to surf within his limits. But the ocean was always moving the goalposts. His worst experience had been at Sunset when he had taken off on the first wave of a big set. Betty had told me: 'Leave the first wave alone. That way if you don't make it you don't get hammered by the waves that follow.' Bodo didn't make it. He was held relentlessly under by the wave. Then, when he thought it was all over, he was sucked up and rolled over again by the next one. 'That's pretty rare. Even rarer for the third wave to get you too.' After he'd been annihilated for the third time, he looked for the light and started swimming towards it. When you lose consciousness underwater you see great blobs of nothingness mushrooming in your head, more like black holes than stars. After six strokes, Bodo was seeing black holes. He was on autopilot for the last six strokes that took him to the surface.

'What were you thinking while that was happening?'

'I was thinking: God, this is going to be embarrassing: "Lieutenant of Lifeguards Drowns". It would have made a bad impression.'

Bodo warned that the main cause of accidents was inexperience. But even experienced surfers got into trouble. He told me the story of three surfers back in the fifties who had paddled out at Sunset in five- to six-foot waves. Then the sea picked up and some big sets started breaking on the outside. They paddled out further to get beyond them. They had settled into the new line-up when some still bigger sets broke even further out. If they didn't want to get mopped up by more than ten feet of tumultuous whitewater every few minutes, they would have to go out further. They went out further. But the swell kept on increasing. Soon they were over a mile out and the sets were twenty-foot plus. They calculated there was no way in at Sunset any more.

They weren't novices. They didn't panic. They paddled south, parallel with the shoreline, searching for an easier re-entry, just as I had at Chun's Reef. Pipeline was impossible: a mad chaos of turbulence. By the time they reached Waimea, they had paddled four miles through heavy seas and were running out of steam. Still there was no let-up in the swell. Waimea was as huge as Sunset, but at least it was orderly. The three men stripped off their shorts and vests. They knew that if they were wiped out and held under their clothes would only weigh them down. Then they said goodbye to one another. They had to split up so as to avoid the risk of collision. One by one they paddled into the enormous waves.

Only one of them made it back to shore. The other two were found much later.

'I hate having to bring back a body', Bodo said. The twelve-mile stretch of the North Shore – 'the biggest impact zone in the world', according to body-surfing champ Mark Cunningham – has fewer lifeguard towers than the half-mile strip of Huntington Beach in California. Bodo showed me the motor-driven jetskis and the Zodiac boats built to Australian specifications that the lifeguards sometimes call on. But their main tool is the rescue board: a solid twelve-foot tanker in white, big enough to accommodate two, a compromise between a thruster and a lifeboat. We dropped off one lifeguard and his board and picked him up again four miles down the road. He'd paddled the whole way and wasn't even out of breath. 'It's a bit like being a fireman', Bodo said. 'You have to be ready. You never know when the alarm's going to sound.'

It was part of North Shore tradition to underestimate the size of waves. What was twenty foot to a European was only fifteen to an Hawaiian. But there were exceptions to this rule, and I heard a few angler-like tall tales. Bodo took me into Steamers Restaurant in Haleiwa and swapped reminiscences with the barman. His name was Brian.

'I hear you're researching the North Shore', Brian said. 'We can tell you anything you want to know right here. Do you remember that time we were out in twenty-five-foot Waimea, Bodo? And we only had one board between the two of us? So we caught that massive wave and I stood on your shoulders?'

'That time I was juggling, you mean? Yeah, I remember that.'

'God, what a day that was.'

14

IT WAS on the night of Saturday, 9 December that the Great North Wind struck. It was also the night I left my *Surfing* vest and beach towel hanging on the line. I never saw them again: I imagined Callahan finding them and assuming the worst. I heard a terrific howling in the darkness. It turned out to be Betty, cursing and mopping up the flood that had hit her room. 'What do you expect,' she said with bitter stoicism, 'if you live in a house that faces north?'

Betty lived with a Cuban architect named Rick who worked

at the Turtle Bay. There was one other member of the household, Yvon, a Peruvian shaper who was deaf and virtually mute. He could only mutter a few unintelligible syllables which always came out sounding like 'tomorrow'. But he had a rich and eloquent repertoire of gestures. He would often show me his new boards and run a caressing hand down the rail or slide his hands one over the other to show how smoothly it would move through the water, or take a sight down the rocker line and then kiss his fingers with jubilant pride.

The morning after the Night of the Great North Wind, Yvon gave me to understand that the cause of all the trouble was two cyclonic forces clashing somewhere to the north and blowing down at us. He pointed over the horizon and his hands met and clashed mightily. But there was a pay-off. The storm would bring a big swell in its wake. Just wait and see (he hooded his eyes with a hand), tomorrow (was he saying *tomorrow*?), tomorrow: he formed a cylindrical wave with his arms and then looked up at something way over his head and quivered with terror.

I went out to buy some breakfast and ran into Callahan, who was taking shelter at Foodlands. I told him what Yvon had said and explained he was deaf and couldn't speak properly. Callahan listened a while and then said: 'He's not deaf, he's crazy. Look at that surf – there isn't any. You've seen the North Shore at its best – now you're seeing it at its worst.'

He was right. The surfer-friendly 'Trades' that blew offshore had vanished. The north wind kept blowing and the waves were choppy. Over the next few days, whenever I saw Yvon he would give me an apologetic look, point to the north, and croak, 'tomorrow, tomorrow'. Eventually he stopped saying anything at all and simply put his hands together in prayerful supplication and lifted his eyes to heaven.

On the North Shore, people hibernate during the long flat summer and wake up for winter. They don't say to you 'How many years have you lived here?' but 'How many winters?' It was as if they packed all their living into this one short season. For three months of the year their lives were greatly intensified, the pressures increased, the highs heightened and the lows abysmally depressed.

The North Shore was like a monastery in which everyone worshipped the god of the ocean. The difference was that here the monks expected god – in the shape of a perfect Pipeline barrel or a Revelations cloud break – to put in a regular appearance. When he kept them waiting too long, their faith was put to the test.

After the north wind started to blow, opinion divided into two main schools. There were the pessimists and prophets of doom who saw this as the beginning of the end. 'It's last year all over again. Once the wind sets in like this, it never stops. You can kiss goodbye to the waves for this winter.' And there were the breezy never-say-die optimists. 'This year is going to be the big one. *El niño* is on its way back again.' *El niño* (the 'Little One' or 'Christ Child') was the name given to a Pacific weather system producing giant winter surf that had last hit ten years ago. Local evangelists were convinced the Day of Judgement was at hand. 'These things work in ten-year cycles. This is the year, all right.'

Rumour and counter-rumour continually swept the surfing brotherhood. People would stop you in the street and say, 'I've heard there's a swell on its way. It'll hit during the night. Tomorrow it'll be twenty-foot plus.'

At first I took these predictions rather seriously. Hawaiians surely knew what they were talking about. I would leap out of bed at sunrise and rush to the window to find the surf as worm-eaten and windblown as the day before. This recurrent disappointment aroused a certain scepticism in me. 'Twenty foot, you say? Which direction is it coming from? Where did you get this information?'

There was a surfeit of information on the North Shore, none of it reliable. It expanded to fill the vacuum left by the truant swell. The radio broadcast hourly surf reports. Betty phoned around the island every morning at dawn to collect the data she supplied to the stations. If she overslept, there would be a string of irate producers calling in clamouring for news.

Over the phone Callahan never said hello, he said, 'What's happening, Andy?' It was his catchline. North Shore natives always wanted to know what was happening. And Betty always knew. But she had no line on what was *going to happen*. She couldn't predict any better than Yvon. The nightly weather forecasts were vague, although you could usually read between the lines. If you wanted a more detailed picture you could call Wavetrak in California, who had satellites trained on every beach in Hawaii and would give you an ETA for forthcoming waves together with their vital statistics.

The ASP had computer printouts giving a graphic identikit image of every swell within a thousand miles. But as the surf drought inexorably extended and the start of the Marui Pipeline Masters was deferred for day after day, Randy Rarick, between moods of black despair, began to succumb to bouts of North Shore positive thinking. 'Tomorrow', he would say, echoing Yvon.

George Downing, a veteran big-wave rider and contest director of the Quiksilver in Memory of Eddie Aikau (a specialty event separate from the Triple Crown), to some the single most important person on the North Shore, had his own personal system of buoys strung at regular intervals across the Pacific. As they bobbed up and down they would signal back to him the size of the waves way out in the ocean. They were like thermometers in a sick man's mouth. People used to ring him frantically. 'What are the figures, George? Is it looking good?' they would ask, as if they feared for the patient's life. In the week following the Night of the Great North Wind, it looked as if the ocean was a terminal case. The rain had flushed the earth from the mountainside, producing a spreading red stain that incarnadined the sea and made you think someone very large – Fat Eric, perhaps – had died.

15

*N*EAR THE opening of *Moby Dick*, Herman Melville ponders the phenomenon of water-gazing.

> Circumambulate the city of a dreamy Sabbath afternoon. What do you see? — Posted like silent sentinels all around the town, stand thousands upon thousands of mortal men fixed in ocean reveries. Some leaning against the spiles; some seated upon the pier-heads; some looking over the bulwarks of ships from China; some high aloft in the rigging, as if striving to get a still better seaward peep. But these are all landsmen; of week days past pent up in lath and plaster — tied to counters, nailed to benches, clinched to desks. How then is this? Are the green fields gone? What do they here?
>
> But look! here come more crowds, pacing straight for the water, and seemingly bound for a dive. Strange! Nothing will content them but the extremest limit of the land; loitering under the shady lee of yonder warehouses will not suffice. No. They must get as nigh the water as they possibly can without falling in. And there they stand — miles of them — leagues. Inlanders all, they come from lanes and alleys, streets and avenues — north, east, south and west. Yet here they all unite. Tell me, does the magnetic virtue of the needles of the compasses of all those ships attract them thither?

Melville depicts this obsession with the sea as a mystery. It is thought that we, prisoners of the land, are compelled to return to the source whence, eons ago, we first emerged. Pilgrims of the primordial, we go to reflect on our birth. But perhaps, too, we go to observe our death, prefigured in the element in which we cannot survive, and which may eventually cover the earth for all time. It could be that we are fatally drawn to the mysterious: the water is that which we cannot fathom, the unfathomable. Homer referred to the 'wine-dark sea' not because the Mediterranean was the colour of wine, but because it intoxicated with its obscurity. Even those who have never seen the ocean, who live forever landlocked or are blind, would, according to Wordsworth, still have sight of that immortal sea.

Melville's weekend water-gazers were stationed along the east coast of New England, 'from Corlears Hook to Coenties Slip, and from thence by Whitehall, northward.' The North Shore of the island of Oahu is a land of full-time contemplatives. There, water-gazing is a way of life. If you turn your head seawards as you drive along the Kam Highway, you will find a ribbon of water-gazers between you and the sea. They might be surfers looking for surf, or spectators looking for surfers, but mostly they are just wave-watchers, bearing witness to the shifting moods of the ocean, timing the pulse of the patient.

Hawaiians on the North Shore are the exegetes of the Pacific, expert in deciphering the ocean. They have given up reading texts and treat the water as their scripture, their Bible, their Koran, from which they are constantly teasing out ingenious interpretations of hidden, secret messages. If we live on continents, we tend to see the world as land inconveniently dissected by expanses of water. Islanders see it as water intermittently disrupted by unsightly deposits of earth. The sea is their kingdom, water their element. To a cartographer, the North Shore is only a corrugated fractal from Kahuku Point in the north to Kaena Point in the south. But to the surfer, it has no limits. It is the nexus at which the planet converges on itself, the focal point of our universe.

The sun stirs up the winds; the winds suck up the swells; the swells pump out waves that trip up against the jutting kerbs of the land. If you know how to read the ocean, it is like looking at the stars: you can see what is happening not only far away but also long ago. A new blossom of light in the night sky reveals a supernova on the edge of the Milky

Way thousands of years past. A resident of the North Shore will look at a wave and say, 'Bad weather they've been having in Alaska', or 'I see Siberia is in trouble again'. To the Hawaiian eye, waves are light rays bending round the planet from distant lands. They are like Cuvier's heel-bone, a minute particle of the whole from which the entire anatomy of the terrestrial animal can be reconstructed.

Within the collective memory of the North Shore resides an entire history of its natural phenomena. It is an oral history, passed on from generation to generation. The original Hawaiians, emigrant Polynesians from the south, had a sophisticated language but no writing. Parts of Hawaii still frown on the paraphernalia of the text: on printed words, on pens and paper, on portable computers. Such things are tolerated but discouraged. 'Andy,' people would say, 'put that pen away. You don't need your notebook.'

There were no libraries or bookshops on the North Shore. The spoken word was the dominant, almost the only record of events. When the surf was flat, it was like listening to BBC Radio cricket commentators when rain stops play: the lack of action is balanced by a surplus of reminiscence. The North Shore is a nostalgic culture. Its inhabitants are gifted with phenomenal memories. Just as cricket buffs can remember who scored how many runs on this or that ground in a particular season decades ago, so too the Hawaiian can recall who surfed which wave when, where and how.

'Do you remember,' a typical conversation might begin, 'that time back in December of '59 when Waimea was unrideable and Greg Noll caught that wave that must have been thirty-foot plus?'

'That wasn't the biggest, though, that was in January of '65, on outside reef Pipeline . . .'

The Greek miracle-worker or *thaumatourgos*, in order to have his marvels recognized, needed a *martus*, a witness, to observe and to spread word of what he had seen. So too the surf-riding chief of ancient Hawaii kept a surf-chanter among his retinue, who would compose a personal hymn, or *mele*, to his prowess and nobility. One minstrel was supposed to have not just glorified his master but saved his life as well:

Naihe from Ka'u on the Big Island was so expert a surfer that his fellow chiefs grew jealous and plotted to lure him into a surfing contest in which he would die. They agreed on a rule stipulating that no surfer be allowed to return to shore until he had heard his personal chant sung from the beach. Naihe, knowing nothing of the rule until he paddled out, let his chanter sleep and was marooned far off-shore at the end of the contest. His enemies sent out a canoe of men with orders to dispose of Naihe. But a chief from Puna who had greatly admired Naihe's surfing ability sent a servant to wake the sleeping chanter. Learning of his master's plight, the chanter hurried to the beach and sang the following *mele*:

> The great waves, the great waves rise in Kona,
> The ebbing tide swells to set the loin cloth flying.
> The day is a rough one, befitting Naihe's surfboard,
> He leaps in, he swims, he strides out to the waves,
> The waves that rush hither from Kahiki,
> White capped waves, billowy waves,
> Waves that break into a heap, waves that break and
>   spread.
> It is the sea on which to surf at noon,
> The sea that washes the pebbles and corals ashore.

Naihe caught a wave into shore and so escaped his assassins.

I saw myself as a sort of *martus* among miracle-workers, a surf-chanting troubadour. But modern surfers were capable of singing their own praises. Anglers like to talk of 'the one that got away', but at least they occasionally bag a fish to flesh out their claims. The wave is a fish that always gets away. You cannot point to a wave and say, 'that is the wave I rode', as you can say, 'that is the mountain I climbed'. The very transience of the wave, a purely provisional form doomed to decline into formlessness, condemns surfers to be story-tellers, constantly recalling their ephemeral experiences in the water, shaping and reshaping the past, immortalizing fleeting moments of intensity. The wave, like the *mele*, like all music, like the text, is a mental event, since it is never wholly present in any one instant and can only be grasped as a formal pattern existing through time.

The North Shore was full of historians. But these wave-chroniclers, these Xenophons of the surf, often went about masquerading as prophets. Like Laplace's omniscient scientist they claimed, on the basis of their knowledge of the past, to be able to foretell the future.

'Psst. The Eddie's on tomorrow. It's definite.'

16

THIS PREDICTION used to send me into raptures of antici-pation. 'The Eddie, oh God, are you sure?'

'The Eddie' — shorthand for 'The Quiksilver in Memory of Eddie Aikau' — was a collective act of surfing nostalgia, commemorating a North Shore waterman who had died heroically in 1978. The man had become a myth and acquired the definite article. The Eddie Aikau denoted a big-wave contest of a kind that could only be held in Hawaii. Its precondition was that the surf at Waimea Bay should be over twenty feet for the entire duration of the day in which the contest would be surfed. But 'the Eddie' signified more than a mere sporting spectacular: it was a celebration of a way of life.

The Eddie Aikau was supposed to be an annual event, but it had not been held in three years for want of perfect conditions. It was a universal obsession on the North Shore. The less it happened the more important it became. It seemed more important than the Triple Crown and the world cham-pionship put together. It was a matter of pride, of principle, among the faithful that it should be held. The Eddie was as turbulent as its homophone: it gave rise to eddies of contro-versy that swirled up and down the Kam Highway.

Some muttered that George Downing, who had final say

on whether or not the contest should take place, was too fussy. 'You could have held it two years ago, no problem. He just wasn't ready.' There was a hint of sinister commercial pressures being brought to bear. 'The waves were there. It just wasn't sunny enough, that's all. And Quiksilver insisted on good light for the shots.' The most paranoid account held it was all a cunning ploy on Quiksilver's part, a mirage of advertising and hype. 'They're getting all this free publicity every year without even holding it.'

Quiksilver had created the richest prize in surfing for this contest: $50,000 for the winner. This caused a sensation among the surfing fraternity, but dismay in the hearts of Quiksilver's rivals. Billabong quickly matched the figure: now the Billabong Pro, the last of the Triple Crown events, also boasted a $50,000 first prize. Quiksilver responded by hoisting theirs to $55,000. There were at least a dozen big-wave specialists on the North Shore who, if the Eddie Aikau were actually to be held, could reasonably expect to make a small fortune.

The Quiksilver contest was unique.

It was simple: in contrast to the Triple Crown, there were no cut-throat elimination rounds. Three groups of eleven went out twice in succession, once in the morning, once again in the afternoon. The winner would be the surfer who was judged to have performed best overall on the day: to have ridden the biggest waves in the most critical positions. Only your four top waves would count.

It was timeless: other contests set a date and trust to luck that nature will co-operate – the Triple Crown was already distinct in having a much longer window of opportunity than fixtures elsewhere on the Tour. But the Eddie didn't specify a date at all, beyond a vague 'waiting period' that extended from the beginning of December through to the end of February. It had a pre-defined space – Waimea Bay – but it left the time open. The élite group of thirty-three big-wave riders who would compete for the title had been chosen. But now they had to wait until, as the advertising put it, 'The Bay Calls the Day'. The Eddie Aikau wouldn't take on lesser challengers:

it dared the ocean to field its strongest possible team. It was as if it was only when the surf was at its most savage that the ghost of Eddie Aikau could be expected to revisit the Bay.

It was the ultimate submission to the impersonal forces of fate. The Eddie was not called forth by an act of human will. It was not scheduled or given an elaborate countdown and fanfare. Sports editors hated it. It didn't fit on any particular page of their diary. It was like trying to prepare for an earthquake or a hurricane. It was like waiting for the Second Coming. You know a year in advance when the Cup Final, Wimbledon fortnight, or Superbowl Sunday will take place. With the Eddie, you wouldn't know until the morning of the day it was happening. The event demanded the most stringent virtues before it even began: patience, perseverance, reverence. You had to wait. And you had to be ready.

This was the greatest test for surfers, but it was just as much of an ordeal for journalists. It was the story of a lifetime, the story I had been born for. But I knew I would be leaving Hawaii in January. I only had a few weeks. I was ready, but I couldn't wait. The Pacific, though, had already waited three years and didn't seem in any particular hurry this year either. 'I dreamed about this every night during the waiting period', said Clyde Aikau, Eddie's brother, after winning in 1986. He was still dreaming about it, and so was every other surfer on the North Shore, and so was I. But would this dream become a reality? Would the curtain go up on the world's greatest surfing spectacle before I had to leave – or would it all go ahead without me?

The story of Eddie Aikau began a long time ago:

In the second half of the first millennium, a canoe set out from an island in the Tahitian chain and steered due north for two and a half thousand miles by the light of the stars and the ocean currents till it reached Hawaii. The crew of that canoe were believed to be among the first human beings to set foot on the Islands. A folk tale told of a Tahitian chief, Moikeha, who sailed to Hawaii and, largely thanks to his prowess on a surfboard, married two princesses and became king of the island of Kauai. When his sons returned to Tahiti and were asked the fate of their father they said:

> He is dwelling in ease in Kauai,
> Where the surf of the Makaiwa curves and bends,
> Where the kukui blossoms of Puna change,
> Where the waters of Wailua stretch out,
> He will live and die on Kauai.

On 16 March 1978, another canoe, the *Hokule'a*, sixty feet long and double-hulled, set out from Honolulu, steering south towards Tahiti, seeking to mirror that original expedition, using the same techniques of astral navigation and water-knowledge. There was no radio and no motor. The deep hulls of the *Hokule'a* were loaded with dried and canned food and three hundred one-gallon containers of water. If all went according to plan, the voyage was expected to take a month. All the sixteen-man crew were as trained and tested as astronauts. Among the sixteen was Eddie Aikau.

He was a Polynesian Hawaiian, thirty-two years old and already a legend on the North Shore. He worked as a lifeguard at Waimea Bay; but he was more than a lifeguard: he was the Bay's presiding spirit, its faithful genie, its ruler. The newspapers called him 'Mr Waimea'. He was supreme among big-wave riders, paddling out on his traditional wooden board when no one else dared. There is a photograph that preserves him forever racing down the face of a twenty-five-foot wave. The sun picks out the muscles in his back. He is wearing long white shorts with a black band, he is perfectly poised, arms outstretched, slightly crouched, his arrow-like board barely carving the water with one rail, spraying out a tail of whitewater behind him like a comet moving through space.

Waimea was an arena of combat to some, but to Eddie it was a temple and playground. He surfed the most savage seas, smiling from ear to ear and hooting with joy, and he saved many lives. He was a benign man. 'I never once saw him get upset or angry', said Ken Bradshaw, one of his circle of disciples. Eddie thought Bradshaw's name was Brad Shaw and called him 'Brother Brad'. Once, when native Hawaiians were out for blood after a visiting Australian had abused a local, he brought the two sides together and persuaded them to settle peacefully. 'You've got to learn to live together', he would say. 'The ocean is for everybody.' When he surfed Waimea he wasn't competitive. He loved to see others catching waves too. 'Come on, brother! You and I! I'll be on your inside.'

Eddie called the crew of the *Hokule'a* 'his second family'. He was not the oldest on board, he was not the captain, nor the navigator; he was the canoe's spiritual father and guardian angel. Eddie was their good luck charm.

The wind and currents were set fair when the *Hokule'a* paddled away on that sunny afternoon in March. The canoe moved swiftly south from Oahu, west of Molokai, towards the Big Island at the southernmost tip of the Hawaiian chain. But after several hours' hard canoeing, when the *Hokule'a* was due west of the island of Lanai, in the channel known as Kealaikahiki, or 'The Path to Tahiti', a vicious swell blew up. Soon, the craft was making its way through the darkness over twenty-foot waves and taking on water. The skipper steered the vessel at ninety degrees to the waves, careful to tackle them head on. But the multiple currents passing around and between the islands were treacherous. A twenty-five-foot wave flung itself at the canoe from an unexpected angle and before the crew could turn to absorb the blow, the *Hokule'a* rose up the face of the wave at forty-five degrees, and was capsized as it flew off the peak.

The crew swam out from under the canoe and attached themselves to the upturned hull. It was impossible to right the craft. The hours went by and no one panicked, but they got cold and tired and dispirited. The sun had not yet risen when Eddie Aikau said he was going for help.

'Are you crazy?' said David Lyman, captain of the *Hokule'a*. 'It must be twenty miles to land.' One of the cardinal rules of the sea was to stay by your boat.

'It's okay. I'll take my board. It'll be the longest ride ever.' Eddie had brought his twelve-foot rescue tanker. It was on this board that he had saved so many lives at Waimea. He was used to paddling it for miles at a stretch.

Eddie dived under the canoe and unlashed his board.

'Don't worry,' he said, 'I can do it. I'll get to land.' Then he pushed himself calmly off from the *Hokule'a* and paddled away with quick firm strokes and vanished into the half-light.

The crew were picked up later that day. 'Did Eddie make it?' they asked. There had been no word from Lanai. The helicopter trawled back and forth across the channel. They found the big white board with the word RESCUE painted across it. The search continued for a fortnight. But Eddie Aikau was never recovered.

There was no body to commit to the deep. But over a thousand mourners gathered at Waimea Beach Park for the funeral service. Surfboards were planted upright in the sand like tombstones and decked with leis. The minister said that the Pacific Ocean, for the Hawaiian people, was like the desert for Moses and the Israelites: 'The open sea is the place where we go to meet God.' An urn of Waimea sand, representing the ashes of the dead man, was voided on the sea. The rescue helicopter strewed thousands of blossoms on the waters of the Bay. The orange lifeguard tower where Eddie used to keep watch was empty; a sign on the side announced: NO LIFEGUARD ON DUTY.

There was a sticker you could stick on the back of your car. It said simply: EDDIE WOULD GO. Everyone knew what it meant.

17

*H*ALEIWA IS the only town on the North Shore, fifteen minutes up the Kam Highway from Sunset, fifty out of Honolulu. In the city they call it 'Country'. It is the kind of American small town that Steven Spielberg might have invented in one of his more whimsical moods. The inhabitants have structured their lives around the ocean. They not only surf and swim in it, but paint it, photograph it, worship, contemplate and consult it. The ocean is not just their livelihood but their life. Without it they wouldn't exist.

Haleiwa means 'the house of the frigate bird (the *iwa*)'. A mission had been established there as early as the 1830s and the Liliuokalani Protestant Church, named after Hawaii's last queen, was still standing. The hands of its clock pointed not to numbers but to the twelve letters of its patron's name. At the turn of the century the town expanded to accommodate the sugar cane workers, and a railway line led to the Haleiwa Hotel. Now the hotel, the railway, and the labourers had all gone. Hodads from Honolulu still think of the place as the Wild West and venture up the H-2 to stare at surfers as if they were herds of buffalo grazing on the sea.

The Haleiwa Theatre was a pink, art deco pleasure dome built by the sugar barons which by the sixties had become the hub of social activity, screening nightly surf movies. Everyone spoke of it with affection. Some even had photographs of it on their walls. I wanted to go there, but it turned out that it didn't exist any more. It was demolished in a hurry one night in 1983 to make way for a McDonalds. As a conciliatory gesture, the restaurant was built like a large shack, so as not to be too obtrusive.

The simple plantation-style wooden buildings, with their crooked façades and creaking boardwalks, now included a bank, a post office, a café, a health food store, and several surf shops. These seething emporia of boards and beach-gear were outnumbered only by the healing parlours of various persuasions – 'Back and Shoulders', 'Healing Hands', 'Acupuncture', 'MD' – where you could put in for repairs. Astrologers, psychics and crystal-ball gazers ministered to the North Shore passion for prophecy, and elaborate charts detailing the movement of the moon and planets could be drawn up to ascertain the prospect of waves on any given day of the year.

Dave Jerrome and Shelaine, my born-again Christian friends, disapproved of the mystic fringe. 'If it's God's will there will be waves.' They took me along to a service at the North Shore Christian Fellowship on the Sunday after the Night of the Great North Wind.

The church was a whitewashed barn owned by the Haleiwa Community Association. As I walked in I was handed a leaflet bearing the image of an apocalyptic Pipeline wave and above it a line from Psalms 93:4: 'The Lord on high is mightier than the mighty waves of the sea.' The Bible frequently invokes waves as the measure of nature's power and the limit easily transcended by God. God could part the Red Sea, Jesus could calm the storm or walk on the water. But the shapers of the Old and New Testaments only had the Mediterranean as their model of what the ocean could do. And in Hawaiian terms, the Mediterranean wouldn't even register on the swell scale. I doubt that any of the Israelites wandering in the desert and occasionally venturing down to the water would have written those lines about God being mightier quite so confidently if they had seen big Waimea. For the Hawaiians, the god of the ocean did not move upon the face of the waters: he was not pre-eminent over the ocean, he was indistinguishable from it. Kane, in creating the world, did not, like Yahweh, *make* light: he *made himself* into light. Hence the god of the ocean *was* the ocean, the god of the volcano *was* the volcano and so on. Polynesian holy water, used for purification and sanctification, for driving away demons and diseases, was simply sea water, as saturated with divinity as with salt. Traditional Hawaiian society only began to fall apart when the godhead became detached from the environment: when Captain Cook arrived and ushered in a foreign idol, ubiquitous, omnipotent, immortal, but disembodied, absent, invisible.

There was a four-piece band of two guitars, drums and bass. We sang along to a rousing tune while particularly enthusiastic members of the congregation waved their arms about like stalks of corn blowing in the wind. The minister, who had red hair and fire in his eye, started on an upbeat note. 'Hey, praise the Lord, man! He loves you guys! We lift the North Shore up to you, Lord.'

There were many surfers among the flock, limping, scarred, sunburnt, dressed in their Sunday best of Rip Curl tee-shirts, Billabong shorts and Oakley shades. They were hoping and praying, on this blown-out Sunday, that the Lord would lift the North Shore up to them.

A peach-faced woman who was on her way from Amsterdam to Fiji 'to share', sang sweetly of how good life was. A pastor exhorted each of us to be a rejoicing person, to be an encourager, to be solution-oriented and not problem-oriented.

The minister thanked God for his beneficence, citing Deuteronomy 1: 'The Lord will improve your lifestyle.' But he concluded his sermon with a prayer. 'We ask a blessing of you, O Lord, as we go out on the beaches, and we pray for a really neat time and some big swells. Amen.'

18

IT TOOK a while to adjust to the demanding sartorial standards of the North Shore. Whenever I wore my brown leather shoes, people would stop me and say, with genuine amazement, 'Hey, what are those *things* you've got on your feet?' When I needed some black shoes for the annual ASP banquet in Honolulu, Bodo van der Leeden dug out a pair he'd bought fifteen years before. 'You can break these in for me', he said.

I had a pair of tennis shoes, but Callahan vetoed these along with my 'suit'. 'You've got to have thongs for the beach. The cool thing to do is buy two pairs, then wear odd colours.'

I bought just one pair and, sure enough, they gave me nothing but trouble. The straps were fabric instead of rubber, so they kept flopping. 'Did you buy *those* in Hawaii?' Callahan said when he saw them. 'Kinda on the large size, aren't they?' They extended a half inch beyond my toes but the way he spoke you'd think I was John A. 'Snowshoe' Thomson. I half expected five-year-olds to be making funny remarks about them behind my back. 'There goes the jerk with the shoes.'

Michael Willis never wore shoes at all. 'Andy, if you wear shoes, you're not *grounded*. You're out of touch with the earth. With all that rubber between you and it, it's like riding around in a car and never getting out. You might as well be on Mars.'

I met Michael the day I moved into Betty's. I found him sitting on the bench to the side of the house gazing out over Backyards. He had freckles, a wide-eyed look, and a permanent grin.

'Take off those shoes, you'll thank me for it later. Barefoot, you can absorb vitamins and minerals and the magnetic field.' Back in England, I had always looked on people who went round with no shoes on as crackpots and show-offs, on a par with youths who wore shirtsleeves in midwinter. But in Hawaii, where nature was kinder to your feet, it seemed somehow out of step to be wearing shoes. I took them off and rode into Haleiwa with Michael. As we sat in the garden behind his surf shop and talked I could feel the long grass beneath my feet with a sensual awareness I'd never experienced before. Walking, or just standing still, had become a pleasure.

It was Michael who introduced me to his twin brother Milton. Physically they were almost identical, but psychologically they were worlds apart. If Michael was the artist of Willis Brothers Boards, Milton was the scientist. Michael was loose, vague, susceptible; Milton was serious, discriminating, professional. Michael blew with the wind; Milton had objectives, an agenda, a timetable. One twin listened to psychics and astrologers; the other relied only on weather charts. We tried to fix up a time to talk about the Willis Phazer board. 'You and me, we're real flexible', said Michael. Then he jabbed a finger at Milton. 'Let me speak to Mr Cement here.' Milton was wearing deck-shoes. 'He's not grounded', said Michael.

'A Phazer is not a miracle design that can take a junk board and make it a killer', Milton said.

'That's true,' Michael said, 'but it can take a killer board and make it magical.'

'What we Willis Brothers try to do,' Milton said, 'is take the magic out of shaping and apply number to art. It's no longer voodoo and mumbo-jumbo to us. We've got a science now.'

'You see that symbol?' Michael pointed out the Phazer logo on one of the boards: it was the sign of the atom. 'The basis of all Creation.'

Within two hours of returning home, my feet and ankles were stippled with mosquito bites. Great itchy red lumps were popping up everywhere. I caught Michael sitting unashamedly on the bench again. 'Look at these feet. I won't be able to walk for a week, with or without shoes.'

Michael looked at me with compassion. 'Andy, that's the best thing that could have happened to you.'

'How do you work that out?' I said bitterly.

'Listen', he said, as though trying to teach a child some simple truth. 'Once a mosquito's bitten you in one spot, it'll never return. It's like lightning − never strikes in the same place twice. So the more you're bitten, the better off you are. A couple more sessions like that and you'll never have to worry about mosquitoes again.'

19

WE WERE watching the sun go down beyond Kaena Point when Michael asked me how my book on the North Shore was coming along. I told him it was easy: all I had to do was quote the people who lived there.

'You're quoting us?' He looked doubtful. 'We're just parasites.' He pointed out at Backyards. 'Look out there. That's the real star. If you want to write a book about the North

Shore, you've got to quote the ocean, you've got to quote the mountains, you've got to quote the air.'

Whatever I wrote, I knew that Michael would not read it. He had given up reading. 'There's an inside to things,' he explained, 'and print only gave me the outside. I had the crust, but I wanted the meat. So I closed all those books and it was then that I opened up my eyes and looked around me and said, "Now I'm reading".'

I wanted to quote the ocean. Living at Betty's house, I had been listening to it speak for long enough. But what language would translate what I heard? What words would describe the *inside* of the waves?

Callahan had advised me to devote myself to one simple and perhaps impossible mission: to discover the etymology of the word *cowabunga*. *Cowabunga* was an exclamation of joy or approval among the surfing fraternity. You uttered those syllables at the sight of a big wave or in acknowledgement of a good ride or, like a war-cry, to arouse aggression. It had become dated and out of fashion, but was still occasionally heard. It wasn't until much later that Sidney E. Berger, curator of manuscripts at the American Antiquarian Society in Worcester, Massachusetts, explained to me that the word had made its début in the *Tarzan* movies. When Johnny Weissmuller swung through the trees, the African natives would mutter in amazement, 'Cowabunga!' It was an imaginary Swahili *Holy Cow!* invented by Hollywood scriptwriters. I liked the word, but it was a late accretion. I wanted something authentic.

Rousseau, in his *Essay on the Origin of Languages*, interpreted the first sounds uttered by our ancestors as 'the cry of nature'. Humanoid bipeds shaped their vocal chords to reproduce the noises they heard about them. In Hawaii, likewise, it was said that, casting off its Indo-European moorings, the language had evolved in unison with the rise and fall, the ebb and surge of the ocean. The *mele* and dances echoed the modulations and music of the all-encompassing Pacific. Students of chanting practised their art on the beach, with one ear attuned to the waves. If you listened closely to certain words, it was like

75

putting your ear to a conch shell: you could hear the sound of the sea breaking on the shore. It was as though the waves had chosen Hawaiians to act as their mouthpiece.

I had once read a story by Arthur C. Clarke about a Tibetan sect which believed that God had nine billion names. In Hawaii the ocean had almost as many. Just as the Eskimos had countless words for snow and ice, so too the Hawaiian language abounded in wave nomenclature. Each type of wave attracted a different noun, and the nouns incorporated adjectives, verbs, whole narratives. Instead of *terrible, death-dealing, curling* wave, you said quite simply *kakala*; a high wave, formed by the meeting of two crests, was *huia*; *lauloa* was a long wave that broke from one end of the beach to the other; a *calm, unbreaking* wave was known as *opu'u*.

I consulted Lorrin Andrews's *A Dictionary of the Hawaiian Language* on the Hawaiian for surfing, *he'enalu*, which split into two words, *he'e* and *nalu*.

He'e (he'e), *n*. 1. A flowing, as of a liquid. 2. The menses. 3. A flight, as of a routed army. 4. The squid, so-called from his slippery qualities.

He'e (he'e), *v*. 1. To melt; to run or flow, as a liquid. 2. To slip or glide along. 3. To ride a surfboard. 4. To flee; to flee through fear.

Nalu (na'lu), *adj*. Roaring; surfing; rolling in, as the surf of the sea.

Nalu (na'-lu), *n*. 1. The surf as it rolls in upon the beach; sea; wave; a billow. 2. The slimy liquid on the body of a new born infant.

Nalu (na'lu), *v*. 1. To be in doubt or suspense; to suspend one's judgement. 2. To speak secretly, or to speak to one's self; to think within one's self. 3. To talk or confer together concerning a thing. 4. To think; to search after any truth or fact.

The wave is the universal metaphor, a summary of the world. So said the Belgian poet Henri Michaux: it was pure form, like a poem, nothing in itself and yet containing everything. Similarly, the Hawaiian vocabulary of the surf was infinitely rich in *kaona* or hidden meanings. Surfing was not just 'wave-sliding' (as *he'enalu* was typically translated): it was a flowing and a fleeing; it was communing with yourself and talking with others; it was regeneration and the pursuit of truth.

20

IT WAS the middle of the week when the Marui Pipeline Masters should have been on and wasn't that I ran into Pottz in D'Amicos. The north wind was still blowing, Randy Rarick was still biting his nails, and surfers patrolled the Kam Highway, boards poking out of jeeps, strapped to cars, balanced on bicycles, searching in vain for rideable waves. I was eating a lasagna and reading the latest number of *Surfing* when Pottz cruised in with his entourage.

Most surfers travelled on their own. Martin Potter boasted not just a manager, coach and partner in the shape of Peter Colbert, but an adviser, an agent, and occasional heavies and bureaucrats who hovered around him as if they were guarding the crown jewels. We arranged an interview for noon the next day at his house on Rocky Point.

Callahan and I arrived at twelve, Pottz at one. For an hour we were closeted with Colbert. He was accompanied by a tall, dark-haired girl with pale skin and blue eyes whom he introduced as his fiancée. Stephanie turned out to be an Australian model who had thrown in her job to follow Colbert to Hawaii. The last time I had seen Peter, in Biarritz, he had been accompanied by a tall, fair-haired girl whom he had introduced as his fiancée. Stephanie made coffee while Peter talked.

There was a mystery concerning Peter Colbert. Up until a

couple of years ago his name had been Peter Manstead. What no one knew was why he had changed it. One theory held that he was fed up with being called 'Manstead' and wanted to confuse people into using his first name instead. Now everyone called him 'Colbert'.

Colbert had curly red hair and an aptitude for getting into scrapes. During contests he was as jumpy as a schoolgirl and gave off a static charge of nervous energy. Barton Lynch's manager had once picked a fight with him. Lynch was held technically responsible and fined $500. The story runs that someone then offered Lynch a further $500 with the words: 'Get your manager to finish him off – it'll be worth it.'

Colbert had an ego robust enough to stand a lot of punishment. When I was writing an article on Pottz he sent me three large studio portraits: one of Potter and two of himself. He was loud and self-confident, but he had a right to be: he had a knack for picking winners.

There was a Christmas tree in the living room and a surfing video on the television. Outside you could see invertebrate waves expiring on Rocky Point. I turned on my tape machine.

COLBERT: Do you know who has coached most world titles?

AM: You?

COLBERT: Do you know how many world titles I've coached? Four. Kim Mearig. Tom Carroll twice, and now Martin Potter. Do you know who was the first to coach the men's and women's champions in one year?

CALLAHAN: You?

COLBERT: Right. I'm telling you as a fact that I'm the only person in this industry who's done it.

CALLAHAN: That's a fact.

COLBERT: Fact, fact. Fact: a year ago, we worked out a repertoire to win the world title: forehand snap, floater, and figure-of-eight.

AM: A kind of choreography really . . .

COLBERT: Yeah, it was choreographed. We planned to go full belt, we planned for 1989 to be either win or retire.

CALLAHAN: That's a serious decision.

COLBERT: It had gone on for too long: this is his ninth year on the Tour. It wasn't a fluke. One seventeenth all year. Two ninths all year. Five fifths. Two seconds, one of which should have been a first. And six firsts. Plus a first in a specialty event. I try to tell everybody, this was planned, like a war-strategy.

AM: How did the two of you come to team up?

COLBERT: We met under a bet. I wanted him badly and he hated my guts, and I said all right, I'll leave you alone if you can beat any of the guys on the Australian spring tour. If not, come over to me and I'll make you a world champion in five years. And that was the bet.

AM: When was this?

COLBERT: Five years ago.

CALLAHAN: Oh wow, good timing.

AM: So what makes a world champion?

COLBERT: Surfing is self-expression – it's how you feel. Hardman and Lynch are very plateau-ish personalities, and their surfing's plateau-ish. Compare them with Carroll, Curren and Potter – they're the raw world champions.

[Australians Tom Carroll and Damien Hardman and Californian Tom Curren had all preceded Lynch as world champions. But Hardman was dismissed as a small-wave specialist and Lynch was condemned as a pleasant and industrious journeyman, while Carroll and Curren had acquired the status of living legends among the surfing fraternity.]

CALLAHAN: Those three are communicating on another level.

COLBERT: Oh man, they're so far out they've seen Pluto, those guys.

CALLAHAN: A couple of years ago, Potter was the hottest guy on the North Shore.

COLBERT: Carroll was storming last year. And then he blew it all at the last minute with that interference.

[An interference is deemed to have been committed when one surfer 'drops in' on another, that is, takes off on a wave on which the other has already established priority. In a four-man contest, priority is decided on a first-come-first-served basis; in a two-man, by alternation. In surfing's ten commandments, dropping in was high on the list of thou-shalt-nots, and it was as popular as adultery. I did it all the time, more by accident that design.]

AM: I remember reading that the Carroll camp let out a shriek of despair and I thought, that's got to be Colbert.

COLBERT: I was sitting next to Bob Mcknight, and five seconds before it happened I said to Bob, the only person who can fuck this up is Tom Carroll. And then the interference came. That interference came about because of greediness. There's a grudge against Tom because he drops in on everyone. And he comes back out with a grin.

AM: He's been paid back, you mean?

COLBERT: He's been paid back for dropping in on every human being possible.

CALLAHAN: Is that karma?

COLBERT: I think so.

CALLAHAN: That sixties hippy concept of karma.

COLBERT: Yeah, I believe so.

AM: Poetic justice.

CALLAHAN: A lot of people said that. Straight out.

COLBERT: It's just karma.

CALLAHAN: Tom's copping his karma right now.

COLBERT: He won't recover. It's like: the gods are against me, what can I do?

AM: The fire's gone out of him?

COLBERT: No, because Martin Potter burnt everyone off. What happened this year is what every surfer feared about Pottz. The moment he was going to get his head together, that was it. It was going to be all over for everybody.

CALLAHAN: But there was always a question of when and if.

COLBERT: Yeah, especially if. But now, when the video comes out, he's just going to break down doors.

[The video was *Strange Desires*, a study of the life and times of Pottz, shot by Jeff Hornbaker for Gotcha, his sponsors.]

CALLAHAN: He has an unusually high charisma level.

COLBERT: He's certainly a lot more marketable than Damien Hardman.

CALLAHAN: Or Barton Lynch, for that matter.

AM: Barton's a good guy.

CALLAHAN: Nothing against him. But he doesn't excite anyone. You wouldn't mind if he married your daughter, but you wouldn't want to put him on the front page.

COLBERT: Yeah, you wouldn't take Pottz home to dad.

21

A PROPHET almost without honour in his own country, Martin Potter is a national celebrity in Australia. Based in Whale Beach in Sydney, he has featured in (Australian) *Penthouse* and *Playboy* and been named among the country's fifty most eligible bachelors. A television sports presenter once said he makes Rambo look like a wimp, while legend has it that even Mel Gibson envies the Pottz physique.

He has the classic surfer's build: shoulders like an American footballer, legs like a ballerina. With his deep-set eyes, Desperate Dan chin and uncombed quasi-Rasta locks, he is the photographer's dream: not beautiful but brooding, his deep shadows and craggy contours flattering the lens. He was the first man in nearly twenty years to have a full-face mug-shot on the cover of *Surfer*.

Recent champions have projected a clean, wholesome image. Pottz marks a reversion to unreconstructed virility symbol. Ever since the days when Hawaiian nobles played out tribal and sexual politics in the ocean, surfers have been the beneficiaries of a semiotic hyperinflation conferring the virtues of naturalness, freedom, potency, on the simple juxta-position of a man and a board and a wave. Perhaps I was in thrall to an illusion, but to me Pottz looked natural, free, and potent.

He reckoned he had picked the wrong waves at the Hard Rock at Sunset, and was worn down by the sheer hard labour of surfing so long in such arduous conditions. But he was impatient for Pipeline.

Pipeline is a hollow left-hander which, with its right-handed twin brother, Backdoor Pipeline, turns into a double-barrelled shotgun of a wave that blasts its victims over a shallow, razor-sharp reef. Pipeline put more surfers in Kahuku Hospital than any other break. As Pottz said, 'Anyone who paddles out at big Pipe and says he's not scared is either lying or crazy.'

I'd heard North Shore *aficionados* reminiscing about the ten-point tube Pottz had caught here back in '82. That was the wave that earned him respect in Hawaii. It was his first Pipeline Masters. In the opening rounds the waves had been small, four to five feet. Now they were steep walls of water dropping like guillotines onto the reef. Potter felt his throat run dry. He was only sixteen. He wasn't ready to die.

In his quarter-final heat, he was surfing against four times world champion Mark Richards, another Australian, Rabbit Bartholomew, and Hawaiian Michael Ho. Each had caught his share of rides. Then a wave formed, the like of which had not been seen at Pipeline that winter. It was a full fifteen feet and the offshore wind was holding it up like a crystal tower. Potter made straight for the peak and plummeted down the perpendicular drop: the lip curled over him and he was inside the tube. At first it seemed big enough to drive a train through. Then he saw that his exit had begun to narrow. The mouth was closing and the roof was caving in. He crouched down and clung to the rail with his right hand and reached out with his left as if to punch a hole through the wall. As the wave started to collapse, the air it had sucked in, now compressed, was ejected in a single violent snort. Potter was blasted through the eye of the needle in a cloud of spray and the wave snapped shut behind him.

'It was one of those waves,' he recalled, 'that either make or break you. Pull it off and you're a hero, back out and you'll always be remembered as the guy who let the perfect wave go by.'

Mark Richards won the heat, with Ho and Potter tied for second. Ho and Pottz were sent out for a sudden-death surf-off. Pottz wiped out three waves in a row and crept back in with his tail between his legs.

Pottz felt he had 'paid his dues' on the North Shore. There is still a widespread superstition among surfers that, in accordance with ancient Hawaiian tradition, you have to make some sacrifice to placate the bloodthirsty gods of the ocean. And the sacrificial victim is yourself. Potter's bid for martyrdom came at twenty-five-foot Waimea in the winter of '86–7 when the early rounds of the Billabong Pro were held at the Bay. It was so big that some of the ASP surfers refused to go out. Pottz was pressured into taking off because he'd waited too long. 'As soon as I stood up I knew it was going to be bad. I ended up going over the falls and being held under for a long time, and thinking there was no way I was going to come up before the next wave came across. A one-wave wipeout I can handle, but two waves, that's when it starts to get marginal.'

As a wipeout specialist myself, I could see him being torn apart by the turbulence, I could feel his bursting lungs and taste the fear of blacking out. When I get 'taken out to lunch' I'm in a state of shock for a week. On the North Shore, surfers consider it a matter of pride to go straight back out and reassert their dominance and exorcise their demons.

'That was the worst wipeout ever', Callahan said. '*Surfing* ran two pages on it. A special on the wipeout of the year.'

'I got pretty badly worked. But the way I look at it, if you can't have a spectacular manoeuvre, have a spectacular wipeout – it's good for the public.'

Pottz was confident of taking the world title, but less sure about the Triple Crown. 'That would be a dream come true. But the Pipeline and the Billabong are probably the hardest events there are. Hawaii's different. If you want to be anyone or get anywhere, you've got to go for it here.'

Callahan took his shots while Colbert and Stephanie sketched out designs for next year's Pottz Australia wetsuits. Then we left. Callahan was impressed by Stephanie. 'What has Colbert got to get girls like Stephanie?' Without waiting for an answer he said, 'I'll tell you what he's got. Brashness. Either that or a dong the size of a surfboard.'

22

'*I'M NOT* asking for preferential treatment. Only for what I deserve.'

Most surfers were worrying about whether there would be a swell or not. Ted Deerhurst was still worrying over whether, assuming there were a swell, he was going to be given a shot. I went to visit him in his room at Crazy Joe's Plantation Village on the north end of Waimea Bay. He was living on the wrong side of the highway. His room was no bigger than Fat Eric's, but the people in the house were friendlier, slimmer, and didn't boast of spinal surgery.

Ted was beginning to feel everyone was against him. 'I was in the British amateur team for three years – which Pottz never was. I never came worse than third. And yet I haven't had one penny of sponsorship out of Britain.' Nor had he ever been offered a wild card at the Hot Tuna in Newquay, the only World Tour contest to be held in the UK.

He had been based in England up to the age of twenty-two before going abroad to earn his living as a surfer. It grated with him when people insinuated he wasn't really British. 'I've never been anything but British and proud of it. Look at the book I'm reading.' It was Winston Churchill's *Memoirs of the Second World War*. 'It's only the condensed version – not the six-volume job.' You got the impression he would have liked to have brought all six volumes with him if he could. Ted was the only surfer I knew who read history between heats. In fact he was the only surfer I knew who read – at least, anything other than surfing magazines.

On the floor of his room Ted was masterminding the fate of Europe. He was re-enacting the Battle of the Bulge. 'The way I see it,' he said, strategically deploying troops and artillery around a wall-to-wall map, 'with a little more armour the Germans could be really kicking ass.' He was also planning Operation Sea Lion – the German invasion of south-east England. 'With better air support they could have got across. Of course, we'd have pushed them right out again. It didn't matter what our defences were like. It was a question of attitude.'

Ted thought we'd have made short work of a mere hundred thousand Hun. 'Churchill knew a thing or two about the British. He said that when everything was easy we were hopeless. But when we had our backs against the wall . . . '

Ted was a child of the sixties, but he sounded as if he'd been born in the Blitz. He'd been brought up on a steady diet of blood, sweat and tears and Douglas Bader. The first music he ever heard was *The Dam Busters*. 'Churchill and I have a lot in common – we both have American mothers.'

His mother was crucial in forming Ted's outlook on life. 'My father taught me the value of manners and being a gentleman. But my mother taught me never to give up.' When he was only seven, his horse threw him and hammered him with his hooves. His mother put him straight back in the saddle. 'I guess I've been getting back on that horse ever since.'

On the other side of the road lived another Brit I'd met in France. The house overlooked Off-the-Wall, the break next door to Backdoor. In fact, the wall Off-the-Wall was 'off' was *its* wall. Carwyn Williams was sitting out on the balcony watching the waves. The swell was picking up and the wind turning around. 'I love it here. Look at those down-the-line barrels. Very roomy. It's the shallow reef that produces the hollowness, see.'

He was from Mumbles on the Gower Peninsula and had retained his melodious Welsh accent. He was twenty-four – Martin Potter's age. He had a reputation for brilliance and inconsistency. He was a nice guy and a poor competitor. Now it was the end of a disappointing Tour, he was somewhere around the 50 mark in the rankings, running out of money, and talking about going home. He hadn't done well at Sunset, and was planning to pass on the Billabong.

The high point of his year had been winning an 'expression session' (an out-of-competition contest) in Japan. For his winner's speech he sang the opening lines of *My Way*. The low point was sitting out the European contests with a broken arm. In his pre-sponsorship days he used to be known as 'the surfer who lived in a car'; in France he had a tent on the beach.

Carwyn looked on Off-the-Wall as virtually his home break. 'There's only one wave every ten minutes that's perfect. But if you catch that perfect one ... Last Thursday I caught a classic A-frame triangle and bopped straight into the biggest barrel. The size of a house.'

I hadn't caught too many tubes myself so I asked him what it was like in there. 'It's like a tunnel. Sometimes it bends a bit and you can't see out. You're completely locked in. Then you turn the corner and you're out again. It's heart-stopping. I don't breathe. You have to rely on your instincts to pull you through. Go too high and you've had it. Go too low and you've had it as well. You've got to stay in the sweet spot. You use the compressed air to pull you along. It's like a turbo. The sun shines through. It emphasizes everything around you. They say time slows down in the barrel. It does. It can be the noisiest thing – like a building crashing down right next to you.'

One of his worst experiences had been at Sunset just a few days before. 'I had fifteen feet of water land on top of me.

You've got to relax in that situation. I know that. I was relaxing for a long time. I was relaxed. Then I was nearly panicking. Then I was panicking. I was struggling and I wasn't going anywhere. I wasn't coming up. Then I was up for a second – and the next wave hit me.'

Eventually he limped into the channel, recovered his breath, and went back for more. 'You've got to paddle out again after a bad experience. Unless you can't.'

Carwyn pointed out Pipeline, less than a hundred yards away. 'Fifteen-foot Pipe – it took me a long time to psych myself up to it. But the waves were fantastic. I'll never forget any of them. So steep, so fast. When you take off you're weightless. Sometimes you lose touch with your board. Sometimes your board loses touch with the wave. It's like going into a ninety-mile-an-hour spin on a cliff road in a Ferrari – and still not dying.'

Carwyn desperately wanted to come through a few heats of the Pipeline Masters. 'There's no other wave like it: when you surf Pipe, you've got to be ready. Your body's got to be in harmony with your brain.'

'So are you ready?'

'It still scares the shit out of me. Last year, my board hit me underwater. It wouldn't stop hitting me. My fins hit me in the chest. I had blood coming out of my tits. My whole body was in pain.'

He paused to relive the sensation. 'It felt good, though.'

Carwyn was a homesick nomad. After Pipeline, he was thinking of catching a plane back to Wales. He had missed three Christmases in a row. The year before he'd had scrambled eggs for Christmas dinner and no presents. He even cried. Carwyn seemed like a castaway on a desert island. He gave me an orange card that advertised his status as PROFESSIONAL SURFER, but he was still a child at heart and surfing was still a game. He wasn't going in for the Eddie. 'That stuff's not for me. You just want to tuck the board under your arm, run down the beach, paddle out and have fun. And if it's big and scarey, you still have fun. But that – that's not fun – that's death. If you fall off, you drown.'

Carwyn recalled an occasion when he was fast asleep in his ground-floor bedroom, dreaming about a great wave coming straight towards him. He woke up, and lo and behold, a great wave *was* coming straight towards him. 'It came right in through the window. Dumped a ton of sand on the floor.' There had been a wooden bench in the garden outside. 'A big fat wooden bench – really heavy. Never saw it again.'

On my way back to Sunset I stopped at the press trailer. The line-up for the Pipeline Masters had been posted. Ted was down as eighth alternate in the heats.

23

TED AND Callahan and I had agreed to meet at Jocko's at 8.30 in the morning. When I got there they were already out on the beach sizing up the surf.

'Killer board, dude', said Callahan.

I was carrying my brand new Willis Phazer under my arm. It was an eight-foot rocket spraygunned in swirling blue and yellow and stamped with the sign of the atom. Ted admired it too.

'I guess you won't be needing the old Excalibur any more', he said sadly.

I anointed its curves with wax. 'Race you to the line-up', I said. On that immaculate morning, I felt as if I could do no wrong. This would be the day that I finally cracked the North Shore.

Sure enough, the channel was as smooth as silk. I cut effortlessly through the water with Ted and Callahan tagging along at my heels. The waves were whipped up like ice-cream and frothing like champagne and there was no one else out. Maybe it was too early for the crowd. We would have first bite at the cake: ours would be the first footprints in the snow.

We came up behind the break and manoeuvred into position and sat on our boards. I knew no fear. It was as if what had happened at Jocko's and Haleiwa and Freddie's was all a bad dream.

'Do you think we should let this guy go first?' said Ted.

'If he's ready', said Callahan. 'Are you ready, Andy?'

'I'm ready', I said.

A set showed. I span my Phazer round, the wave lifted me up towards God, and I rose to my feet. I wafted down the face and traced out an elegant arc with my bottom turn, squirting a fountain of spume from my rail as I flew back up and pirouetted on the lip. Now I had the hang of it, I racked up a handful of top to bottoms with plenty of vertical. When I pulled out Callahan and Ted were waiting for me. They must have caught the next wave.

'Jesus, Andy,' said Callahan, 'I didn't know you could surf like that.'

'Neither did I', I said.

'Keep surfing like that,' Ted said, 'and you'll be ready for a shot at the title soon.'

I raced back to the line-up and picked off a few more waves. I was a gambler on a winning streak: it didn't matter what number I placed my bet on, it always came up a winner.

A bigger set broke on the outside and we dived under it, then paddled out to get beyond the break. Still another set broke on the outside so we kept on going out. Now we were almost a mile from shore. On the horizon, to the south, beyond Kaena Point, I could see what looked like a shadow or a cloud. We paddled out another hundred yards just as a precaution. Our strokes, at first casual, became faster, then frenzied. The horizon had jumped up to where the sky used to be. Coming straight at us was the biggest wave since Krakatoa. Callahan had turned the colour of flour with all the wheatgerm kicked out of it. Ted looked as if he was about to be personally bombarded by a squadron of Messerschmitts. We were too far out now to risk heading in: we were bound to be caught smack in the impact zone. We barely had time to exchange a glance – a glance which said despair, courage, delirium – before pointing our noses at infinity and pulling for dear life.

We were nearly a mile and a quarter out, the set was another quarter away from us, and already it was fleecy at the top, throwing up spray a hundred yards in the air. I put my head down and kept stroking. It seemed to take forever to get up that face, like climbing the rungs of Jacob's ladder. When at last I broke through the lip and parachuted into the void beyond I turned my head and looked behind. The wave had had its ropes cut and was erupting in an avalanche of fury that would bury everything in its path. Of Ted and Callahan there was no sign. I wondered if I would ever see them again and silently said goodbye.

The second wave was fifty yards away and bigger than the first. But it was only when I punched through the thick, creamy crest and the rainbow mist cleared from my eyes that I finally gave up all hope. Right in front of me was the Absolute, the *ens perfectissimum*, a metaphysical colossus that had strayed into reality. It towered so far above me I couldn't even see the top of it. There was nothing left in the world but this vertiginous wave. I had a chillingly clear picture of its abominable face: it had so many wrinkles and boils it looked as if it had lived for centuries. And now it was looking for a graveyard. As I came up out of the trough, the wave was pouting out a lip like the deck of an aircraft carrier.

It started to suck me up the face. As I looked down a tube as empty as Outer Space, I pushed away from my board and dove for the bottom. But there was no bottom: it was like going through the Star Gate, with whole galaxies reeling by me. The concussion of the exploding wave drove me down like a steam hammer. There was darkness below me; above me, yet more darkness. I could no longer tell which way was up and which way was down. I was drowning and it didn't hurt. I felt a momentary regret for all the waves I would never ride, when I had only just learned how. Then I died. Death was warm and embracing like porridge. I saw an infinite and never-ending wave: whether it was heaven or hell I knew not.

It was nearly eight when I woke up. I pulled on my shorts, sank half a pint of yoghurt, and grabbed my crippled Excalibur. By 9.15 Callahan and Ted still hadn't showed at Jocko's, and I'd forgotten my webbed gloves. I couldn't go surfing without my gloves. I turned the car round and headed home. Maybe I'd drop by Michael's place and see how my Phazer was coming along.

24

ON THE morning of Sunday, 18 December, exactly one week after the Great North struck, Pipeline came back from the dead. The beach was swarming with photographers. Surfers were waxing down their boards. The Marui Pipeline Masters was on.

This was my first Pipe. I had come to Mecca and now I was seeing God. And I was sitting at his right hand. For this was the extraordinary thing about Pipeline. It wasn't just a sheer and hollow left-hander: it reared up and rolled over right in front of your eyes. Even when you were on the beach it seemed to land in your lap. Sunset had been grand but remote, like listening to a radio signal from some distant country with only a weak transmitter: when a surfer caught a wave or came to grief, you had to filter out a lot of static and strain to follow what was happening. At Pipeline, you could see the whites of his eyes, you were out there with him, in the tube, on the reef, feeling the adrenalin rush, getting your teeth kicked in.

Backdoor was breaking too, a mirror-image of its sinister partner, a back-to-front *doppelgänger*. While the left-hander twisted and turned up towards Ehukai Beach Park, the right-hander spiralled away in the direction of Off-the-Wall. 'Look at this guy', said Callahan, peering through the viewfinder of his yard-long lens, targeted on the snarling peak like a sniper's rifle. 'He's getting barrelled out of his mind.'

It was at Thurso in Scotland that I'd first seen surfers riding tubes. They would take a lazy bottom turn, stall as they climbed up the wave, then disappear behind the curtain for a second or two, reappearing like actors at the end of a play to take a bow. That was in a bay overlooked by a ruined castle straight out of *Macbeth*. The tubes at Pipe were bigger, meaner, longer, bluer, warmer. When someone went into one, you had time to go and buy an ice-cream before they came out again. If they came out.

To pass unscathed into the inner sanctum of the wave is the categorical imperative of surfing. Every surfer who is swallowed up by one of the blue-ribbed behemoths of Pipeline re-enacts the legend of Jonah and the Whale. Many myths of the hero retrace a common narrative: a sea journey; battle with a monster; descent into the belly of the beast; and, finally, triumphant re-emergence into the light of day. A Polynesian folktale tells of Rata, who travelled across the ocean and ingeniously outwitted a hungry whale by jamming open its jaws with a broken oar; venturing in through the mouth he came face to face with his parents who had been gulped down before him. So too the yawning depths of the wave, even while threatening annihilation, hold out the promise of rebirth. A poem by Hölderlin, 'Patmos', puts it succinctly: 'Where danger is, there/Arises salvation also.'

Until recently, Pipeline was thought to be unrideable. The wave was *kapu*, as the Hawaiians said, a forbidden zone you visited at the cost of your life. It was a holy virgin: untouchable. The first men known to have flouted the taboo were Bob Sheppard and Bill Coleman from California, in 1957. For their sins, they were both nailed and all but crucified on the reef. Fred Van Dyke, a pioneer of the North Shore breaks, recalls a time in the late fifties when he and Pat Curren (Tom Curren's father) were sitting on the beach at Banzai and Pat said, 'Maybe in two thousand years this place will be surfed.'

But the sixties were a time for breaking rules, transgressing limits. Rumours began to circulate that Banzai had been conquered. The first photographic record dates from December 1961, when film-maker Bruce Brown shot Phil Edwards – considered by many at the time to be the best surfer in the world – on a six- to eight-foot west swell. 'We always wondered,' Edwards said, 'could you get in and make the drop? That was the question. It was so fast. We knew if you could catch it, it'd be a great wave.' Edwards caught it, rode it, and emerged intact. It was on that day that 'Pipeline' was added to the name Banzai. Edwards's trailblazing feat opened the way to others: by the time he'd strapped his board on the roofrack of his car, he claimed, three other men were already out. He was known as the 'Columbus of Pipeline'.

What stopped people surfing Pipeline was only in part the wave itself – not so much perpendicular as concave, bent over like the hook of a question mark or a twitching scorpion's tail. It was largely the prospect of what lay just beneath the surface: the coral reef. This was what made Pipeline a killer. Pipeline could suck the coral dry and dump a solid fifteen-foot wave on it. You could crack your skull on that intractable stone, or it could scoop out spoonfuls of flesh. On calm days people dived to inspect the bottom contours. They returned, like astronauts from the moon, with stories of immense craters and chasms. What everyone feared was getting slammed into one of the Pipeline cavities like a golfball into a hole and not being able to get out again.

Mark Cunningham, who was lifeguard for the Masters and regularly bodysurfed big Pipe, was offhand about the danger. 'It's all mystique', he said. 'It's like a parking lot out there, rolled smooth by rocks and wave action.'

I began to regret I didn't have a board with me. I mentioned I was doing a bit of surfing myself. Mark looked at me with wild surmise and then spoke in capitals: 'THE NORTH SHORE IS TWELVE VIOLENT MILES OF SURF. And Pipeline is the most violent of the lot. I lose count of the fatalities. Last winter I fished a kid from Santa Monica out of the water. Before that it was a local. This place kills and maims more than any other. I'm just surprised the toll isn't higher.'

Just as well I didn't have my board after all. I didn't want to wind up permanently parked on the Pipeline reef.

25

TED'S POSITION as eighth alternate meant that eight men who had qualified for the heats would have to drop out before he was summoned. He wouldn't know he was on till he was on. He clued me in to some strategy. 'Out of every five or six guys going for the wave, three are bluffing.' Just then the Tannoy cleared its throat and made an announcement. 'Ted Deerhurst – pick up your competition singlet from the beach marshal.'

Ted jerked up like a man who'd been zapped with a thousand volts. He scrambled to his feet, hesitated for a moment, then clasped his 7 ft 3 in Excalibur to his bosom. 'You and me', he said to it lovingly.

'Any last words?' I said.

'Right now, I don't want to talk, I just want to surf.'

Ted marched away into the competitors' zone, the glint of battle in his eye. Kristin and Sabine were sitting on the beach. Kristin said, 'The Excalibur man is in this? I don't believe it.'

Barton Lynch, sitting out the qualifying rounds and waiting for the main event, recalled the 1988 Billabong, which for the first time had been held at Pipeline. Something of an intellectual among surfers, Lynch has a weekly column in a Sydney newspaper and an air of philosophical detachment.

For years, the ASP bureaucracy had annexed the closing stages of the annual circuit for Australia. But there had long been a feeling that Hawaii, birthplace of surfing and home of the biggest waves, should have that honour by right. In 1988, after a decade of wrangling, the surfing year would finally culminate with the Hawaiian Triple Crown.

But that winter was a dismal season on the North Shore. People were cursing the Greenhouse Effect and swearing that it had put paid to surf in Hawaii for all time. The pre-season dispute over which contest – the Eddie Aikau or the Triple Crown – would have priority if the surf topped twenty feet at Waimea seemed about as relevant as an argument over how many angels you could fit on a pinhead. Randy Rarick had once said that 'to be declared world champion after a two-foot day at Manly just wasn't significant.' But it looked as if the title might yet be decided on the flip of a Manly-sized wave after all. The reputation of Hawaii was at stake.

At last, on 2 January 1989, only forty-eight hours before the waiting period was scheduled to expire, the rollers returned, rising up like submarines out of a smooth blue sea and snapping shut like mousetraps. The Billabong had been saved at the eleventh hour. Everything hung on this final event of the year. The world title was still a three-horse race between defending champion Damien Hardman, Tom Carroll, and Barton Lynch.

Barton was the only one of the three to make it as far as the quarters, but he still had to come through another two heats to overhaul Hardman's tally of points. His semi-final against fellow Australian Glen Winton – known as 'Mr X' for his unpredictability – would be the crunch. This was the moment Lynch had been building for all his life. He was riding a stick shaped by George Downing on the pattern of an old balsa board George had crafted thirty years earlier. He had hired George's son, Keone Downing, as his coach in Hawaii. He had even bought a house up the road from Sunset.

He dropped into the spinning vacuums of Pipeline with apparent nonchalance. 'Looks like he's on Valium', cracked one photographer. The issue was settled when Winton dived into a black hole and didn't come out again. Barton had clinched the world title – his subsequent victory in the Billabong was almost a formality.

He was eerily coherent afterwards. 'I think it'd be fair to say this is the best day of my life.' There was a risk everything else might seem an anti-climax, a series of footnotes. 'If I had written a script for myself I wouldn't have changed a thing', he said. Winning the title and the Billabong at the last minute on the most cut-throat wave in the world – that was the perfect ending. But what could you do for an encore?

In his own way, Ted had been building for this moment too. He didn't have a house here, he didn't have a coach, he'd shaped his own board. It wasn't the final. But he'd been practising his backhand all year, mentally preparing himself for the North Shore. Lynch was a goofy so he surfed Pipeline with his eye on the wave. Ted was a natural, so unless he managed to find a right-hander to take him through the Backdoor, he was always looking over his shoulder.

Callahan was still in bed: he didn't bother with trialists. I rustled up a friendly Australian to take a shot of Ted in action. As luck would have it, the light wasn't good enough and the shots didn't come out.

Ted was wearing a fluorescent green competition vest. You couldn't miss him. It was a six-man heat, so there was plenty of scope for the wily strategist. A couple of surfers caught waves Ted didn't even move for. He probably thought they were bluffing. Then a wave came through that was earmarked for him. He stroked firmly, looked over his right shoulder, stroked some more, looked over his left, then he was reversing up the stomach-churning Pipeline elevator. He made a clean take-off, skidded down the face, and tracked the wave into the hazardous zone known as the 'Bermuda triangle', somer-saulting as his board stalled on the sandbank.

Some of Ted's opponents were finding the Backdoor. But Ted stuck with the left-handers. His next two waves were close-outs. On the first he could only straighten out to stay ahead of the whitewater; on the second he bailed out as the roof caved in. A mile out to sea Outside Pipeline was breaking. The swell was still coming up.

Ted hadn't set Pipeline alight, but he had acquitted himself honourably. In ASP contests you are allowed a maximum of ten waves in any one heat, but are scored on four (in finals it is five out of fifteen). When the siren signalled the end of the twenty-minute period, Ted had only three waves under his belt. But on my reckoning most of the others had fewer, and none better than his first.

'One good wave and two close-outs should get me to advance.' I agreed with Ted. He only needed to make third to go through to the next round. We sat on the sand and waited for the placings to come over the Tannoy. When the names and numbers were read out it was a long while before we heard the name of Deerhurst. He was given sixth.

'I won't ever quit!' he said.

Ted wasn't the only casualty at Pipeline. But Carwyn Williams at least had the consolation of winning the Wipeout of the Day Award. On his second wave he took a steep drop and his nose dug in. He came briefly back from the dead a few minutes later, pulling into a Backdoor tube and getting fried on the reef.

I didn't see Ted for a while after that. When I finally caught up with him at Crazy Joe's Plantation Village, he was in a resigned mood. He was playing the mouth organ, a plaintive lament which seemed to say 'I've got those didn't-get-through-my-qualifying-rounds-again blues.' I denounced the judges who only gave him two (out of ten) for his best wave, but he said, 'It was fair. I should have caught some more waves so they couldn't underscore me. They're used to perceiving old Ted as a loser.'

He was searching for something positive in the experience. 'Going out there on a new board and catching my first wave when I hadn't surfed Pipeline for a year only reaffirms my confidence.'

Technically, there was nothing wrong with his surfing. But he was choking when he should be charging. He had lost so many times, he had forgotten what it was like to win. He had to start thinking of himself as a winner again. He had put away his Churchill and was reading a new book. I looked at the title. It was *How to Increase Your Self-Esteem*.

26

*T*ED COULD only enlist the spirit of Churchill to his cause.
Richie Collins had an unfair advantage: he had the Holy
Ghost on his side.

I'd run into Richie twice in France. Twice he had come
second to Martin Potter, once at Lacanau and again at Biarritz.
He achieved notoriety in the first final by turning up ten
minutes late for the start. His excuse was that he had been
praying. He was still praying when he got in the water. While
Pottz tacked to and fro energetically seeking out the elusive
peak, Richie dropped anchor and contemplated the horizon.
While Pottz came to the mountain, Richie waited for the
mountain to come to him. He adopted the same tactic in
Biarritz, with the same result. I asked him if after his second
second to Pottz he didn't feel history was repeating itself. 'No,'
he said with a grin, 'today I turned up on time.'

He hadn't been joking or speaking metaphorically when he
talked about praying. He was actually addressing God when
he should have been in the water. He reminded me of this as
we sat on the beach watching Ted and Carwyn having their
hopes dashed on the Pipeline reef. 'God said to me, "Richie,
you're going to be late for your contest, it's on now". And I
said to the Lord, in my pride, "No, it's okay Lord, it's not for
another twenty minutes".' He said he had learned his lesson
at Lacanau: God was the better time-keeper.

But God was more than a heavenly speaking clock to Richie.
He was a friend, a confidant, an adviser, a business manager,
a collaborator. God was to Richie what Peter Colbert was to
Pottz. But He had at least one advantage over Colbert. He
could look after His protégé in the water as well as on dry
land. He could serve up waves in the right place at the right
time — or not. 'I pray to the Lord to bless me with a good

wave.' That's why Richie was in no hurry in Lacanau. He was waiting on God's will. 'Jesus told me to go to France. He said, "Richie, you can be a good witness on the Tour. You can save people".'

At Biarritz, he again failed to heed advice from above. 'I knew I needed a good right to win. And a right came. Potter paddled for it and could have made it. I paddled for it and caught it. I was going for my usual roundhouse and the Lord said, "Don't finish that roundhouse." But I finished it anyhow. And I came right off the wave.'

His best result in 1989 was winning the Ocean Pacific Pro at Huntington Beach, California, the most high-profile event on the mainland. 'But I'm not going to get a big head about it or anything. Everyone knows it's the most important contest on the Tour. Everyone knows about you if you win it.' That victory was all thanks to God. 'I wouldn't have won the OP without Him. I said, "Thank you so much for letting me win". You look on Him as a father telling you what to do.'

Richie Collins faced the same theoretical conundrum that affected Michael Chang when he congratulated God on helping him to win a tennis match. Did he think the devil was on the other side of the net? Why hadn't Tom Curren won the OP Pro? He was a good Christian, too, wasn't he? 'Yes, but I'm a better *witness* than Curren on the stand. He probably wasn't following God the way I was.' Richie thought everything was a test of worthiness. He was always on trial in some celestial courtroom.

Richie Collins was twenty, with short curly hair, a wispy chin beard, and long beanpole legs. In France teenage girls would squeal at his floaters. Sometimes he went semi-shaven-headed and looked like a monk. His father was a California shaper and Richie was one of the few top ASP surfers who shaped his own boards. His logo was 'Wave Tools'. He favoured swallow-tails. 'I tried bobs and square-tails. I don't like 'em.' Like Ted, he had created a whole new quiver of boards specifically for Hawaii, and he too was planning to use a 7 ft 3 in at Pipe. Unlike Ted, he had risen rapidly up the ranks, was voted Rookie of the Year in 1987, made it into the

Top 16 at the end of '88, and was tipped to become a challenger for the world title.

His recent history — which sounded as remote when he spoke of it as a previous incarnation — had enacted a traditional surfing scenario he wasn't particularly proud of. 'I went totally over the limit. Me, myself, and I.' After losing in the Gotcha Pro early that summer on the South Side of Oahu, he went off on a self-destructive bender. 'I went completely nuts. I was literally breaking things over my head. I'd been wanting to break a board over my head for a long while. So finally I did. I knocked myself out.' But everything changed for him on 12 June 1989 when he eventually came to. 'The Lord said, "You're coming home". He took me back to the past and showed me the future. I said, I don't want that to happen. I just asked Him to have grace and mercy on me. So I dedicated myself to God. No going after girls, no going off on drugs. I strive to live like the Lord Jesus on earth.' He wasn't perfect, though. 'I still freak out and go off and do things', he added enigmatically.

I didn't have to ask Richie any probing questions. He was probing himself for me. He was writing his autobiography in his head. He had been coming to Hawaii since he was thirteen and competing since he was seventeen. But he'd never done well there. This year he went out in his first heat at the Hard Rock. 'I got skunked at Sunset', he said. 'The Lord said to me the day before, "You're not going to make it out of your heat tomorrow". The Lord puts you through these trials.'

He confided that Hawaii was the most difficult place in the world for him. He had a fear of heights and was claustrophobic, so he hated being held under. 'A lot of people like to get worked because it knocks the fear out of them. With me, it only makes things worse.' Richie's worst experience at Sunset was also in a way his best. It was ten to fifteen feet, it was getting dark, he had lost his board, and he couldn't get in and he couldn't get out. He thought he was going to die. 'I started crying. And I called out, "Lord, have mercy on me". And I looked up and the sea had gone calm. And I swam straight in. The Lord has complete control over the sea.'

Richie had no time for Hawaiian polytheism. 'There's no ocean god, there's no tree god, there's just One God – He takes care of everything.' He wasn't really watching Pipeline any more. Behind his Oakley sunglasses his eyes were focused on the inner drama of his own existence. 'I give most of the prize money I earn to the Church. I say to God, "Here's my pay cheque, Lord, you want the whole thing?" And sometimes the Lord will say to me, "Richie, you need that money more than I do. You need it to pay the rent. You keep it".' God was with him every day, worrying over the smallest details of his life. 'I went to look for a new car and the Lord said to me, "Richie, you buy this car. I know you're going to like it. This is the right car for you".' God moved in mysterious ways – to Richie he manifested himself as an extremely successful car salesman.

Richie was afraid I was going to do a hatchet job on him. 'Why is everyone always picking on us Christians? We're always getting drilled on TV. That must mean we're right. All the atheists know there is a God.' He asked me not to misquote him. I promised I wouldn't. 'I get misinterpreted. The last magazine article came out on me, I had a lot of Christians writing to tell me I had it all wrong. I still don't live up to my standards. Because they're perfect. They're God's standards. All I can do is try to live up to them – try to be like God.'

The King James translation of the Book of Genesis renders the first line as *In the beginning God created the heaven and the earth*, confident that prior to God there was nothing, that Yahweh created the universe *ex nihilo*. But the phrase beginning *bereshith* in the ambiguous Hebrew might equally well be read as *In a beginning*, or *In the beginning of creating the heaven and the earth* ... On this second interpretation, Yahweh summons order out of a pre-existing primeval soup: *when the earth was without form, and void; and darkness was upon the face of the deep*. Some translators of the Bible have gone so far as to postpone the main verb until the divine fiat: *And God said, Let there be light*. But it may be that God's primordial action occurs in the previous verse: *And the spirit of God moved upon the face of the waters*. This line carries two compelling implications. On the one hand, God is a wind (*pneuma theos* in the Septuagint) stirring the ocean into life, and the rest of Creation flows from the movement of the waters. On the other, simultaneously, He moves across the surface of the sea: upon the face, riding the waves even as He creates them, surfing the world into existence. A bottom turn: the spray turned into birds. An off-the-lip carved out the Himalayas. One great cutback: and there was Africa. Out of the spinning vortex of a tube came Adam and Eve. Paradise was a riverbreak in Mesopotamia. There was a theory that the Ten Lost Tribes of Israel begat the Polynesians and, hence, the Hawaiians. The gospel of surfing was not far removed from the Old Testament account of Creation: *In the beginning was the wave*: God was both shaper and surfer.

Small wonder then that surfing was Richie Collins's way of trying to be like God. And he wasn't the only one. It seemed to me that all surfers aspired to the condition of divinity. They all wanted to be mightier than the mightiest waves. I knew that during those brief immortal moments when I was standing up on the board, walking on water, I too felt like a supreme being, until the ocean cast me down again and turned me once more into a creeping thing that creepeth upon the face of the earth. Richie had picked up an almost invisible speck and said, 'I'm just this tiny grain of sand.' That's how I felt too, being tossed about at the behest of the currents and waves.

Eventually Callahan turned up. He was complaining of an aching neck and rubbing it gingerly. 'Damn girl', he said. 'Got my head in a leg-lock and wouldn't let go. Whiplash, that's what I've got. Whiplash.' Callahan liked the sound of the word *whiplash*. It could have kept him going for hours.

I told him I'd been talking to Richie. He thought Richie was a great surfer but a poor human being. 'He's inhaled too much resin – sends you crazy after a while.' He paused. 'I guess that's what makes surfing so interesting. You have all these weirdos.'

27

*D*ON KING gave a party during the Pipeline Masters to celebrate the completion of his house on Ke Iki Beach. The house was like Don himself: tall, imposing, tranquil. It used only natural materials: wood and stone and glass. I had seen Don sloping about the beach, still not satisfied with the surf, not enough to swim out and take shots, anyway. He was just as fussy on the North Shore as he had been in France. Callahan said Don was more interested in the waves than the surfers. Some of his best shots were of unridden waves. One of the most famous enabled you to look right down a spitting Pipeline barrel through the snake's eye at the far end towards the mountains in the distance.

I left Kristin and Sabine in the garden talking to the body-boarding champion of the world and went down to the beach. The moon lit up the roof of the breaking waves. It was a cool night and someone had made a bonfire on the sand. Betinna and Liese were sitting by it, their faces half shadowed in darkness, half aglow from the flames. Liese was Bodo van der Leeden's wife, Betinna was her daughter. I sat down with them. You could hear the gentle strumming of two guitars from the house.

Liese was a still point in a giddy universe. She had fled Europe two decades before and qualified in Chinese medicine in Hawaii, spending seven years of her life in a monastery, absorbing the lessons of the Tao, science, philosophy, astrology, and martial arts. She told me that 'Ke Iki' meant 'Struggle little'.

I considered this. 'Does that mean it's a good beginner's break?'

Liese laughed. 'No, it means that once you're caught in those waves you might as well give up.'

I hadn't heard of anyone surfing Ke Iki. They didn't, Liese said. People just drowned there. Once, four girls were collecting shells when a big swell came in and swept them away. Another time, a photographer had ventured onto the reef that rose up from the sea at the far corner. He stood mesmerized by a giant wave, shooting picture after picture until it came right over and dragged him out. Liese made the ocean sound like a hungry beast that demanded to be fed with human flesh. I was still nursing my Freddieland injuries, and the way she was looking at me with her unflinching gaze gave me a queasy feeling I'd only narrowly avoided providing lunch.

Surfing Hawaii was like being in the Blitz, and it may have been the thought of death that made me think of love. Or perhaps it was the combination of moon, surf, and acoustic guitars. Like everyone else, I'd come to Hawaii for the waves, but some clandestine part of me had been plotting all along to make love on the beach beneath a palm tree. I had read too much Captain Cook. I knew how willing and sensuous Hawaiian *wahini* were. They flung themselves at sailors in a bid for immortality. I liked to imagine that the tradition of free love had never died.

According to Hiram Bingham in 1820, the Hawaiian Islands were 'waiting for the law of Christ'. In the following decades the missionaries stripped the Islanders of everything: their gods, their culture, their land, even their nakedness. It might have been better had they looted, pillaged, raped, and left. But they stayed to erase every vestige of paganism. The Hawaiian tongue was given a written form for the express purpose of translating the Bible. The East Coast Puritans refused to alter their garb or touch the native food. They rejected bananas and held on to buttoned coats. The One and Universal God should be mirrored, in their view, by a monolithic human culture, in which all worshipped, dressed, and ate alike.

Hawaiian society collapsed in the face of such ironclad convictions. Callahan's theory was that 'there was a need for something hard and rigid, no matter what. And that's what the missionaries were.' Hawaiians would henceforth cover their shame, refrain from exhibitions of public indecency on the beach, and put aside their boards. I had already come across a congratulatory account of this transformation in Jules Verne. On its whistle-stop tour of the Pacific his *Floating Island* – an Oahu with propellers – found Polynesian gentlemen in waistcoats and wing-collars instead of savages in feathers. His travellers appeared on the whole disappointed not to be cooked by cannibals.

Surfing was an integral part of traditional Island society: not just a sport, but a rite of passage, an initiation, an act of worship, a demonstration of power, and a form of courtship. One missionary, Sheldon Dibble, observed that surfing led to the loss of life and limb, the neglect of the land, gambling and starvation. 'But the greatest evil of all,' he complained, 'resulted from the constant intermingling, without any restraint, of persons of both sexes and all ages, at all times of the day and at all hours of the night.'

In the twentieth century surfing has been appropriated by the advertising industry and invested with enough sexual connotations to sell anything from soap powder to condoms. But it was from the beginning an erotic exercise. One legend taught that if a man and a woman caught the same wave they would be joined in physical union. Sharing the wave was a prelude and an incitement to copulation. Wavesliding, *he'enalu*, was to water what the *hula*, the dance of love, was to land. The modern obsession with the tube – that evanescent twist of the wave as it curls itself up into the form of a vagina to lure in unwary youths like bees into the mouths of flowers – perpetuates the equation of surfing and sex.

The *kapu* system of priestly prohibitions and sanctions had finally disintegrated in 1819, but new taboos rushed in to take the place of the old. In 1825, acting under missionary influence, a group of chiefs issued an edict exhorting people to give up their games and turn instead to Christian teachings. 'The decline and discontinuance of the use of the surfboard as civilization advances,' wrote Hiram Bingham, 'may be accounted for by the increase in modesty, industry and religion, without supposing as some have affected to believe, that missionaries have caused oppressive enactments against it.' There was no need to ban surfing outright. As the old ways were forgotten, it simply disappeared or went underground.

Certain nineteenth-century paintings – Manet's *On the Beach at Boulogne* and Degas's *At the Seaside* – obliquely reflect the colonization of Hawaii. In the Victorian era you wore exactly the same clothes on the beach as you wore in the city, with the simple addition of a parasol. Gauguin, in his evocations of life in Tahiti, was the first to show that there could be a completely different culture – more sensual, less strait-laced – more fitting to the beach. But in the South Pacific as in the North, that original idyll was fading away even as Gauguin paid tribute to it. His naked riders on the beach and bare-breasted women laden with flowers and fruit were nostalgic celebrations of a vanishing world.

Now, to a degree, the tables have been turned. Not only do we strip off at the beach, but we have brought the values of the beach inland. Beach culture, a third force wedged between town and country, imposing its own norms and practices, has spread across the globe from Hawaii like sand blowing in the wind. Grey city streets enlivened by boldly patterned boardshorts and shirts present a feeble parody of a lost paradise: fashion and tourism have together unmoored a raft of signifiers from their origins. Images of that immortal sea, of children sporting on the shore and the mighty waters rolling evermore, are not so much allusions to what brought us hither, as Wordsworth would have it, but reminders to book this year's holiday to the Costa del Sol or the Bahamas. But, since the heyday of the missionaries, the collective consciousness has nevertheless undergone a sea-change. And surfing is the most potent symbol – even stimulus – of that shift. Now that the sport was re-established in its place of origin, was it right to suppose a return to the pagan ways of unbridled pleasure and carnal gratification?

I had detected some promising signs. Women orbited about surfers on the beach; they clung to them in cars; they occupied their houses in loose liaisons. There was a myth that surfers were irresistible to women. It wasn't a myth: they were. I wasn't sure I qualified as a surfer yet, but I hoped I might benefit from this general disposition.

I never found any hula girls. There were no grass skirts, no bare breasts. There were even self-appointed morality patrols, recruited from the ranks of the born-again Christians, who would blow the whistle on indecency on the beach. But I was sitting on the sands of Ke Iki at midnight with a fairy-tale princess, a Botticelli Venus whose long blonde tresses reflected golden glints from the fire. I wanted to ride a wave with her. And the only trouble was, she'd brought her mother along as well.

Liese said, 'I'd better be going now. I expect Bodo is wondering where I am. You can stay, though, Betinna.'

'No, I'll come with you', she said. 'I don't want to be left here all alone.'

28

*D*OLLY SPELLED her name 'Dolle'. I met her sitting out on the bench where Michael Willis always sat, water-gazing. 'This is the best place in the world', she said. 'That ocean is the source of universal energy. It's our playground. The sea is our friend.' It hadn't been all that friendly to me, but I let that pass.

Dolle was a woman of all ages and none. Her voice had the pubescent innocence of a junior high school majorette. Her streaky blonde hair and skimpy bikini were those of a nineteen-year-old beach belle. When she fluttered the long lashes of her baby blue eyes she had the timeless charm of Olive Oyl or Betty Boop. But her deep tanned face had been lived in for a fistful of decades. She was a veteran nymphette who had been kicked out of Shangri-la for seducing the monks.

She occupied a tiny apartment hidden away beneath Betty's house, and she had a habit of materializing unexpectedly as if she'd sprung up through a trapdoor. 'Hi, Dolle', I'd say, hopping about with one leg in my trousers. She was the mother of Mike Latronic, a hot North Shore surfer who effortlessly outshone visiting pros. The surname, from her first husband, had been Polish, but she had adapted it to fit the modern age.

Dolle described herself as a dancer (she had worked in Las Vegas) and a traveller. She was a nomad who was finally taking root in Hawaii. It turned out she was a writer too. I was reckless enough to ask her what she'd written. She hauled me down to her lair to find out.

She showed me a pamphlet entitled *Gourmet Dining for Hot Place Living —with Tid Bits for the Essence of Life*. As far as I could tell from a quick skim through, every meal was designed to act as an aphrodisiac. She'd also written two or three books of poetry, although I didn't see them. But she was preparing a longer and more ambitious work, an imaginary autobiography called *The Boyfriends*.

The Boyfriends haunted my stay on the North Shore. The title was perfect. As it stood, it consisted of a multi-volume jumble of *vers libre*, written over many years, some in the form of letters, especially to her mother – 'if I sent her a letter she sent me some money – so I kept on writing' – listing the men she'd known. Dolle had spent her entire life obsessed with but ill-used by men. Men were to her what waves had become to me. The book was the story of her wipeouts. Now she wanted me to help her edit it into shape.

I looked at some of it. I'd expected to find a vacuous mess. But instead it was intermittently lyrical, funny, sad, and incisive; it was also sentimental, confused, and cliché-ridden. My advice to her was simple: cut the sentiment, leave in the sex. There would still be enough to make a good-sized book out of it.

I jotted down a few extracts from *The Boyfriends*:

There were plenty of men in big cars riding around
the neighbourhood, 'Come here little girl'

Fell in love with an Italian,
a punk Mafia dude
his tomato red convertible
and all his bull

Had the New York Yankee ball team
as my clientele

Occasionally she tried to rationalize what she was doing. It
never came off. I told her all the justifications and apologies
had to go. All she had to do was be more herself and less
what she thought she ought to be.

John Lennon filmed us for his movie, *Up your legs for Peace.*
I got an autographed dollar bill and Viral Hepatitis

I started bullying her. She had to be strict with herself: ruthless. But I was the one who was being ruthless. Confronted
with Dolle I felt myself becoming a punk mafia dude. I came
within an ace of slapping her around. She was all soft and
loose and self-indulgent. I told her she had to be hard, tight,
self-critical.

He says 'I love you more than anything in the world'
I believe him

Fortunately, it didn't have any effect. In the time I was
there she did pencil out a few passages, and got me to red ink
a lot more. She bribed me with pasta and blackmailed me
into writing a synopsis on my last night in Hawaii. But mainly
she kept on bodyboarding on the quieter waves between
Sunset and Backyards, going to parties, hanging out at the
Sugar Bar, and talking to her friends on the telephone.
Her techniques were not subtle but they were effective.
'Andy, do you think you could drive me to the Sugar Bar?'
'Come on, Dolle, I'm trying to work!'
'Oh, of course, I don't want to interrupt. Forget I asked.'
She would dematerialize. Five minutes later I would be

shouting downstairs, 'All right, damn it, get your shoes on.'

'They're on.'

I knew she'd never finish that book. I knew I would never finish a book so long as I was on the North Shore, either. It was a place to live in, not write in. Writing was a sign of the Fall, it was a kind of punishment; Dolle was still living in the Garden of Eden or at least the Sugar Bar. Writing was a substitute for surfing. If you could surf who would ever bother writing?

29

*O*N MONDAY, the second day of the Marui Pipeline Masters, the waves were glassy and tubular and the local hotshots were setting the pace. The ASP rule-book asked the judges to look for the most radical manoeuvres in the most critical section of the wave (that is, nearest the curl). All other criteria – wave selection, length of ride, style – were secondary. Pipeline was easy to judge since it was basically a one-manoeuvre event: what everyone was after was the tube. A good tube-ride might score anything from 8 to 10. After you'd knocked off the highest and lowest assessments of the five judges, three scores still counted. Three times that day the judges awarded the maximum 30 points for a single ride. One 30 was rare; three on one day was unheard of. Part of this record-breaking hat trick was pulled off by Johnny Boy Gomes.

Johnny Boy Gomes was the July pin-up on my surfing calendar back in Cambridge, and now he was picking up more barrels than a beer-truck. This was the first time I had seen him surf in the flesh, but for an entire month I had contemplated him pulling fearlessly into a vicious Pipeline tube when I should have been writing lectures. When I mentioned his name in Hawaii an informant who asked to remain anonymous said: 'Johnny Boy Gomes is the meanest, heaviest dude on the whole of the North Shore.'

He had a reputation for being tough in the water and was alleged to be a champion of 'localism' – the attitude of resident surfers who guard their break jealously and resent the intrusion of outsiders. Hawaii was notorious for localism. Johnny Boy, according to some reports, was seething resentment in bodily form. Stories of his mean streak were legion. If you dropped in on him you were history. Jodie Cooper from Australia told me that she had been out at Haleiwa when Johnny Boy got it into his head that she had robbed him of his wave. He swam up to her and said, 'If you want to surf like a man you're going to be treated like a man.' Jodie retired hurt.

In the public mind – in their own minds – surfers are the modern equivalent of outlaws. The surf is their Sherwood Forest, their *maquis*, their snarling Harley Davidson. Martin Potter's press photos made him out to be a cross between James Dean and Marlon Brando. Surfing was like a photographic negative of normality, inverting good and bad, and turning madmen and monsters into heroes and saints. There are sporadic attempts to rehabilitate surfers and integrate them into society, but it never sticks: they belong on the margins, in another dimension where things are *unreal*, where *outrageous* and *insane* are terms of approbation, and all non-surfing humans are ridiculed as *hodads*. They are sandwich-boards for Oedipal tendencies, eagerly disposing of the father – they reject authority, law, the land – and reverting with fervour to the embrace of the all-mothering sea. You could admire them from a safe distance, but you wouldn't want to run into one of them on a dark night at the crossroads. Even apparently respectable citizens, family men and pillars of the establishment (one old-time big-wave rider had been elected to the House of Representatives and was running for Hawaii State Governor) become teenage rebels again when they wax down their boards.

I mentioned the stories I'd heard about Johnny Boy to Michael Willis. He didn't answer straight away. His artist friend James William Berthrong III said, 'Johnny only surfs like he's mean. He's fairly mellow most of the time. The meanest guy on the North Shore is Perry Dane.'

Perry Dane was my August pin-up.

Michael decided the name Johnny Boy Gomes had become a convenient shorthand, a symbol. 'Guys come in with board injuries and they say, Johnny Boy did it to me. He's the bogeyman of the North Shore. An alibi.'

For Michael there was no such thing as insiders and outsiders; he hated the idea of nations and nationalities. 'Fish don't have passports. The air permeates everywhere. We're all one. This guy's a local and that guy isn't: all these labels come from limited-thinking man in 1989. Whereas proleptic man, futuristic man . . . ' He went off into a reverie, dreaming of proleptic man. 'You know, surfers are probably the first human beings to travel around peacefully, not to conquer. It's a non-colonial thing. That looks like the future to me.'

According to Michael, surfing was the fount of all virtue:

It was freedom. 'It liberates you mentally – opens people up. There's no boundaries and no stop light. You don't have mandatory seat belts or helmets. There's no policemen out there.'

It was courtly love, ennobling and uplifting: it purified the soul. 'They call Johnny Boy bad – well, if he didn't surf, he'd really be bad. Who's going to get into a fight after surfing for eight hours?' Surfers were tranquil. 'Swimming and surfing give you long loose muscles. Weight lifting and construction give you tight bulky muscles. Take your pick. When you're tight – you get uptight.'

It equipped you to cope with everyday life. 'I'd rather depend on a surfer in an emergency than anyone else. If you can face a fifteen-foot wave at Banzai Pipeline, you can handle anything.'

Above all, it heightened your consciousness. 'When you're surfing big Waimea, you can't be thinking about anything – except for the moment. Which means that you're just there, in harmony with the universe.'

'Only for a moment?' I asked.

'That's all there is – moments connected to moments. If

112

you've got that moment, that's all you need. If you know that feeling of being here, now, you're set.'

I still hadn't had that moment of awakening, *satori*, enlightenment. But I was working on it.

Michael promised to help. 'Human beings have been on an ego trip for centuries. We've gone round looting and raping, we've got to learn to just *be*.'

I was contemplating the truth of these words as I drove up Pukea Road, a turning off the Kam Highway past Pipeline heading towards Waimea on the hill side. I'd met Kristin and Sabine that morning and they'd told me to come over and described where they were now living. They said it was about three houses up on Pukea. I pulled into the driveway of the third house on the right-hand side. I got out of the car and a large brooding man with close-set eyes and farflung shoulders came up to me.

'Move your fucking car out of my drive', he growled.

'I'm looking for Kristin and Sabine', I said politely. 'Do they live here?'

'No.' It was only a monosyllable, but it had all of ninety kilos behind it.

'They mentioned the name of a shaper they were staying with – Hector, I think it was.'

'You want the next house up the street.'

I walked back to my car. Just as I was about to get in, the man spoke again. 'And move your fucking car out of my drive.'

Later that day I phoned Callahan. 'I considered saying something like, "Is there anything the matter with you, mate?" But somehow it didn't seem worth it.'

'Where did you say this was?'

'Pukea. Third house on the right.'

'Jesus, just as well you kept your mouth shut. That's Johnny Boy Gomes's house. No one messes with him. He would have *dismembered* you!'

The stretched-out, salivating way Callahan said 'dismembered' made my blood curdle.

'But I've been reading an interview in *Groundswell* where

Johnny Boy says that he's misunderstood and really he's got a heart of gold.'

'Want to know how they did it? They sedated him with Southern Comfort. He had to drink half a bottle before they dared even ask him a question.'

Johnny Boy turned out to be an old friend of Betty's. She introduced me. He had forgotten our first fleeting encounter. I fixed up an interview with him. But I never went. Somehow it didn't seem worth it.

30

TUESDAY WAS the third and last day of the Pipeline Masters. Carwyn was flying home, Ted was working on his self-esteem, Richie was nursing a broken nose. Johnny Boy was waiting for someone to pull into his driveway. I saw the biggest, steepest cylinders of water I'd ever seen from the relative sanctuary of the beach, and Pottz finally landed the world title. He barely had to get wet.

Hawaii is ten hours behind British time. I filed reports around midnight to catch the sports desk the following morning. They appeared twenty-four hours after the event, but then no one back in England seemed in much of a hurry for results. The surf was crashing outside my window and I was caressing a sentence at around 1 a.m. when the phone rang. It was Tom Clarke, Sports Editor of *The Times*.

'Do you know,' he inquired with deceptive gentleness, 'that this morning's newspapers are already reporting the Potter victory?'

'Er, no.'

'How is it that *The Times* is the only British newspaper with a man in Hawaii, and yet has been scooped?'

For a moment, the sinister thought occurred to me that there might be another more efficient British reporter lurking on the beach. Then I realized what had happened. The PR team in the Triple Crown press trailer faxed out releases at the start of the day which had hit England in time for the next morning's edition. Suddenly my short journalistic career looked as if it would stay short. I clutched at a straw.

'Tom,' I said, 'all they've got is the bare fact of his winning the title, but did he win the Pipeline Masters? They've got no idea. I can put the whole thing in context. I've got 500 words all set to roll.'

'We've got to stay on top of this story', said Tom. 'Give me 700 words – make that 750. As soon as you can.'

Another 250 words may not sound much in the great scheme of things, but after a heavy day at Pipeline and an end-of-contest thrash at the Turtle Bay Hilton, it felt like being asked to dash off another chapter of *War and Peace*.

The report appeared the following day under the heading

POTTER IS NAMED RULER OF THE SURF

The new world champion is crowned at Pipeline

This was part of it:

Martin Potter of Great Britain yesterday clinched surfing's world title at the Marui Pipeline Masters in Hawaii without progressing beyond the quarter-finals. The elimination of Australian Dave Macaulay and Hawaiian Derek Ho, who would have had to win to keep their hopes alive, means that with one contest still to run in the Hawaiian Triple Crown he can no longer be overhauled.

This year's Pipeline Master is Gary Elkerton of Australia who attacked the most demanding conditions with impunity.

The Hawaiians once practised human sacrifice. That tradition lives on at the Banzai Pipeline, not so much the

Wembley Stadium of surfing as its Coliseum. Helmeted, armed with long, spear-like boards, the surfers looked like gladiators going out to engage in mortal combat. But sometimes it was more like seeing Christians fed to the lions. The pipe lures surfers in but seldom lets them out again. The jaws open, then clamp shut, occasionally spitting out the remnants of a broken board. Potential contestants sat on the beach with limbs encased in plaster, crutches by their side.

On the fiendishly tricky 10–15 foot sets of the final rounds, resident Pipeline specialists began with a huge advantage. But in the four-man final it was the Hawaiian goofy Ronnie Burns who, despite riding the longest tube, finished last. Veteran Australian Cheyne Horan took third place, while Tahiti's Vetea 'Poto' David, a popular favourite with the crowd, who stylishly hot-dogged the biggest waves on the shortest board, was only narrowly pushed into second.

In the end it was the regular-footer Elkerton's ability to hit for six every type of wave – leg-breaks, off-breaks, googlies, head-severing bouncers – that the Pacific could bowl at him that gave him supremacy.

Having already come runner-up at the Hard Rock Café World Cup, Elkerton is now favourite to win the Triple Crown. The last event in the series, the AAAAA-rated Billabong Pro, is scheduled to open today. Offering the richest purse on the Tour – with a $50,000 first prize – this is a mobile contest that can take its pick among the numerous world-class waves of the North Shore.

An account of the more melancholy destinies of Ted and Carwyn, and the hopes and fears inspired by the Eddie, completed my quota.

So far, although Pottz was now officially *numero uno*, he still hadn't actually won in Hawaii. There was speculation at the Masters that he was no longer trying. In Pottz's quarter-final, Tom Carroll had yet another interference call against him. He stupidly took off on the outside of a wave when someone else had already established priority on the inside. It looked as if his karma was working overtime. The punishment for this crime was to be docked his best wave, so his tally would be reduced to three against the other surfers' four. Normally, as at the 1988 Billabong when Lynch went on to win, that would be enough to ensure his automatic exit. But Carroll went on to harvest three high-scoring waves, putting the pressure back on his opponents.

The final set was decisive. With four waves to choose from, each of the four surfers had a chance. Liam McNamara (a North Shore surfer riding a Willis Phazer) took off on the first, followed by Tony Moniz (another local) on the second and Carroll on the third. McNamara already had the first spot in the bag and Moniz was out, so the battle was on for second place. Two men only would advance to the semis. Carroll rode his wave irreproachably all the way in to shore. As the last wave periscoped up, with only a minute or so left in the heat, Pottz knew he had to take it: he needed a fourth wave to beat Carroll. This one was maybe fifteen foot, the most difficult of the set, pitching and rolling like a drunk.

Pottz drove for the peak and was winched irresistibly upwards. Now he was teetering on the edge of the parapet. He was peering down from the leaning tower of Pisa like Galileo testing his theory of gravity. He took one last look into the abyss and slid back. The wave spiralled forwards into a flawless but bone-crushing tube. Carroll took second; Pottz was out.

When I caught up with Pottz later that evening, I asked him what had gone wrong.

'Just didn't catch enough waves, mate.'

'What about the last wave in the heat?'

'Oh yeah, that one.'

'Did you hesitate and pull back?'

He grinned conspiratorially. 'Can you blame me?' he said.

'He's smart', said Callahan. 'You don't want to wind up on crutches when you've just won the world title.'

31

'*IT'S DOG* eat dog out there.'

'In the water, you mean?'

'No, on the beach. Those photographers would cut each other's throats for a shot.'

I thought Callahan was exaggerating. It was true that photographers swarmed around surfers like ducks around a crust of bread. But they seemed on good terms, always fraternizing and joking together: a team of workmates on the assembly line.

'Don't let that fool you', said Callahan. 'They're just trying to psych each other out. They don't want anyone sneaking off and getting the shot of the decade.' He told me about two photographers who used to work together. One of them always got the better shots. The other couldn't figure this out until one day he found his friend jiggling the settings on his camera, systematically sabotaging his work.

We were at the Café Haleiwa for breakfast. It was packed at 8.30. 'Yeah, they love it here when it rains', Callahan muttered. He laughed at me for missing out on perfect Pipe the day before. I couldn't yet hear the jungle drums that told you where to go on any particular day. Chang could. Aaron Chang was *Surfing*'s top photographer. He was 'Senior Photographer' while Callahan was only 'Photographer'. 'For years he wouldn't even talk to me. Thought I was just a wannabe nobody.' Chang was muscular, unemotional, self-contained, with a smile that flickered like a defective light bulb. Callahan called him 'the enigma'.

He had found Chang browbeating a bodyboarder. 'Don't you ever feel the need for real speed, for that acceleration you get when you dig your rail into the face of the wave? You're never going to get that lying down.' Surfers despised bodyboarders for not standing up on their boards: they weren't walking on water, they were wallowing in it. But bodyboarders knew they could do things with waves board-walkers could only dream of.

Callahan said to Chang: 'Yesterday you were talking about your shaper like he was your priest, as if you were having communion together. Now you're preaching the sacrament of the foaming fibreglass, and digging your rail into the face like it was some kind of religion. Why don't you leave the guy alone?'

'Why don't you shut up, Callahan?' was Chang's response.

'It was like he was trying to save souls.' Callahan wasn't religious about surfing. That was one of the things I liked about him. He respected it, he loved it, but there were limits. He didn't worship it, or surfers either. But there was one thing Callahan was religious about: surfing photography. Whenever we arranged to meet anywhere he would invariably let me down and his excuse was invariable too: 'I was taking shots for *Surfing*.' I got the impression that if he was found guilty of robbery, rape and murder, his plea in mitigation would be: 'I was taking shots for *Surfing*.' And he would expect it to get him off the hook.

Chang lived just a couple of doors along from me at Back-yards, sharing a house with Barton Lynch, so we often ran into each other on the early morning surf check. He said the profession of surfing photography was like a pyramid. There was only room for one at the top and he was it. He rejected the claims of Hornbaker. I had met Jeff Hornbaker in France. When Callahan heard that Hornbaker was on his way, he was as jumpy as Gary Cooper waiting for Frank Miller and his gang to ride into town in *High Noon*. He warned me to be on my guard. 'He looks like a pirate — acts like one, too.' Whenever I ran into him he would ask, 'Seen Hornbaker yet?' Hornbaker was shadowing Pottz, shooting a video for Gotcha. He was another senior photographer for *Surfing* and reminded me of a more weatherbeaten Errol Flynn. In France he was courted by publicity-conscious surfers; people asked him for his autograph. In Hawaii Chang said, 'Hornbaker? He wants to be *me*.'

I'd heard from a sceptic that there were only six basic shots in surfing photography and everything else was just window dressing. This opinion enraged Chang. 'There are infinite possibilities. We've hardly begun to explore them. Nobody ever gets the same wave – even when it is the same wave. Photographing waves is like photographing women. There's no end. You just keep looking for another beautiful woman.'

The water shot stood as the quintessence and pinnacle of the photographer's art. Don King was famous for swimming one-armed into the most critical positions, taking his shots, then melting away into another dimension until the danger had passed. At Pipeline he was like Daniel in the Lions' den.

Chang had produced some seemingly impossible shots too: not just decapitating waves as they curled over and scimitared down, but the underbelly of the wave as well, shot through the turbulence; the lip from behind and below; the inside of the barrel taken from the inside looking out. It was the photographic equivalent of sawing a lady in half, except the photographer was also the lady.

Callahan's speciality was what I thought of as the 'establishing shot': the picture that put everything into context. Even before I met him I'd admired a North Shore picture of his which showed the Kam Highway as it meandered out of the hills and down into Haleiwa, flanked by pineapple plantations and clumps of trees, and in the distance the Pacific, rippling with big waves. But he liked water photography too. Once Chang pulled rank on Callahan at Sunset and ordered him out of the water. 'I'm taking the shots here', he said. 'You'll have to wait your turn.' Callahan shot a roll for me at Lacanau. They were some of the best he'd ever taken, he said, but it was difficult to tell since he'd dropped them in the water when he was changing film.

One of the worst things that could happen was getting water in your camera housing. It happened to Sarge. 'It was my first time here and I wasn't used to the power. I could see the lens just swimming around in there. I kept on taking shots anyway so as not to lose face.' Sarge – his real name was Paul Sargeant – was an Australian who had modelled himself on John Belushi and disapproved of good language (he once took me to task for using the word 'carouse'). He used to be a surfer and dreamed of being one again. He was always talking about the board he was having shaped back in Sydney. Once in Hawaii he was hit by a wave and lost all his equipment. 'I borrowed some other guy's gear and went straight back out and lost his too. He was pissed.' Now Sarge stuck to the beach and was fanatical about covering every angle on land.

Photographers were vital to the development and promotion of surfing, publicizing its beauty and drama. Their pictures were the memory bank of the sport, canonizing the ephemeral in magazines that surfers collected like relics. But now they threatened to desecrate the temple. 'Sometimes there are so many in the water,' said Chang, 'they destroy the wave. All they do is set up an obstacle course for the surfer.' It was a test of manhood to get as close as possible to the board without a fin raking across your back. Some who had failed to get out of the way in time bore the scars like war wounds or medals which they paraded for public admiration. During contests, photographers were policed and only two were allowed in the water at any one time. But at Pipeline on a non-competition day there might be over twenty in a scrum around the peak as if they were shooting Marilyn Monroe. 'Like rats in a cage', said Callahan.

Chang had got his start when Dan Merkel went into cinema. Merkel had worked on *Big Wednesday*, probably the best film about surfing ever made. Merkel was small and irascible with brillo-pad hair. He was as cranky as a bad-tempered goat, always putting his head down and charging into things that annoyed him. Almost everything annoyed him, but especially other photographers. 'Fucking photogs. More of 'em on the beach than surfers in the water.' He was like the man in a traffic jam who curses all the other cars for taking his road, but he didn't see it that way. 'There are only two serious magazines in the States,' he said (*SurfING* and *SurfER*), 'a handful in the rest of the world. Surfing can only sustain about a dozen photographers. So what are the rest of them doing? I'll tell you. They're tourists.' 'Tourist' was about the worst term of abuse you could use. 'This place has lost a lot of lustre.'

Merkel had come up with a sinister final solution to the population explosion. He cackled as he told me of his plan. 'I'm going to give all my shots away free this year. The magazines will be printing nothing but Merkels. All the others'll be nowhere. They won't be able to sell a thing. I'll starve 'em out.' Extermination was a form of altruism, he argued. 'I'll be doing 'em a favour – magazines pay a pittance anyway. Next year, it'll be me and a couple of others and that'll be it. It'll be like paradise all over again.'

32

IN THE winter of '88 Betty had been fleeced by an Australian photographer. His name was Bruce Carver. He stayed for weeks, ran up astronomical phone bills, and then vanished. One evening there was a call from Bruce Carver. He was sorry he'd forgotten to pay Betty any money last year, but could he come and stay for a while and pay her then? Betty said that would be fine.

He had an unshaven anvil chin, glittering eyes and a blonde-haired schoolteacher whose name was Maya. It was her first trip to Hawaii. They took over Yvon's room while he was away in Peru. Carver explained that he was expecting a friend in Australia to wire him $1,500 any day.

Bruce Carver reminded me of Bill Murphy. Bill was an American photographer I had met in Nicaragua. He didn't know you had to change $60 into cordobas at the official rate before you could get into the country. All he had was $30: he'd blown everything else on a crazy night in Miami. I loaned him the other $30. He would have a lot more wired down the next day. I didn't have to worry. He was a Vietnam veteran from Rhode Island who had also been a drug enforcement agent in Pennsylvania and a cosmetologist in Palm Beach, and he was in Nicaragua to take combat photos. When he decided to head north to enlist in the Sandinista army, I felt I had to tag along just to protect my investment.

On the last day of the Marui Pipeline Masters, Bruce Carver and Maya went up in a helicopter to take some aerial shots. Carver wanted me to send a picture to London. Maya was bubbling with excitement afterwards. It was her first trip in a helicopter.

When I went to bed at around two o'clock that night, everyone else was still out partying. I woke up when someone shook me by the shoulder. Maya was sitting on the bed next to me. She was babbling something about helicopters.

'America has invaded Panama.'

'Really?' I looked at my watch. It was 4.30.

'I've just seen all these Chinooks taking off. It was amazing. I've got to write a story on this. Can you send it to *The Times*?'

It sounded like a nightmare. An Australian schoolteacher in Hawaii wanting to write a story on the States invading Panama for *The Times* in London. It got worse.

'Can I borrow your computer?'

I explained at length that I didn't think this was such a good idea. She didn't know how to use it and I didn't want my memory wiped. In *2001: A Space Odyssey* there is a poignant scene where the computer, Hal, has his brain disconnected in retaliation for un-user-friendly conduct. As each of the memory discs is unkeyed in turn, his intellect drains away. 'It's going,' says Hal, 'I can feel it going.' I identified deeply with Hal's predicament: there were many moments when I could feel my brain going – especially in Hawaii. This was one of them.

'Maybe you could just get it started for me.'

I dragged myself out of bed and set the machine up on the kitchen table. With one tentative finger, Maya started tapping out the opening of her story. 'There were ten Chinooks . . . '

Then she paused, searching for inspiration. I left her to it and retreated to my room.

Half an hour later, unable to sleep, I got up again. She was on the second line. 'Still more Chinooks whirred their propellers and . . . '

I told her I thought *The Times* would probably have a man on the spot and it was late, and I prised my Toshiba away from her grasping hands. As I closed my door she was still sitting there, wide awake, but dreaming of Chinooks.

I slept fitfully. When I wandered out for a surf-check in the morning, Michael was sitting on the bench.

'Did you miss it?'

'Miss what?'

'Only the biggest drama of the winter. There were police cars, fire engines, helicopters – oh yeah, and a naked woman. What more can you ask for?'

Carver and Maya had been fighting. She had caught him flirting with another woman. The invasion of Panama, curiously summed up for her in the shape of Chinook helicopters, had served as a convenient diversion. After her abortive attempt to break into journalism, she had gone down to the beach, flung off her dress, and plunged into the water at Backyards. It was six to eight and heavy. Betty saw her swimming away into the darkness and called the emergency services.

Maya cut through the breakers into the line-up and then steered towards Sunset. Hooded waves sprang out at her like muggers from underwater alleyways.

The helicopter found her in the vicinity of Kammies. She was still stroking and heading for Waimea. She was a strong swimmer. As she looked up into the spotlight and the rope ladder unfurled she thought the Chinooks had come for her.

There were American military bases scattered all over the Islands: they were there to protect the Pacific. Camouflaged trucks patrolled the Kam Highway and US Army grunts invaded the beaches in their time off. When the States took over Panama, the troops stationed in Hawaii were put on full alert in case of a retaliatory attack. Perhaps they feared another Pearl Harbor. Panama was five thousand miles away, but you couldn't be too sure: it was still America's backyard.

'You're worse than Noriega', I heard Maya yell at Carver.

She thought of him as a drug-running tyrant.

'I've paid all this money to come to Hawaii and all you can do is screw around.'

Noriega had gone into hiding. The might of the armed forces searched in vain for some trace of this elusive enemy of freedom, originally shoehorned into power to guard American interests.

'He hasn't been paying his dues', was Michael's comment.

Bruce Carver and Maya ran to ground, too. He'd run up another massive telephone bill and hadn't paid Betty a dime. 'The skunk. What a sucker I am', she said.

I never got my money back from Bill Murphy, either. I even had to loan him some more to get out of Nicaragua. After being rejected by the Sandinistas, he resolved to become a flying doctor and ferry medical supplies to war-stricken *campesinos*. As far as I know, he never returned.

I saw Bruce Carver on the beach once or twice after that. He tried to sell me a Pottz picture. Maya said, 'You ever been up in a helicopter?'

33

'*ANDY, THAT'S* the best thing that could have happened to you.'

That was Michael Willis's line whenever I told him about some fresh disaster in the surf.

I often watched Michael at work in his shaping room. All he wore was a pair of shorts and a mask. He gave me a mask too. 'Is this dust bad for you?' I said.

'There's dust at the centre of the universe', he said. 'We're all made out of dust, aren't we?'

He didn't want me to worry about my health. 'Check those lights', he said. I looked at the tubular lighting in the roof. 'They emit vitamins. The more you work in here the healthier you get.'

He listed all the variables of a board: length, width, thickness, bottom curve, nose, tail, fin configuration, rocker, rails, V, stringer. 'I've shaped all the shapes', he said.

'So there is an almost infinite number of possible combinations?'

He looked pensive. 'Yes. But they don't all work. An eagle flies better than a pelican even though they've both got wings.'

Michael's parable reminded me of Jules Verne's *Albatross*, a flying machine with seventy-six propellers, which was supposed to be modelled on the flight of a bird. But the *Albatross* was superseded in turn by a still more extravagant vehicle – at once spaceship, submarine, and racing car – called *The Terror*.

The requirement of mimesis compelled inventors to find a model for their designs in nature. In this I was no different from Michael, but where he thought of eagles, I thought of dolphins. Arion, son of Poseidon and master of the lyre, was sailing to Corinth when he was put overboard by the captain, who coveted his wealth. His last song attracted a school of dolphins, one of which ferried Arion on his back all the way to Corinth. Now that the rounded nose of the old malibu had been sharpened to a point in the thruster, the benign image of the dolphin had dissolved into the leering grin of a shark, inverted, its fin trailing in the water. Boards could maim as well as protect: they had to be muzzled with noseguards.

'Here, look at this rail.' Michael pointed out how he had a long curve along the top of the board's edge, and only a small curve at the bottom. 'You can make it fifty-fifty. But I prefer eighty-twenty. Why? The more you have on top, the more it lifts you; the more you have on the bottom, the more you're pulled down. I prefer to go up rather than down, don't you?'

I did. I wanted a Willis board. I wanted a Phazer. 'The board

I'm going to make for you will be a masterpiece', Michael said. 'It's going to fit you like a glove. You see, I know what you're like. So I know what your board should be like. I'll sign it, but it'll have your name written all over it.'

He carried on sanding the blank into shape. 'But you want to know my dream? To produce boards the way you produce record albums. From a master copy. I want everyone to have a board like yours.' It was only the fact that boards were expensive, Michael thought, that kept some people out of the water.

He stood back to admire his handiwork. His next words astonished me. 'There's an ugliness to boards,' he said, 'an extreme ugliness. And I'll tell you why. The material. This idea of being in harmony with nature on the wave – isn't that the biggest crock of shit you ever heard?'

'So you don't think surfers are in harmony with nature?'

'With a polyurethane board? Impossible. You're destroying nature. Polyurethane is plastic. The whole thing is toxic. You breathe a burning surfboard and you die. To me it's a crock of shit to go out and harmonize with nature on my resin polyurethane surfboard.'

Michael loved the surfboards he shaped. But he hated what he loved. He confided his second dream to me. 'What I want is a biodegradable board – like the husk of a grain of wheat. That way, when you bust your board, you don't just toss it in the garbage. You bury it in the earth and fertilize a tree – that's what I call harmony with nature. It's the only way to go: the mass-produced organic biodegradable surfboard.'

'Do you think it's technically possible?'

'Do you think God would give me the vision and no way to make it come true? Everything is possible. Show me something that's not possible. Where were you when they put a man on the moon?'

I told Callahan about Michael's ideas. 'You don't think surfers are worried about feeding the plants, do you? All they want to know is: am I going to get a good bottom turn?' He thought Michael was a dreamer.

But Michael was undeterred by scepticism. 'The nineties will be the decade of the board builder. I have plans, I have a myriad projects.'

I hoped his plans included building a board for me. In the meantime, I kept using what was left of Ted's Excalibur. Then I met Alan, who worked for Olo Surfboards. I gave him a lift into Honolulu one night when his car had broken down. He was a shaper, too. It was almost an hour's drive, which gave him time to elaborate his philosophy. He told me I should never use a leash. They were the work of the devil. I told him a leash was all I had. What I needed was a board to go with it.

'You don't have a board?' The idea struck him as somehow absurd, as if I had told him I didn't have a head or a heart. 'Come on over to my place. I've got loads of old boards just lying around. Pick one up to suit yourself.'

He gave me his number. I called several times and spoke to his wife. Finally we arranged to meet in Foodlands at six. I waited until 6.30 and then left.

'Alan?' said Bodo. 'You don't mean Bullshit Alan, do you?'

'Well, he didn't call himself Bullshit Alan.'

'No, but everyone else does.'

I never heard from Alan again. Bodo said he'd take me out and loan me one of his boards. I met him at Laniakea (familiarly known as *Lani's*), a long, multi-peaked break past Jocko's heading towards Haleiwa. He had Damon with him. Damon was a nineteen-year-old student from California who was staying with Bodo and Liese for a month. He was a great surfer. I would have two great surfers with me. This time I knew I couldn't fail.

There was a brief debate over which way we should paddle out. Half a mile from the beach there were three breaks: from right to left as you looked out, big, medium, and small. You could paddle out from the right alongside a rock jetty, or you could go from the left. Before Bodo arrived I'd already decided in favour of the gentler angled approach through the rip from the left, with an eye on building up gradually from the small to the not-so-small.

128

Damon said, 'I'm taking the short-cut', and dived in with his board by the rocks. Bodo said, 'You might as well come with us.' He drew me a map of the route with a stick in the sand. 'There's a path through the break here, where it's not so strong.'

The first few hundred yards were deceptively smooth. But accelerating towards us was a row of sharp, jutting, foamy peaks, like a set of upturned shark's teeth wreathed in toothpaste.

'Where's the path?' I yelled to Bodo above the grinding of jaws.

'It's right in front of us. Follow me', he said.

It had seemed clear enough in the sand. Now all I could see was spray. I tried ducking under broken sections, but they just ducked right down after me. When Bodo saw I was in trouble, he said 'We'd better turn round and go out the other way.'

'No, come on, we can make it!' I cried.

My overriding desire at this point was not to do any more paddling. We were only twenty or thirty yards from the line-up, albeit divided from it by a thin blue line of helmeted, truncheon-tipped breakers. The paddle in, around, and out again, was at least a mile. I knew I wasn't up to it. Bodo mistook my cowardly calculation for gutsy heroism.

'Yay,' he cried as a wave broke over his head, 'that's the fighting spirit! Andy, you're a credit to British surfing. Pottz look out!'

I scrambled frantically up the face of another eight-footer. Miraculously, we were out the back. Damon was already up and running; Bodo was champing at the bit.

'I'll check out the smaller break for starters. Catch up with you later.' I crawled off. By the time I reached the furthest peak I was feeling distinctly sick. I'd been yo-yoing up and down a rollercoaster for the best part of an hour and I was still hung over from the phial of 'Renshenfengwangjiang' – a potent blend of panax ginseng and royal bee jelly – that Michael Willis had persuaded me to drink for breakfast. Then it started raining. I drove into the mouth of a carnivorous wave with the reckless abandon of a man who has just been given a week to live.

It wasn't the best possible trial for Bodo's eight-foot mini-tanker. It was like test-piloting a plane and crashing on the runway. I still hadn't made a clean take-off.

When Michael asked me later 'Are you ready for Sunset yet?', I said I didn't think so, but I would be soon. Every day I went to see him I hoped I would be fitted out with my bespoke Willis Phazer. I knew it took a while to finish a board: there was not just the shaping, but the painting and the glassing. When it came to within a few days of my scheduled departure date, I said to Michael, 'I suppose it's too late now.'

'Andy, what's my last name?'

'Willis.'

'And how do you spell it?'

'W - I - L - L - I - S. Isn't that right?'

'Yeah, but in two syllables.'

'Will . . . '

'You got it. WILL IS.'

34

*B*ODO'S EPIC misinterpretation of my failure at Lani's established itself as the authorized version of events.

Betinna said, 'I hear you've been a hero.'

Liese said, 'This has been a day of great accomplishments.'

I could have wept with frustration.

Liese made me dinner in the Chinese style: miso soup, stir-fried vegetables, sweetsap for dessert. Afterwards she fixed me a potion she promised would tone up my whole system. She had a cupboardful of Chinese remedies. I asked her if she had any medication that would make me a better surfer.

'No. There is nothing that will make you a better surfer.'

'I need more control. I've got no control.'

'You mustn't seek control. You must be like a piece of wood

in the ocean: wood always floats to the surface, even though it is rolled over and held under.'

Her hallucinatory voice, creamy as cappuccino, soothing as Valium, anaesthetized my instinctive resistance.

'The wave cannot be mastered – you can only move with it, not against it. It is the same with your Self: don't struggle to impose your will: let your mind be your body and your body be your mind.'

She prescribed a massage. Strands of wispy Chinese music looped themselves around my brain like a spider's web. Liese rolled a sheaf of a Chinese root which she grew in her garden and put a match to it. The smoke wafted up my nose like incense. She blew on the cigar and held it next to my skin. I thought I was on fire but the cigar left no mark.

Liese scoured my body for tension. 'These hands are like X-rays. They are like magnets, drawn to those parts of your body that need healing.' Whenever she found a knotted muscle she would say, 'Here we have a coconut', and then pound the spot into insensibility. Then she would say, 'That is better.' When I cried out, I didn't know whether it was with pain or pleasure. I saw nothing but her deep brown legs as she knelt beside me, felt nothing but her strong hands kneading me like dough.

I told her I suffered from headaches. She squeezed my ankle and said, 'There, this will help your head.'

Liese told me the two centres of the *chi* – the life force – were located an inch or two above and below the navel. She gave a few tentative prods.

'How is my chi?' I asked.

'Pretty sleepy', she said. 'But it will wake when you need it.'

When she had finished she shook her arms, as if trying to dry her hands. 'I absorb your tension', she explained. 'It is like a glass of dirty water. To clean the water I must take the dirt out. It does not help just to stir it around.'

Liese thought the ocean could teach me many things. 'Listen to Lao-tzu in the *Tao Te Ching*', she said:

> Under heaven nothing is more soft and yielding than
> water.
> Yet for attacking the solid and the strong, nothing is better.
> It has no equal.
> The weak can overcome the strong.
> The supple can overcome the stiff.
> Under heaven everyone knows this,
> Yet no one puts it into practice.

'You must watch and imitate. That is how my master taught me. He used to say: "I cannot teach you. But you can learn".'

It was on that night that we consulted the *I Ching*. Liese explained how I could look for answers; but first, silently, I had to formulate my question.

'It has to be something important to you.'

I thought: 'Will I get to surf Sunset before I leave?'

I tossed the three discs. The combination of different faces produced a score which required me to inscribe a divided line or a single unbroken line on a sheet of paper. After six throws I had a hexagram which looked like this:

I checked my hexagram against the index, which led me to the pages headed *Ta Kuo: Preponderance of the Great*. I read them with a kind of terror.

> The hexagram represents a beam that is thick and heavy in the middle but too weak at the ends. This is a condition that cannot last; it must be changed, must pass, or misfortune will result . . .
>
> It is an exceptional time and situation; therefore extraordinary measures are demanded. It is necessary to find a way of transition as quickly as possible and to take action.

This promises success . . . the time when the great preponderates is a momentous time.

I read on and learned that a nine in the second place means:

A dry poplar sprouts at the root.

An older man takes a young wife.

Everything furthers.

Wood is near water; hence this image of an old poplar sprouting at the root. This means an extraordinary reanimation of the processes of growth. In the same way, an extraordinary situation arises when an older man marries a young girl who suits him. Despite the unusualness of the situation, all goes well.

From the point of view of politics, the meaning is that in exceptional times, one does well to join with the lowly, for this affords the possibility of renewal.

This, I felt, was the story of my life. If I interpreted it correctly – 'Nothing is definite, you must interpret the words', Liese said – I had only to keep lying on my bed of North Shore nails for it to turn ultimately into a pillow of foam.

Betinna lay curled up like a long-haired cat on the sofa. I asked the *I Ching* one more question. I found my hexagram under the rubric *K'un – Oppression (Exhaustion)*. I had a six in the third place:

He butts his head against a wall and in consequence feels oppressed by the wall . . . Thereupon he turns back irresolutely and returns to his house only to find, as a fresh disappointment, that his wife is not there.

I needed no further warning. I fled into the night.

35

I WANTED to meet some 'real' Hawaiians, but they were hard to find. I knew there was an island reserved for racial Hawaiians. But I never went there. I knew there was a strong Hawaiian community on the west side of Oahu, in Makaha. But on the day I went to Makaha I got distracted by a shapely wave and a firm offshore and met no one apart from a lifeguard in the tower and a girl on the beach.

Captain Cook's third and last voyage was a dismal echo of the first two. Cook was suffering the effects of a debilitating illness that had killed many of his earlier crew; his ship had been poorly repaired and took in water constantly; the North-West Passage was impassable. He was sobered to find that many Tahitians were already dying from the venereal diseases bequeathed to them on a previous visit. Cook may have sensed that, like a cloud of anti-matter, he was fated to destroy whatever he discovered. He foresaw the decimation of the Hawaiian people; perhaps he had some premonition of his own end too.

The Puritan missionaries thought the heathens didn't deserve to exist and the heathens were so compliant that they duly dwindled towards extinction. The population of more than 300,000 at the time of Cook's arrival had plummeted to less than 40,000 by the end of the nineteenth century. Many sought refuge in intermarriage, with Chinese, Japanese, Filipinos, Thais, as well as Americans and Europeans. While we in other countries had become Hawaiianized, the Hawaiians themselves had melted away. They were everywhere and they were nowhere.

On the North Shore, racial disharmony found a hook in the simple division between *locals* and *haoles* (pronounced 'howlies'). Haoles were white people. Locals were almost everyone else. The word haole meant 'without breath', lifeless; it could also mean 'ignorant'.

The feeling that Hawaii had been unlawfully possessed by the United States was still a potent force. Hawaii was *of* the United States but it was not *in* it. It often looked askance at the mainland. When the States invaded Panama, the typical reaction was 'why don't we keep our noses out of other people's business'. Panama seemed to many like a re-enactment of Hawaiian history: the States had needed a reason to take over and it had found one. The Americans turned the Islands into a plantation and Honolulu was now the business centre of the Pacific. But it was always the newcomers who did well: the older families, the Hawaiians, were always the losers.

'Without welfare,' said Callahan, 'there'd be an Hawaiian liberation army camped in the hills, armed to the teeth with machine guns. Economically and politically, they've been completely disenfranchised. Genetically, they've been wiped out.' He said there was a protest movement, similar to that among American Indians, which had had some small success in winning back some of the lands that had been taken over. The sense of dispossession sustained an underworld of thugs, drug pushers, and thieves (I wanted to write about crime in Hawaii, but the godfather of the North Shore let me know that he'd rather I didn't). The ASP had once had to pay protection money to prevent disruption to the Triple Crown. 'But surfing is the main way out for Hawaiians. It's about the only thing that hasn't been sold off to the Japanese – yet.'

The Hawaiian surf club, the *Hui o he'enalu*, had become a focus and a forum for dissatisfaction and dissent. In certain quarters the members of the club were known as 'the Black Shorts' on account of their surfing costumes. The name accidentally recalled the pseudo-fascist organization run by P. G. Wodehouse's comic villain, Roderick Spode. I felt that Bertie Wooster might not have approved. But the *Hui* was essential to the orderly running of the ASP contests. Formidable members of the Black Shorts, more formally known as the 'Water Patrol', policed the contest areas, warning off errant outsiders.

There was no chance of my winning the women's event here.

'Surfing is what you do when you've got nothing left', said Hailama, one of the contest beach marshals. His name meant 'old warrior' (I remembered it by thinking of the High Lama in *Lost Horizons*). I had a theory that Hawaiians had the same kind of relationship with the sea as the Australian aborigines had with the land. The sea was their patrimony, their past, their reservoir of stories about themselves. 'We'd like to have a relationship with the land,' Hailama said, 'but we ain't got no land. All I've got is my surfboard. I was practically born and raised on a surfboard. The beach is my back yard.' He hankered after a lost Golden Age. The North Shore wasn't the way it used to be. 'It's got so heavy here. There's so much shit come up. I used to know everybody. Now there's guys like you around.'

I was the whitest human being on the island. I stood out like Moby Dick. I was chief haole, a direct descendant of Captain Cook.

In the Bishop Museum in Honolulu, I found the sixteen-foot board that George Freeth used to ride. Freeth was the surfer of Hawaiian and Irish ancestry who tried to teach Jack London to ride the breakers of Waikiki in the first decade of the century. The board was supposed to have been given to him by his uncle, an Hawaiian prince. It was Freeth who introduced surfing to California. Henry Huntington, who would give his name to Huntington Beach, had built a railway from Los Angeles to Redondo. But no one wanted to go there. An article in a national magazine by Jack London on 'The Royal Sport' inspired him to devise a publicity stunt to pull in the crowds. He invited Freeth to demonstrate the art of surfing at Redondo Beach. In the spring of 1907 Freeth, billed as THE MAN WHO WALKS ON WATER, became the first surfer to ride a wave on the mainland coast, while Californians rode Huntington's trains to go to watch him. Freeth stayed on to become the first lifeguard too, and when he died during an influenza epidemic at the age of thirty-five it was said that he had exhausted himself rescuing swimmers.

Terry Ahue worked as a lifeguard at Pipeline and was

President of the *Hui o he'enalu*. I saw him a lot at the Ehukai Beach Park where he was based, but only managed to talk to him at any length at a party in the hills. As we swung in a hammock by the fire he explained that far from being a subversive organization, the *Hui* was actually a preserver of traditions.

Surfing had a symbolic value for Hawaiians. It was like a barometer whose health or *malaise* reflected the state of society as a whole. 'What's happening to surfing is happening to everything,' Terry said, 'that's progress for you.' For the *Hui*, Hawaii *was* surfing – everything else was superficial and transient. But superficiality had crept into surfing, too. On the one hand, Hawaiians were proud that the climax of the Tour was back where it should be. 'Australia, who wants to go to Australia?' one lifeguard sneered. On the other hand, there was bitterness at the exploitation of surfing in Hawaii. 'What has Billabong got to do with us?' Someone was making money out of Hawaii, but it wasn't the Hawaiians. Hawaiians who weren't even competing felt it most of all. 'Let's all go to Burleigh Heads [in Queensland] and take over the place for their best month. And see what they say.'

Duke Kahanamoku was one of the founders of the first Hawaiian surf club, known as the *Hui Nalu*. It was said that the Kahanamokus were the descendants of Kamehameha the Great, but Duke inherited his name from his father, a Honolulu police captain who was named after the then Duke of Edinburgh following his visit to the Islands in 1869. Born in 1890, Duke lived his early years in the waters of Waikiki. It was the dream-time of surfing, the creation, when everything was still possible. There were no skyscrapers, no bikinis, no suntan oil; you lived off fish, fruit and *poi*. In those days no one surfed the North Shore. The waves of the South Shore were long in forming and slow to break and the water was a constant seventy-six degrees. Waikiki was where the bygone chiefs of Oahu had surfed. Princess Kaiulani had defiantly ridden her big *olo* board in the bay in the last decade of the nineteenth century, but the old skills had been lost. Now Duke and his brothers began trimming sideways across the face of the waves, as their ancestors had done, rather than riding them straight into the beach. Photographs of the period show a grinning Duke with his ten-foot board looming up behind him like a tall wooden tombstone, his name engraved on the deck like an epitaph.

36

FOR THE better part of two decades, Duke Kahanamoku was the best swimmer in the world. In a timed swim across Honolulu Harbour in 1911 he covered 100 yards in 55.4 seconds, shattering the existing record by 4.6 seconds. The judges were so incredulous they twice remeasured the length of the course. Mainland officials rejected the claim in disbelief. In 1912 Duke represented the United States at the Olympic Games in Stockholm and won the gold medal in the 100 metres freestyle, losing it again only in 1924 to Johnny Weissmuller: 'It took Tarzan to beat me', he used to say. When he returned to Hawaii he was more than a hero, he was a saviour, a messiah. He would tour the world quietly preaching the gospel of surfing. Those who met him never forgot it.

There was a debate among anthropologists over the question of origins. In pre-European times, surfing was practised from Easter Island to New Guinea, in Micronesia and Melanesia, although it was only in Hawaii and Tahiti, whence the Hawaiians had come, that riders stood up on their boards. Dieter Schori in *Das Floss in Ozeanien* argues that occurrences of surfing elsewhere can all be traced to Polynesian influence. Ben R. Finney, on the other hand, in *Surfboarding in Oceania*, favours the hypothesis of independent invention, drawing attention to the different names for *he'enalu* in different places (*wahakaheke ngaru* among the Maoris and *fakapapa* in Uvea). But what is beyond question is that, in the post-contact era, it was Hawaii that colonized other countries with surfing.

In 1912, C. D. Paterson of Manly in Australia returned from Hawaii with a heavy redwood board which a few local bodysurfers tried in vain to ride. In 1915 the New South Wales Swimming Association invited Duke Kahanamoku to the Domain Baths in Sydney where he beat his own world record for the 100 yards with a time of 53.8 seconds. When he arrived at Manly beach with a board he had carved out of sugar pine, many were those who said that riding a wave on a board was pure myth, a legend of the South Seas brought back by drunken sailors. On 15 January 1915, a bright Sunday morning in summer, while in Europe men were digging trenches to die in, Duke paddled out at Manly. The lifeguard boat offered to tow his board out through the pounding break. Duke laughed good-naturedly and turned them down. He powered through the water, leaving the boat and the other swimmers who had escorted him far behind. Soon he was in the line-up in the northern corner of the bay. He swivelled the board round, moved effortlessly into a wave and stood up, cutting diagonally across the break and finishing with a headstand.

Duke's miracle caused a sensation. Young Australians clamoured to become his disciples. By the time he left Sydney surfing had taken root in another continent. Claude West, who had watched Duke that day, won the newly inaugurated national surfing championships from 1919 to 1924, and once saved the life of the Governor-General, Sir Ronald Munro Ferguson. Many years later, it would be said of Australia that it was not a sea-going nation but a surf-going one.

Duke Kahanamoku begat surfing: he was the origin, the first cause, the primordial father of all. He created the cult of the beach boy. Surfers traced themselves back to the Duke as if he were Adam. He seemed to embody in his person the entire history of the sport: he symbolized the Hawaiian spirit. He saved twelve lives when a pleasure boat capsized in heavy surf at Corona del Mar in California in June 1925. He played bit parts in Hollywood, acting alongside John Wayne in the 1948 *Wake of the Red Witch*. He mellowed into a white-haired wise man. He knew everybody. A friend was changing a light bulb when Duke said, 'I knew Tommy.' *Tommy?* The friend was baffled: *Who the hell is Tommy?* Then it dawned on him: Duke meant Thomas Edison. *Duke had met Thomas Edison.*

President Kennedy, who as a young competitive swimmer had learned the Kahanamoku Kick, asked to meet him. He became Sheriff of Honolulu, Official Greeter, and Hawaii's unofficial ambassador. After he died of a heart attack in 1968 on the dock next to his boat at the Waikiki Yacht Club, his ashes were scattered over Kalahuewehe break.

In the early years of the twentieth century, hardly anyone surfed Kalahuewehe First Break, off Diamond Head, now known as Outside Castles. These were the biggest waves on the South Side, like surfing the North Shore in Waikiki. In 1917 Duke had ridden a Kalahuewehe wave half a mile till it died in front of the Royal Hawaiian Hotel, where now the ASP annual banquet is held. It was hailed as the longest ride, but Duke was convinced a still longer ride was possible. It was in the summer of 1932 that Duke paddled out alone into the biggest swell he had seen in his life, with a stiff offshore from the Koolau mountains pinning back the peaks, which he estimated at thirty feet, as big as the storm waves off Kaena Point. The night before, a rumour had swept Waikiki that the 'Bluebirds' were coming: the giant tsunamis that thundered in only on very rare occasions. Sometimes years would go by and there would be no sight of the Bluebirds. Now the Bluebirds had come.

Duke wrestled with the torrential whitewater, spinning his *Papa nui* – a sixteen-foot, hundred-and-fourteen-pound semi-hollow Tom Blake board – upside down in an Eskimo roll to let the broken waves pass over him. The sound as they smashed on the upturned bottom was like 'a string of freight cars roaring over a trestle'. At last in the line-up, rising and falling with the ridges and troughs, he wondered whether even he could withstand the force of the mighty impact zone. This is how, in his partly autobiographical *World of Surfing*, he described the wave for which he is still remembered:

Strangely, it was as though the wave had chosen me more than I had chosen it. It seemed a very personal and special wave – the kind that I had seen in my mind's eye in a night of tangled dreaming. There was just this one wave and myself – no more. Instinctively, I got to my feet when the pitch, slant and speed seemed right. Left foot forwards, knees slightly bent, I rode the board down that precipitous slope like a man tobogganing down a glacier.

I shifted my weight, angled left, and shot into the big Castle Surf which was building and adding to the wave I was on. Spray was spuming up wildly from my rails in a way I had never seen before. Diamond Head was leaping at me from the right. Then I was slamming into Elk's Club Surf, still sliding left, still fighting for balance, for everything and anything that would keep me upright. Then I skidded and slanted through into Public Baths Surf. Three surfs combined into one, big, rumbling and exploding. A curl broke to my right and almost engulfed me, so I swung even further left and shuffled back on the board to keep from pearling.

Left it was; left and more left, with the board veeing a jet of water on both sides and making a snarl of speed and stress and thrust. Borrowing several hundred yards from the Cunha Surf I steered the board into the now towering Queen's Surf. One mistake would spill me into the maelstrom on my right. I teetered, caught control again, and made it down that last forward rush, sliding and bouncing through the lunatic water.

That ride, from Castles, across Elks, Cunhas and Public Baths, as far as Queens, was the longest in the history of surfing, the ride of rides. Duke reckoned it at a mile and three-quarters; the most conservative estimates put it at over a mile. Duke never repeated that achievement, and now such a ride is no longer possible. The bottom contours of the bay have changed and the lighter, shorter surfboards lack the momentum to connect the rider across the flat intervening sections to the next break.

But if surfers could no longer make those connections through space, they made them through time. Surfing was all the Hawaiians had left: it was their last living link with the past. The ancients had surfed while other nations floundered in the water or built unwieldy vessels to keep them precariously afloat. They had established an intimacy and an affinity with the ocean which we can still only envy. When the haoles took everything, surfing became a gesture of revolt, a symbolic reassertion of power over superior forces. More than that, it was the Hawaiians' way of retaining a sense of dignity and worth, it was their way of staying alive. And now the haoles were stealing their waves. Martin Potter — from Captain Cook's own country — was taking over. It was no accident that when Pottz won the world title one of the tabloid headlines in England ran: 'Britannia Rules the Waves'.

But Hawaii had a natural defence against this brand of surfing imperialism: the big waves of winter and the Eddie Aikau. David Kahanamoku, Duke's nephew, had already broken his ankle in the November swell at Waimea and been fished out of the Bay by Michael Willis. As Hailama said, 'You don't need a contest to have a contest here.'

37

*O*N THE North Shore I often heard people say 'there are no two waves alike'. They were like fingerprints, like snowflakes. Surfers could describe individual waves as well as their friends or enemies. They thought there was one wave that was meant just for them, in the same way that marriages were supposed to be made in heaven.

The Hawaiian wave is born thousands of miles away, awoken by the rotation of the sun and the moon, the circulation of the wind and the spinning earth. It dies when it runs out of water to breathe and pump round its body. When water-depth decreases to 1.3 times wave-height, the wave is compressed, its steepness rises, and the orbital journey of a wave particle is squeezed into a tilted ellipse. The onrushing crest dips below the critical 120-degree angle and falls forward in uncompleted cycles, thumping out its agony on the out-stretched limbs of the land.

The wave, a creature of the sea, seems to suffocate and gasp when it is beached on the shore. It is hardly surprising that it should occasionally wreak vengeance on its executioner. A wave 10 feet high and 500 feet long can pack a punch of 400,000 pounds per linear foot of its crest. Waves organize themselves into trains so that, as one of their number expires, a memory of its strength is bequeathed to its successors, consolidating their length (the distance between crests) and speed and height. Sometimes converging swells will syn-chronize to produce a peak that is higher than any of the separate peaks that preceded it.

It is then that rogue waves appear, devouring other waves in their path to grow still larger. Statistically, they are inevitable. Waves cannot exceed a seventh of their length in height without breaking; but they can stretch to as much as a thousand feet. The average ocean wave is five feet in height. One wave in 23 is over twice the height of the average wave. One in 1,175 is over three times the average. But the totality of waves in the world is incalculable: who knows how many there are? Giants stalk the waterways, day in, day out. Odys-seus met with them in the wine-dark sea of the Mediterranean and called them Cyclops, Scylla and Charybdis. But those mythic monsters were as dwarves to the waves that inhabit other oceans. Lieutenant Margraff was the watch officer aboard the USS *Ramapo* patrolling the North Pacific on the morning of 7 February 1933. It was then, after a storm that had blown for seven days at speeds exceeding seventy knots, that the *Ramapo* encountered the biggest wave ever reported by a ship at sea. Lieutenant Margraff estimated it to be 112 feet from base to crest. The vessel survived.

Bigger waves undoubtedly occur, but those who witness them do not return to tell the tale. Flying saucers and kidnapping aliens have been postulated to explain the disappearance of whole vessels, supposedly spirited off to distant stars. And giant waves are indeed like alien presences, as big as the Death Star, erasing ships and sailors as effectively as Martian ray guns. They are a rigorous mystery, governed by unfathomable equations.

Waves ignore frontiers and time-zones as they echo round the world. They can penetrate far inland in the form of tidal bores, funnelling incoming tides up a narrowing channel with increasing power and destructiveness. People on the North Shore identify particular waves as 'Ken's wave' or 'George's wave'. There was once a wave that was Victor Hugo's wave.

For over twenty years, Hugo had masterfully deployed the metaphor of the wave: he had bent the wave to his own ends, he had coupled it to revolution, to love, to Napoleon, to centuries, pinning it to the page in alexandrines and rhymes. On 4 September 1843, while Hugo was travelling with his mistress, his newly married daughter Léopoldine and her husband Charles took to the river at Villequier in a small sailing boat. On the same day, the *mascaret*, a river-bore which had been known to reach as far as Paris, was sweeping up the Seine. According to one account, by the time it hit Villequier, it was a wall of water several metres high moving at fifteen miles per hour. What is certain is that the boat capsized and all on board were drowned.

Following his daughter's death, Hugo ceased writing for several years. When he took up his pen again, it was as if he had assumed the annihilating impact of that wave: his books, he said, 'must be read as if they were the books of a dead man'. He divided his career into two phases, *Autrefois* (Before) and *Aujourd'hui* (Today); the dividing line was Villequier. When he exiled himself to Jersey, it was to surround himself with 'the sinister sheep of the sea', 'the hydra-headed dragon', which had become for him an image of the abyss, of fate, and of God. The last line of one of his last novels reads: *There was nothing left but sea*.

According to Hugo, everything speaks; everything has a soul. Like Michael Willis, all he had to do was quote the wind and the sea, flames, trees, reeds, rocks. The ocean spoke to Hugo with its own distinctive voice:

> Do you think that the ocean, which swells and struggles,
> Would be happy to open its mouth day and night,
> To breathe into the void a vapour of noise,
> And that it would roar, beneath the hurricane above,
> If its roaring was not speech?

Michael Willis, the ancient Hawaiians, Victor Hugo, had all been affected by wave-fever; all of them had abjured the text. It seemed to me that there was a law relating in inverse ratio the experience of waves and the production of writing. The bigger and more frequent the waves, the less scriptural the culture. The biggest waves in the world generated a wholly oral society. Waves washed away the words on the page as they swamped islands, ships, sailing craft and poets' daughters.

This theory would illuminate one lasting mystery. Throughout his three great journeys of discovery and exploration, Captain James Cook had been the most assiduous of diarists, keeping an almost daily record of thoughts and observations. The closing pages of his journal speak repeatedly of the 'high surfs' and 'great waves' crashing against the Hawaiian littoral and preventing the *Discovery* and the *Resolution* from docking. On 17 January 1799, nearly a month before Cook's death in Kealakekua Bay, the journal breaks off. There are no rough notes for the succeeding weeks, and there is no explanation of his silence. Cook was worshipped as Lono, god of peace and of surfing, and priests prostrated themselves before him. Lono, who came forth from the waves, did not write.

38

THE HIGH priests of the North Shore, the ayatollahs of this surfing Mecca, are the big-wave riders. When the swell rises to twenty feet plus and the high surf warning siren sounds and everyone else is evacuating the water, these are the men who paddle out.

If Sunset Beach, Banzai Pipeline, and Waimea Bay are the holy trinity of the thirty-odd North Shore breaks, Waimea is the Father, the holy of holies: slow to rise, but majestic and terrible when it does. It can elevate and glorify, or it can crucify you. Those who ride the Bay are surfing's acknowledged aristocracy. Sponsored by sports companies and worshipped by women, these modern *ali'i* are torn between the claims of tradition and media-exploitation, divided in their approaches and personalities.

Ken Bradshaw and Mark Foo, two of the main pretenders to the crown, are a study in contrasts. At the age of fifteen Ken ran away to California from his Texas home when his parents locked up his surfboard. He kept on heading west, lured by the magnet of Hawaii. After a succession of jobs as bellhop, waiter, car-park attendant, like a bit-part actor who finally made the big time in this aquatic Hollywood, he has built a career out of surfing big waves. At thirty-six, he has the raw machismo of Burt Reynolds, the biblical authority of Charlton Heston, the classical physique of Johnny Weissmuller. He jumps off waterfalls to pass the time of day.

Mark Foo is more in the mould of Bruce Lee, a Zen master among big-wave riders. Born in Singapore thirty-one years ago, with a dash of French blood in his Asian veins, brought up on Hawaii, he did two years at the University of Hawaii, but concentrated on attending some of the tougher colleges of the North Shore before finally graduating from Pipeline and Sunset to take his PhD at Waimea in the early eighties. The student quickly claimed pre-eminence over his professors. His sudden rise ruffled the feathers of the old guard, 'the men with beards' as he contemptuously called them. They disliked his aggression, his finesse, his lack of respect for tradition, his obsession with media coverage. No photos, no Foo. There was no love lost between Ken Bradshaw and Mark Foo.

But there was a joker in the pack, too, a fool at this court of kings, a jester, a clown, pure showman and extrovert, the big-wave riders' answer to Evel Knievel. His name was Alec Cooke, but he preferred to be known as Ace Cool. A real estate agent and descendant of one of the old missionary families, he set out with only a minimal grasp of technique to achieve the simple objective of riding the biggest wave in history.

On 18 January 1985 there were plenty of old scores to settle. By noon, the swell at the Bay had built to eighteen to twenty feet. This is when it qualifies, in the phrase of its disciples, as 'real Waimea'. Ken Bradshaw was holding court among a handful of Waimea veterans. By three o'clock, the twenty-five to thirty-foot sets were not just immense, but increasingly gnarly and hard to handle. One of the beauties of Waimea is that, for all its size, it is regular and predictable, almost like a machine-wave, breaking at virtually the same spot every time. But now Waimea had become as shifty and treacherous as Sunset, a churning vortex that would suck in the over-audacious.

Big Waimea has been described as a 'lunatic washing machine'. On that day, Bradshaw said, 'it was more like a toilet. Guys were getting flushed away.' Bradshaw himself got picked off by a thirty-footer and lost his board. He charged the half-mile to the narrow exit lane at the eastern end of the Bay, wedged between the point and the beach, but got trapped in the surging rip current that dragged him towards Coffin Corner, the shipwrecking rocks at the west end of the Bay. He angled out to sea, carved round, then tried again, his huge arms working like steamshovels. Again he was swept away. Now he was on his third circuit of the Bay: he'd been ducking under bulldozers for almost an hour. Bradshaw's technique, his whole life, was built on the twin pillars of strength and stamina; he was used to taking on an unbeatable opposition and winning. Now even he began to look defeated. Betty, who was on the beach at the time, said: 'We thought he was a goner. No one had ever been more than twice round the Bay in those conditions and survived.'

Bradshaw knew he was running out of energy. This time he hugged the point, coming in as close as he dared to the rocks, and felt the gut-wrenching tug of the rip as he approached the shore. But then, as if Waimea had prematurely taken its gloves off, the waves all round him eased and he took advantage of the lull to belt the last thirty yards to the beach. A lifeguard ran up to him, as he strode up the sand amid applauding spectators, and said, 'Hell, you're not even out of breath, are you?'

In the oral history of the North Shore, 18 January 1985 is remembered, in part, as the day Ken Bradshaw swam three times round the Bay. But it would become legend for other reasons, too.

No one was in a hurry to pick up where Bradshaw had left off. Then James Jones, who had pioneered tube-riding at Waimea in the seventies, paddled out. Foo and Cooke decided to join him. They played cat and mouse with the Bay, now scrambling for the outside, now sneaking back in. They flew over a thirty-foot tube which Foo described as 'a huge cavern with half the ocean as its roof and sides'. Jones taunted Cooke: 'Hey Alec, if you'd caught that one you would have had the record.'

Bradshaw was getting ready to go out again when he caught sight of what he later called 'indisputably the largest wave anybody has ever had to deal with'. Out at the line-up, the three men were climbing over a routine thirty-five-footer when they heard screaming and the toot of car horns from the beach. They looked up and the mammoth wave of all time, a titan among giants, a lumbering dinosaur of a wave, had rubbed out the sky. It was still a quarter of a mile beyond the line-up and it was already feathering.

Estimates of the size of that wave vary. Foo says it was twice as big as anything else that day, which would make it sixty to seventy feet from base to crest; some called it eighty feet. Everyone agrees it was the most monstrous wave that had ever appeared on the North Shore. To Foo it seemed so unreal, like a cartoon, a caricature of a big wave, that his initial reaction was to laugh.

The freak wave broke top to bottom across the entire length of the Bay. The surfers bailed out and dived for the bottom. Twenty-five feet down, Foo rolled over and saw an upside-down steam train puff by above him. When he came to the surface, by some obscure miracle his leash had held, and his board was bobbing about a few yards away. 'It was destiny,' he says, 'all part of the Plan.' While the others started looking for land, he slid back onto his gun.

James Jones was picked up by helicopter. Alec Cooke elected to keep swimming. Within minutes, he was getting pulped by the shorebreak. Three times pilot Bogart Kealoha lowered the cage to him. Three times Cooke was pitched out by the pounding surf. 'I was about to become hamburger on the rocks', he admits. At last he emerged from the maelstrom dangling from the bottom of the cage, safe from everything but ridicule and humiliation.

Foo was alone. At this stage his main objective was to catch a wave all the way into the beach. Colossal close-outs kept him sprinting for the horizon. Unable to get far enough inside to catch one of the more amenable waves, Foo at last resolved to attempt an outside set. With the helicopter hovering overhead, he drove for the peak of the leading wave, but then backed off. The next wave was perhaps thirty-five feet, sucking inwards to produce a concave face like the inside of a bottle. Foo was beyond the point of no return. He launched himself over the edge, going into free-fall, his feet still planted on his board. He connected up with the wave again another twenty-five feet down, but lost his footing and fell. It felt more like landing on concrete than water. He skipped on the surface, bouncing the rest of the way down the face.

Ted Deerhurst is one of the few Englishmen to have attempted big Waimea. 'It's like jumping off the roof of a three-storey house,' he said, 'and then having the house chase you down the street.' The house chased Foo, caught him and collapsed on top of him, obliterating his nine-foot three-stringer Lundy.

Foo's luck held. He was given the most cathartic laundering of his life, but his reputation – and his earnings from sponsors – shot up when he published the story in magazines around the globe. Bradshaw thought the hullabaloo was unjustified: 'After all,' he grumbled, 'he didn't actually *ride* the damn thing.'

That was the Day of the Biggest Wave Never Ridden. So who should receive the accolade of riding the biggest wave? The consensus was that the palm should go to Darrick Doerner, a sinewy, red-haired Waimea lifeguard. It was 31 January 1988, Super Bowl Sunday, the last day of the holding period for the Eddie Aikau. In the morning, the swell was three feet. George Downing called off the contest for another year. But at noon, fifteen-foot waves started rolling in. By three o'clock Waimea was twenty-five foot with thirty-foot sets. When the biggest set of the day came through, well over thirty feet but still well-formed, Doerner, Foo, and Bradshaw all set off in pursuit. But there is only a tiny window through which it is possible to slide into waves of this size. Doerner alone was in position. He went over the ledge, hit the water again about half way down, skidded unscathed out of the tube, and kept on going. After that the Bay shut down.

Bradshaw, Foo, Doerner, Cooke: each of them had some claim to supremacy. But there was speculation that the sixteen-foot *olos* of their Hawaiian predecessors had been capable of scaling the monstrous waves, fifty feet and more, that boil and boom off Kaena Point and remain untested in modern times. They were like astronauts landing on the moon and finding footprints in the dust, or like the mountain climbers in Jules Verne who, having at last reached the summit of what they take to be a virgin Himalayan peak, find a sign saying: *M. Durand, Dentist, 14 rue Caumartin, Paris.*

39

*I*ONCE asked Ross Clarke-Jones – a laconic Australian who was on the Tour but also liked to surf big Waimea – which would be his ultimate experience: a big wave or a tube?

'Big tube', he replied.

And what did you need to surf big tubes? 'Bigger everything', he said. 'Bigger boards, bigger lungs, bigger . . . '

Callahan cut in. 'Bigger dick', he said.

I'd always suspected big-wave riders had to have more *cojones* than the average human being, and there was at least one of that species who seemed to bear out my hypothesis. The first time I saw Mark Foo he had two girls with him. The last time I saw Mark Foo he had two girls with him – not the same two. He rode women the way he rode waves.

He had a smooth, lean, compact body. Just below his left shoulder was a raised welt, about four inches long. I speculated endlessly about that welt. Was it a reef injury? Or was it a surgical implant that enabled him to endure more terror than ordinary men, a supplementary hypothalamus? He was a handsome man, with neat geometrical features, but it was this mysterious blemish which, I couldn't help thinking, was the secret of his success with women. It was an irresistible lure, like the quack of a decoy duck.

When I saw him dancing at the Saturday night disco at the Turtle Bay Hilton I thought I had discovered how it was he managed to survive those horrendous wipeouts. At some early stage in his evolution he must have been filleted. He didn't have a pre-ordained and immutable structure to his body, but curled and writhed like a cobra. There were no bones to be broken. He was all suppleness and movement, pure elasticity, like a strip of Blue-Tak.

But we shared at least one thing in common: Foo was a

writer. The account he had written of his experiences at Waimea on 18 January 1985 had won a prize. I had once won a prize for French poetry composition at school, so I didn't feel too outclassed in this respect.

Since he doubled as surfer and media man, our paths crossed often enough. He felt he had only come alive when he started surfing. I felt that way myself – the difference was that he had been living longer. Some people said that Mark was an actor, a hype-artist, an image-projector. This was true to the extent that he was acting out a drama of his own inventing, he was the protagonist in a play that was nothing but climaxes and intervals.

In a strange way, big-wave riding reminded me of cricket. You'd be doing nothing for hours, kicking your heels on the boundary, then, without any warning, the ball would be skied towards you, and suddenly the outcome of the entire match would rest on your shoulders. It was a mixture of tedium and terror: lulls and sets. Paddling out at real Waimea was the equivalent of squaring up to an over from Harold Larwood and finding you had forgotten your box and pads. The board was your cricket bat: the only thing that stood between you and castration.

Foo started out on the Tour but narrowed his sights on Waimea and the outside reefs. There were thousands surfing two-footers, but only a handful on twenty. He had climbed the pyramid right to the top. 'But it's like the Richter scale', he pointed out, warning against the idea of simple increments of difficulty. 'A twenty-foot wave and a twenty-five-foot are completely different worlds. Add another couple of feet and it's twice as hard.' Those figures were misleading anyway: 'A twenty-foot wave might have fifty feet of face on it.' Height is measured vertically from base to crest, but the face – what you actually ride – is the shoreward diagonal of the triangle. 'Some of those waves are thicker than they are high. That's what gives them the power. And you're tapped right into it. You're feeling it all through your toes.'

I suppose I'd expected a stunt-man who pulled off hair-raising feats for kicks. Ken Bradshaw probably wrestled with sharks just for the hell of it. But Foo hated heights, fast cars, motorbikes, even rollercoasters. He liked the quiet life. The odd thing was that he considered life to be at its quietest in the midst of the most thunderous, ear-splitting waves.

He had one huge advantage over everyone else. I put it down to that welt in his shoulder. The more awesome the wave, the calmer he became, until, when the swell entered what he called 'the unridden realm' of thirty foot and above, he was virtually catatonic. He was a yogi, a fire-eater, a knife-swallower, with total control over his body. I felt he could stop his pulse if he wanted to and induce his own death. It wasn't training, it was sheer genetic fluke. He was like a prodigy, a ten-year-old who runs rings around the Grand Master, the infant Amadeus composing symphonies in his head and transcribing Bach masses from memory.

He was just over thirty – still a child in Waimea terms. Waimea demands maturity, experience, the wisdom of years of watching and waiting. It was almost an old man's wave. Foo was perceived as the new kid on the block, the angry young gunslinger who had ridden into town to test his draw against the ageing marshal. He strapped on his three-fin (to increase manoeuvrability and performance) when everyone else was still riding single-fins with no leash. He surfed big conditions with disdainful ease, a slightly meretricious casualness.

But now what had happened to the old guard was happening to him, too. He was in danger of becoming part of the establishment and there was a new young punk hungry for his chance: twenty-one-year-old Brock Little had come fourth in the 1986 Eddie Aikau when Foo was second. I could sense how badly Foo wanted the Eddie. Last year he had won the 'expression session' that replaced the main event, surfed out on occasional twenty-foot sets. But that was just a full-dress rehearsal. Now I could hear the throb of impatience in his voice as he waited for the curtain to go up. Even as we spoke he was thinking of nothing else. Like Ted, he was desperate for his shot at the title.

'Am I ready for the Eddie?' he snorted. 'I've been getting

ready all my life. Every day I wake up I pray it's twenty feet.'

The idea of dying didn't worry him, so long as he went out with a bang. 'When the *Challenger* blew up, everyone said it was a tragedy. But I thought: this was the moment they lived for. They died happy. That's the way I want to go. You can die at Waimea just as easy as Outer Space.' Foo saw the waves as a watery pyre, where he would in due course achieve martyrdom. He reminded me of the author in Godard's *A bout de souffle* who said that his ambition was 'to become immortal – and then die'.

We met briefly once in the water on my ill-fated outing at Laniakea: he was planing down a wave, I was scuttling up it, looking for a way out. He gave me an impassive glance before, like passing trains in a relativity experiment, belonging to separate frames in the universe, we went on our opposite ways. 'Are you crazy,' he said to Bodo later, 'taking that guy out in those waves? He's going to die.' It was a perfectly serious prophecy, for which I would have paid good money had I gone to one of the Haleiwa psychics.

We had another encounter like that, this time on land. I had met a couple of girls on the beach at Pipeline. Their names were Rebecca and Joseanne. They were watching the Masters because, as they frankly admitted, they wanted to meet some surfer boys. But they also wanted a lift into town and we agreed to go to the Hard Rock Café in Honolulu together that night. I went to pick them up at D'Amicos at eight. But, just as at Lani's, I backed out at the last minute. There was no shortage of willing chauffeurs. The next morning I went to Mark Foo's house overlooking Waimea. Rebecca and Joseanne were there. Foo was still in bed. They were fixing him breakfast.

40

'*DON'T MENTION* me in the same paragraph as Ace!'
That was what Mark Foo had said to me.

Ace Cool lived at Jocko's. But it was in the Coffee Gallery in Haleiwa that Bodo first introduced us. Bodo and I had been watching a bodysurfing video starring Mark Cunningham, but when Ace found out I was writing some articles about the North Shore he insisted on an immediate full-scale press conference.

He gave me the inside scoop on the Biggest Wave story: the thirty-five-foot mountain he'd ridden on 5 January 1985. Dropped by helicopter at Fifth Reef Pipeline, he saw the mother of all waves rear up out of the water. This was 'Ace's wave', the one he'd been waiting for all his life.

He looked around for some measure of comparison. 'It was as tall as that tree there.' We were sitting under the canopy of a tree that overhung a two-storey building and dissolved into the inky heavens.

Postcards of Ace and the Wave, showing him flying down an infinite green wall closely pursued by an avalanche, were still available in North Shore shops. A video appeared: *In Search of the Biggest Wave*. And yet Ace was unhappy. 'I'd done everything I set out to do. But nobody took me seriously.' The hardcore élite dismissed the evidence of the camera on the grounds that the aerial perspective didn't distinguish between the face and the base of the wave, effectively doubling its size. He hadn't earned the respect of his peers. He would have to go again.

'I'm aiming for forty feet this time. That'll settle the argument. Or maybe forty-five.'

So far Nature had failed to co-operate.

All Waimea veterans speak of the outer reefs as the next frontier: the majestic 'cloud breaks' that erupt a mile and more from shore where the Aleutian juice is pure and unadulterated and waves even bigger than those at Waimea can, theoretically, be surfed. It was at one of these that Ace was planning another assault on the summit. He had lined up assorted members of the crack US Navy team known as the Seals, a 100-horsepower Zodiac boat, a helicopter, and an oxygen back-pack with six minutes of air.

'The Navy are calling it "The Biggest Wave Mission".'

He made a prediction. 'It's going to get bigger. I can smell it. In the coming month, I'm going to surf the biggest wave ever seen. The boat may get wiped out. I may have to save them. But, basically, if we all survive, we're stoked.'

It sounded as though, win or lose, Ace expected to get to heaven. 'Pulling into a thirty-five-foot tube would be as close to a cosmic experience as you can get, short of surfing the Milky Way. My main motivation is spiritual. It's God's playground out there.' I wasn't sure whether he wanted to meet God or if he thought he was God. 'I want to assume the throne of the big-wave maniacs. My rightful place is at the top. No one else is on the outer reef trip I'm on.'

The holder of a degree in psychology and philosophy, he was anxious to explore the recesses of his own mentality. 'My motives are not completely pure, though. I also want to make some serious bucks out of this. I'm going to license my name. I want to be as famous as Snoopy. I'll be all over your tee-shirt and coffee mug. I want to be the most famous person on the planet, a household word.' After Joe Cool, Ace Cool. I saw Ace becoming the toast of the kings and queens of Europe, having an audience with the Pope, shaking hands with Gorbachev; but he, for once, was more modest: 'I'd like to hook up with Jacques Cousteau — we could stay in tune with the global weather patterns.'

COUSTEAU: Are you familiar with the Balinese behemoth?
COOL: That's a left-hander, isn't it?
COUSTEAU: Fully grown, it has been known to reach up to forty feet in size.
COOL: Holy shit! Do you think it's rideable?

Ace wanted to go out and rape the ocean. 'The wave is my lover and she gives me the ultimate orgasm.' Although, like Asterix, he attributed his phenomenal prowess partly to a magic potion, 'Superjuice', concocted by his druidical sponsors, *Body Ammo*, he didn't really need it: 'They say I have three balls – I need an outlet for that extra energy.' But what drove him on was less his outsize libido than his desire to prove a point and win public acclaim: 'Everyone thinks I'm going to die. So it's me against the world – not to mention the wave.'

He was as psyched up as a footballer about to step out on to the field on Super Bowl Sunday – but he would be sustaining this level of feverish anticipation all winter. 'Every day I'm ready. I dream of it. It's always on my mind.' He was handcuffed to the North Shore. 'If I go to Maui for the day, I'm scared I might miss my chance.'

He was candid about his missionary ancestry. 'My family came to do good and they did very well.' He saw himself as in some way subverting that tradition: they told Hawaiians to put their clothes on and stop surfing; he was taking his off and going pagan all over again. His father wanted him to go to Harvard Business School. 'It was the biggest mistake he ever made buying me my first board.' He had his specially built twelve-foot big-wave gun, weighing about twenty pounds, ready and waiting. 'Yea, though I walk through the valley of the shadow of death, I have the biggest surfboard ever built.'

Ace was a touch over 200 pounds and thirty-three years old. 'Jesus's age', he told me. He may have confused himself with the Messiah, but he didn't expect to die. He thought he was immortal. When he'd gone, there seemed to be a large vacuum in the café. Bodo said, 'I worry about Ace. I hope he's mentally and physically tuned and doesn't just think he is. You're really pushing the limit in anything over twenty-five feet. Last time he only just made it. This time he's a little older. He'll be like an old boxer trying to make a comeback. But the ocean – it doesn't get any older.'

I ran into a lot of sceptics on the North Shore. One lifeguard said, 'Ace may not have ridden the biggest wave, but he's sure got the biggest mouth.'

'A boat and a helicopter?' scoffed another old hand. 'That guy's going to need a submarine to scrape him off the bottom.'

41

*K*EN BRADSHAW waxed and waned with the swell. When it was down, he was down; when it was up, he was up. He competed in the early rounds of the ASP contests, but ten to fifteen feet was a millpond for Bradshaw and he sank like a stone. But atop the blue tower blocks of big Waimea, he attracted as much attention as the Pope on the balcony of St Peter's.

He was six feet tall and 185 pounds and had muscles the way a fish has scales. He had a beard. Often he would shave it off, but the next day he would have a beard just the same. He had a beard all over his chest and back, too. My barber Albert wouldn't have known where to stop cutting. I asked Ken about his reputation as a surfing caveman who would bite chunks out of your board if you got in his way. He laughed, revealing powerful white incisors. Like a circus Hercules demonstrating how to tear up a telephone directory, he showed me how I too could dismantle a board with my mouth. It was all a question of catching it at the right angle. 'If you put them together you can take them apart again.'

Ken was a shaper: he didn't only destroy boards, he created them too. His shaping room had the brightly lit intensity of an operating theatre, the mystery of a chemical laboratory. He strapped his patients to a table and wielded an array of tools with practised precision and dexterity. But the shaper is more than a surgeon or scientist or sculptor: he does more than repair or re-form: he energizes inert matter, turning a slab of foam into a fibreglass dolphin. Green-eyed, bemasked, conjuring up the ten-foot plus boards that could conquer the peaks of Waimea, Ken Bradshaw reminded me of Dr Rotwang in *Metropolis* instilling his robot with beauty and life.

A Bradshaw board carries locked within its smooth husk the seed of its begetter. Ken was father, mother, and midwife to his boards. He hated to throw them away when they got old. They were like children to him. On Christmas Day he grieved over the loss of his second board of the season and nursed one useless half of it all afternoon. He'd seen a kid walking excitedly away from Coffin Corner with a fragment of the Bradshaw cradled in his arms.

'What are you going to do with it?' he asked.

'I thought I'd patch it up and maybe float around on it in summer.'

Ken thought it was going to a good home. 'Keep it, it was mine, now it's yours.'

When Callahan and I visited him at his large house on Sunset Beach, it was like walking around a graveyard: every board was a headstone with memories buried beneath it. 'A good board has a personality, a soul', he said. 'See that one there?' He pointed to a board with a broken nose. 'I mourned it for two whole days when it died.'

Callahan picked on one he recognized from photos. 'This is history right here. State of the art for those days.'

'That was my best board', Ken said. 'I shaped it like a teardrop. But the wide point is too far forward. Those old boards – they were just rockets. I look at them now and think: God, that's prehistoric. But I loved 'em then.' He loved them still. Ken caressed a board fresh from the womb. 'This has more hip to it. Better for pivoting. The trouble is, we sacrificed raw speed for manoeuvrability. Ever since then I've been trying to get the speed back.'

A big heavy man like Bradshaw needs a big heavy board. When it started raining, three of us stayed dry under his ten-foot Waimea gun.

Ken looked like a waterborne Tarzan, swinging through the air from wave to wave. But he had a mild, good-humoured, articulate side, verging on the academic, abjuring the sensational. I'd heard he was vegetarian. 'Lacto-ovo-vegetarian', he corrected. He was as good an advertisement for vegetables as I'd ever come across.

The sixteen-year-old Bradshaw spent the winter of '69 in California. It was the most epic winter the West Coast had ever seen. 'I can remember thinking: that's what it's all about: big waves.' He surfed the reef breaks – La Jolla, Windansea, Swamis – until one day someone came up to him and said, 'With the kind of lines you draw you should go and surf Hawaii.' 'Everything I did was like stepping stones to Hawaii.'

The North Shore was the standard against which all other waves were judged. 'Everyone came to Hawaii to test themselves. That was the mentality I grew up with.' He'd never forget his first experience of Waimea: 'It was 25 March 1974 – a late spring swell, clean and perfect. I went out on a board George Downing had built for me. It was fifteen to eighteen. At the end of the day James Jones came up to me and said: "What's your name?" Man, I was stoked.' Jones was the first man to tube-ride Waimea.

Bradshaw became apprenticed to Eddie Aikau. Eddie was his hero, his guiding light. But Ken didn't always follow his advice. 'In the winter of '76, Waimea was maxing out and houses were floating down the Kam Highway. We were in a car looking down over the Bay and I said I've got to go out. Eddie says to me: "Brother Brad, when the waves are hitting the bath-house, you don't go out".' The bath-house is a couple of hundred yards up the beach. 'So I went out.'

There were thirty-five to forty-foot sets. It was the first time Waimea had been surfed that big. 'I met Roger Erikson on the beach, and he said, "You're going out?" and I said, "Yep, I'm going out", and he said: "All right, I'm going out too." So we both went out.'

That was the day Bradshaw caught the biggest wave of his life. 'It was a left and then the right cut in so I had to straighten out. And then the whitewater caught me so I proned out and hung on – I was eaten up then I was spat out and then I was eaten up again and spat out again and the beach was right there, so I threw the board away and just rolled and rolled and tumbled, and I ended up in the river on the far side of the berm.' No other wave since has deposited him in the river.

He estimated his wave at between thirty and thirty-five. 'If it walls and closes out but you could maybe ride it, that's thirty. If it walls and closes and you can't possibly ride it, that's thirty-five.' He said he'd stood up on waves that were bigger and elected not to go: 'When you know you have that much whitewater to contend with and a rock-lined bay in front of you, it's a deterrent.' That explained why so many of the big-wave riders were focusing their attention on the outer reefs. 'If you want to ride a wave that's over twenty-five feet and feel comfortable, you have to go further out. No matter how good you are, you can't ride an unrideable wave.'

Ken didn't believe Ace Cool had surfed a thirty-five-foot wave. He remembered 5 January 1985. 'Waimea was an adequate fifteen to eighteen. Maybe a couple of bigger sets. I was down here at Sunset and I could see him out there doing it. It wasn't Outside Pipeline, it was actually Outside Rocky Point. When I saw him I was laughing, because it wasn't even twenty feet.' Bradshaw was the only man I met to laugh at twenty-foot waves.

Talking of Ace set him off on Mark Foo. 'Mark is the same way. Mark wanted to go out to Outside Log Cabins with me. He says: "I'll get the boat, I'll get the helicopter." I said: "Keep your boat, keep your helicopter. What if the boat sank? Then we have to depend on ourselves and what about the people in the boat – who's going to save them?"'

Real Hawaiians didn't like accessories and add-ons: they eschewed board grips, gloves, rash guard, stretch shirts, anything that would come between them and the wave. Rubber wetsuits they regarded with distaste as contraceptive sheaths that would interfere with the primal experience.

I, on the other hand, was an accessories fetishist: add-ons were all I had. I never went out without my insect repellent and waterproof sunblock. I'd been given a pair of lime green webbed gloves as a wedding present by Roger, my surfing guru in Newquay. I couldn't get by without them. When I left them behind in Cambridge, I got my wife to send them express to the Turtle Bay Hilton. At Lani's, Bodo told me to throw them away. Regretfully, I consigned them to my personal museum of surfing memorabilia along with my Coogee Beach swallow-tail radical intermediate.

Bradshaw and Foo were popularly supposed to be at war.

'If I wanted to go to war with somebody,' Bradshaw said, 'they wouldn't exist any more. I would win. I think of Mark as my younger brother. Just sometimes his ego gets out of line.'

Ken was a proud traditionalist, a purist, almost a puritan in his stern insistence on standards. But he wasn't a hypocrite. He regularly swam a mile or two out, surfed, and then swam back in again. He didn't mind losing his board and slogging in through the breaking waves. But where I thought of this part of the game as the worst, Ken positively savoured it. 'You have to pay money in an amusement park to get that kind of tumbling.' When I wiped out, it felt like going through a car-wash without a car.

There was one formative element in Ken's youth no one else had mentioned: cinema. As a kid, he had watched the film *Ride the Wild Surf* obsessively. I hadn't seen it, but I recalled the lines in the title-song which went:

> The heavies at the Pipeline are OK,
> But they can't match the savage surf at Waimea Bay.

Ken said, 'Yeah, I remember that too, but what really got me going was the bit at the end:

> It takes a lot of skill and courage unknown
> To catch the last wave and ride it in alone.

Do you remember that?'

It wasn't what I had expected. Ken Bradshaw and I were singing songs to one another like a pair of humpback whales.

Ken's whole life revolved around surfing. 'I've had lots of girlfriends leave me because of it. They would say, "Do you want to do this with me at Christmas or do you want to go surfing?" And I would say: "You're making me choose, don't make me choose." My girlfriend now understands me – she knows my happiness depends on surfing. When I'm happy I'm a wonderful person to be with, but if anyone tries to keep me from doing what I want to do then I'm . . . '

'Unbearable?'

'Unbearable.'

'And if someone makes you choose?'

'Then I'll choose – to surf.'

Ken believed in a supreme being, but said he would never pray for help if he got into trouble. 'I chose to put myself there.' He saw God as a glorified combination of boat and helicopter, not unlike Jules Verne's *The Terror*. Bradshaw wanted nothing to do with either human, mechanical, or divine intervention: he still wanted to catch that last wave and ride it in alone.

42

'*L*OOK AT it: if I'm not working it's blowing up a storm. I'm beginning to think God doesn't want me to surf.'

Banzai Betty had begun to feel things were against her. She'd had a good run on the Tour a few years back and was rated as the best and perhaps the only big-wave rider among women. But now she was suffering from asthma. She worried about having an attack in the middle of a wipeout: 'I'd be gaping like a fish on a gaff.'

Amid the men's Triple Crown events, there was one event for women: the Sunset Beach Sunwear Women's Pro. Betty was determined to compete. She needed the money and there was the lure of the biggest-ever cash prize for women: $11,000 for the winner. But it was more of an existential crisis for her: she had to face her fear. She suspected that the asthma that had put her out of action had psychosomatic roots. She was out of it because, deep down, she didn't want to be in it any more. 'My body is telling my mind I don't want to surf. But I do want to surf. I just can't. I go all to pieces out there.'

'Now you know what I feel like', I said.

She laughed. 'Let's face it, it's no big deal. There are guys around here who take it so seriously. It's a real religion for them. Me, I think it's not so big, compared with God or something.' I thought that was still fairly big.

The contest was called for the morning of 23 December. 'They wait until the waves are shitty then they send the women out.' Now Sunset was only four to five. 'That's not Sunset!' she raged. 'That's Ehukai Beach Park stuff.'

She stormed out with her Willis Phazer under her arm. Her boyfriend Rick thought women were better off on smaller waves and said so. They sniped at each other over breakfast.

'Men just don't understand women surfers', she said to me. 'We're always getting bad-mouthed. First they say you're no good, you're just women, you don't have the power. So you get real tough out there. And then they say: look at you. You're so aggressive, you're not feminine.'

'So you can't win?'

'What I say is, you've got to be tough and aggressive to surf Waimea and Pipeline. You're not going to survive any other way. And to hell with what they say.'

Michael was going to caddy for Betty in the contest, cruising with a spare board. He was in an optimistic mood. 'It's small, yes – but perfect. I can get her through', he said. Then he added, 'You know what I think: judge not that ye be not judged by others.' I had no idea what he meant.

Betty was due to surf in the fourth heat of the morning. She should have checked in by the end of the second and paddled out during the third. As the third heat started an announcement came over the Tannoy: 'Banzai Betty, where are you?' And then again: 'Banzai, this is your last call.' Finally her heat went ahead without her. When I arrived back at the house she was just paddling in at Backyards. 'I missed the heat? So, I missed the heat', she said dismissively.

'It was a good decision', said Michael. 'She's not in the right shape for it. And if you compete and lose, you feel bad. You think negative about yourself. Better to stay positive. She'll have another chance.'

Betty's house was the forum for discontent among the women on the North Shore. Debbie Beecham, the latest in the string of people to occupy Yvon's room, was women's representative to the ASP, which was due to hold its AGM at the Turtle Bay Hilton. One evening, a tempestuous meeting of a dozen of the top women surfers in the world was held in Betty's living room. Feeling suddenly *de trop*, I drifted off with Michael to watch a movie starring Johnny Boy Gomes. Johnny Boy and his beefcake cronies were scouring the South Pacific for waves and putting the wind up pint-sized Samoans.

That night I put a routine call through to Tom Clarke in London. There were no results to report.

'Anything else going on, Andy?'

'Nothing – apart from a women surfers' liberation movement.'

'Sounds interesting. Why don't you do us a few hundred words on simmering mutiny in the women's camp? Phone it through in an hour?'

I thought of saying, 'Tom, it's nearly one o'clock in the morning. I'm tired. I went to a movie instead of staying for the meeting. I couldn't write thirty words on the subject, let alone three hundred.'

But all I said was, 'It's on its way.' Tom Clarke wasn't Johnny Boy Gomes. He wasn't going to dismember me. But nobody messes with the Sports Editor of *The Times*.

What I needed was a source, an informant, a reservoir of indiscretion, whose spontaneous utterances could be shaped into suitable quotations. But a good source can be hard to come by, especially at one o'clock in the morning.

I knocked on Debbie Beecham's door. No answer. I inched it open.

'Who is it?' she croaked.

'It's me, Andy.' Intent on averting editorial displeasure, I'd temporarily forgotten Debbie was an attractive woman with a boyish grin: precisely the kind of woman you might like to drop in on at one o'clock in the morning. For a moment, I felt uneasily like a character in *The Boyfriends*. 'You don't feel in the mood for an interview, do you?' I said.

Debbie explained that the main problem for the women was the lack of media coverage and, consequently, the lack of sponsorship. No pictures, no money, no women surfers. Hardcore surfing magazines — the passport to recognition — were run by men for men; women were allowed in only as bikini-clad groupies draped around their male masters. Debbie had inside knowledge: she worked for *Surfer* magazine, but only in a sales capacity. If women couldn't surf, they couldn't write about surfing.

In a beach shack at Yallingup in Western Australia I had discovered a hoard of old surfing magazines from the sixties. It was like reading a series of dogmatic theological tracts on the evils of the flesh; their recurrent theme was: you have to choose between surfing and sex. Proximity to women would diminish your prowess on the wave. I came across the same monastic anxiety among certain North Shore men. 'You know why sex is bad for you?' Rick said. 'Because sperm contains a lot of lecithin. Every time you have sex, you lose all that lecithin. You have to take a lot of vitamins to make up for it.'

Traditionally, Hawaiian women surfed just as well as the men. Captain Cook had noted their equality in the water. 'It was very common for women with infants at the breast to come off in canoes to look at the ships, and when the surf was so high that they could not land them in the canoe they used to leap overboard with the child in their arms and make their way ashore through a surf that looked dreadful.' Among present-day men, there was controversy about women's surfing. Most thought it was a contradiction in terms. The rest said 'they look good on the beach'. There were various theories to account for the difference in ability between men and women: it was genetic, it was physiological, it was psychological. Girls weren't encouraged to test themselves against danger; their bodies weren't the right shape; they were weak and gutless.

I knew this was all wrong: I had seen Eden Burberry surf.

Eden Burberry wasn't on the North Shore. I had met her in Thurso, where she became 1988 British champion. She composed poems with water, she turned manoeuvres into metre, a twist and turn into a stanza. The wave became a sonnet of surfing style, a ballad of poise and power. Beneath her swift and sensitive board, even Sewage Pipe Break might have been mistaken for Ulu, for Bells, for Malibu. When she finessed a five-footer, passing seals popped their heads out of the water and paused to admire. I had paddled out on a borrowed longboard and found myself competing for the peak with Eden. It was no contest.

Twenty-one years old, with short corn-gold hair, she looked like she would live forever, immune to every mortal corruption, as though she had eaten of the Tree of Life. Her name was enough to seduce me without hope of redemption: a combination of paradise and macintosh. She would provide shade in summer, shelter in winter. She seemed to me vast and inevitable, like the giantess of Baudelaire's poem: I longed to sleep nonchalantly in the shadow of her breasts, like a peaceful hamlet at the foot of a mountain. I realize now that learning to surf was just a way of impressing Eden Burberry. But I might as well try to impress the moon. The last time I saw her she was working in Boardwalk in Newquay: she couldn't remember my name. I couldn't forget hers.

At Sunset Beach, the contest was won by Australian Pam Burridge. Jodie Cooper came in second. Fourth-placed Wendy Botha took the world title for the second consecutive year. Collectively, they constituted a remote reminiscence of Eden Burberry. Eden was the indispensable archetype, the absent mould out of which all other women were formed.

This hidden pattern was lost on other journalists. So long as the Sunset Beach Sunwear Pro was on, most photographers played truant. They turned up in time to see the finalists pose glisteningly on the podium. Callahan spent the day at Rocky Point and Off-the-Wall. 'I've got better things to do with my time than take pictures of clam-bumpers', he said. Callahan divided women into four categories: (1) *slut* – 'hosing every guy in town'; (2) *bitch* – 'hosing every guy in town except you'; (3) *clam-bumper* – 'lesbian'; (4) *the good woman* – 'frigid'.

Betty still yearned to tackle a twenty-footer. 'I'll show those guys one of these days', she said. 'Then they'll have to treat me with respect.' She was single-handedly trying to bust up the male monopoly of the surfing media and big-wave riding. But she was up against a long tradition. Ken Bradshaw, sitting in the line-up at Waimea, once saw Betty paddling out to join the men. 'You're out?' he said. 'I'm going in: it must be too small.'

43

IT WAS on Christmas Eve that I went for a hike in the hills with Liese and Bodo and Betinna. We walked up through Pupukea Park and into the forest overlooking the North Shore. It was probably the first time for almost a month that I hadn't been able to hear the sound of the surf. Through the trees you could glimpse patches of blue piped with white. Even the restless ocean looked tranquil from here.

'This is the best season', Liese said. 'Look at the light. It is too intense in the summer, but now – it is soft and mellow.' She might have been describing herself.

I fell behind the others, distracted by a thousand things. Liese slowed down to keep pace with me. 'Smell this', she said, handing me a leaf. It smelt extraordinarily like lemon meringue pie. 'It is the leaf of a variety of eucalyptus.' She encouraged me to sniff at everything. 'You need to nourish your lungs,' she said, 'you can't just exercise them.' She reminded me of one of that imaginary race, spoken of by Claude Lévi-Strauss, who survive on smell, inhaling the perfume of various life-giving plants.

But she was not beyond eating. The forest was heavy with fruit. As we climbed upwards, we picked guava, mangoes, yellow and purple passion-fruits, and thimbleberries, which were a cross between a strawberry and a raspberry. Liese pointed out the rose apple to me: it had the scent of a rose and the taste of an apple. 'Here, taste this.' She scooped out the inside of a flower and dabbed her finger on my tongue. It was the honey of the hibiscus flower. 'There is only a tiny amount – but it is perfect.'

We came to a ridge overlooking the forest. 'What are you dreaming about, Andy?'

'I was wishing there would be a twenty-foot swell tomorrow.' The surf may have been out of ear-shot but I couldn't put it out of my mind.

'Perhaps you would like the leaves on that tree to turn to twenty-dollar bills, too. It won't just happen. You have to work for it.'

I told her I'd been brought up in the tradition of genies in lamps and fairy godmothers: I expected my wishes to be granted without too much hard labour on my part.

'You wish, you wish. You have too many desires.'

A liana dangled like a bell-rope to one side of the steep path. I said: 'I've always wanted to swing through the trees – like Tarzan, you know.'

The liana was only a yard out of reach, only a jump away. But it was suspended over a yawning chasm. If I missed, it was a long fall. Liese watched me hesitating, torn between my fantasy and reality. 'It is a trap for people like you who cannot restrain their desires.'

I pulled back. 'I'd better restrain my desires, then.'

'But then you will never swing through the jungle.'

It was in just such a spot as this that, six months later, Ronnie Burns, a finalist at the Masters and fearless escapee from the Stalag XIII of Pipeline, would die in a dirt-bike accident.

We stopped at a clearing from which we had a view of Kaena Point to the west. Half an hour later we had a view to the east and saw Kahuku Point.

'You can almost see the whole twelve miles at a glance', I said.

'If you could climb a tree tall enough, you would see it', said Liese.

I looked for but couldn't find such a tree. I craved the omniscient vantage point that would reveal the entire North Shore and all its mysteries to me in a moment of perfect vision. On the beach, in the water, I was blinded by every passing sensation. I had gone up the mountain in search of answers, but enlightenment still eluded me: I had scattered impressions, odd angles, details, but not the single grand sweeping vista that encompassed everything.

Liese told me that all I really needed in life was a coconut palm. The tree would furnish me with food, drink, clothing, shelter, mats, baskets, cups, a bed and even a canoe. My childhood reading had long ago convinced me of the utility of the palm tree. When Peter Duck (in Arthur Ransome's novel of that name) was shipwrecked on Crab Island and besieged by man-eating crabs, he swarmed up a palm and lived there for months. I wanted a tree like Peter Duck's, with buried treasure under it.

Liese and Bodo had little furniture and few clothes. Liese was attached to a chair and a rug; Bodo to a couple of surfboards. They rented their house. Liese said being was better than having, they would rather accumulate experiences than possessions.

'Is there nothing you want?' I asked.

'No', she said. 'I have everything I need.'

'I was forgetting. You've transcended desire, haven't you.'

'No. But I am very patient.'

We came across a forest of paperbark trees. Ragged sheaves of the pale bark, nicotined at the edges, were peeling from the trunks like the pages of a yellowing manuscript.

'That is Lao-tzu's tree', Liese said. 'He loved this tree above all others. It is multi-layered – like us.'

We came back down through the *heiau* that overhangs Waimea Bay. In the days before Cook, the whalers, and the missionaries, a community of Hawaiians lived in Waimea. The *heiau* was where they conducted their religious ceremonies. Liese showed me the tree in whose shade human sacrifices were once made. There was a large stone beneath it with a deep indentation: this was the block where the victim placed his head. He was beaten to death with clubs, then cut up and burned to placate the gods.

Captain Cook had visited one such *heiau* in Waimea on the island of Kauai, and his own lifeless body was dismembered and cremated in another, known as Hikiau, in Kealakekua Bay.

Tumble-down black lava rocks marked out the site of a vast temple. Now it was only a ruin. But the descendants of the Hawaiians continued to treat the *heiau* as sacred ground and people still came here to make sacrifices to the gods. In a clearing looking directly over the Bay we found a coconut-shell urn containing ashes. Resting on the fragmentary foundations of the temple were small offerings – fruit, nuts, bread – wrapped in ti-leaves. I thought of the temple perched on top of the cliffs at Ulu Watu and dedicated to the spirits of the sea, where monkeys watched over the surfers hundreds of feet below. It seemed as if there was a universal affinity between big waves and the godhead.

Liese plucked a ti-leaf – a long green pennant also used in the skirts of hula dancers – from the tree that stood by the temple. 'It is said that if you make an offering then the gods will look favourably on you and your wishes.'

I had only one wish. I found a guava tree and picked a fruit from its branches. I wrapped the guava in the ti-leaf and lodged it among the stones of the temple. A kitten attached herself to me and purred loudly. 'People leave animals here because they think the gods will look after them.' The kitten came back to Betty's with me. I called her 'Sunset' on account of her colouring. She must have been a surfer's cat: she would curl up on the bench where Michael Willis sat and fall asleep watching the waves.

Liese told me that during a lull the surf-loving Hawaiians would seek to summon up swells in the way desert dwellers would try to conjure up rain during a drought. A *kahuna* (sorcerer) would sing special *mele* of encouragement and incitement to the sea. She recited one of them:

> Arise! Arise! You great surfs from Kahiki,
> Powerful, curling waves,
> Arise with the Pohuehue,
> Well up, long-raging surf.

The *pohuehue* was a vine with which you lashed the waters in the surf-coaxing ritual, setting up an undulation which would elicit bigger waves in response.

All four of us picked our way through the dense undergrowth down the tricky path that led to a promontory and a 200-foot drop to the river below and Waimea beyond. I slithered out onto a ledge.

The Bay was perhaps half a mile at its widest point. At the eastern end was a long equilateral of brown rock jutting out into the sea with a house on it. At the western end was a mass of boulders that might have been a ruined temple crumbling into the water. A crescent of golden sand was wedged between them. The sun was slipping down over the horizon, slowly turning the blue sea black.

As I gazed down, it seemed as if someone invisibly far away must be beating the ocean with the strands of a *pohuehue*. Serried ranks of mathematically aligned sine-curves processed across the Bay. The great surfs from Kahiki were arising, the long-raging surf was welling up.

44

I TUNED into Banzai Betty's Surf Report on Kool 83 K–I–K–I:

> Sunset Beach is ten feet and blown out. Pipeline is twelve feet and unrideable. Waimea is fifteen feet and cranking. Merry Christmas, surfers.

Christmas Day on the North Shore. Just another day on the beach.

I jumped into my rental car and drove down Kam Highway. It wasn't every day Waimea was as big as this. Sunset could be fifteen feet and Waimea would still be a dribble. But when the swell gets too big for the other breaks to live with, that's when it starts happening at Waimea.

I drove past Sunset, past Rocky Point, past Pipeline, past Off-the-Wall. Finally I pulled into the Mission car park on the eastern end of the Bay. As I was walking out Mark Foo was walking in with his Willis Brothers Phazer under his arm.

'How is it?'

'It's big. It's getting bigger.'

It was ten in the morning. Foo had already been out for hours.

I clambered along the rocks that take you out on the point adjacent to the line-up and dug in among the throng of photographers and spectators. I stared right down the barrel of the break. It was breathtaking.

The Pacific Ocean was putting on the best free show in the world. Mighty waves reared up in front of me like stallions, spitting foam, then staggered as if shot through the heart, folded over and collapsed under a massive mane of white-water. A dozen big-wave riders were hugging the narrow take-off zone, waiting their chance to get in the saddle. I could feel the earth tremble beneath my feet every time a wave broke.

A set of three or four waves, maybe eighteen feet, came grinding through. The first wave completely erased Ken Bradshaw, snapping his board clean in two. He came up, was worked over by the remaining waves in the set, and struck out for shore.

It was around eleven when the biggest set of the day loomed over the horizon and thundered towards the wave-riders. They let the first one go: too messy and out of control. But it cleared the way for the second: a steep, smooth twenty-foot wall of water, gently feathering at the lip, and ready to erupt like Vesuvius.

Only one of the riders elected to move into position: Hawaiian Titus Kinimaka, from the island of Kauai, one of the front runners for the Eddie Aikau. Killer waves were mother's milk to him. He ran up mountains before breakfast and lived off coconuts which he would pluck from the tree himself. He was hewn out of solid muscle, his black, Rasta-like locks falling down on immense shoulders. This was just a normal day's exercise for him.

He was hauled up the face of the wave, trying to ride the up escalator down. Up and up he went, until it looked as if he was about to fall off the back. But two lunging strokes sent him surging forward. He leapt to his feet and hurtled down the face. He had total control, legs akimbo, crouching, keeping his centre of gravity low, his arms flung out wide to give him maximum balance.

He leaned into a tight bottom turn, and pulled up fearlessly towards the lip. The wave pitched out to form a huge, devouring tube. Titus was swallowed up inside it.

What seemed a lifetime later he broke the surface, clinging to his board and screaming for help. Michael Willis raced over calling others to his aid. A flotilla of surfers quickly formed a human liferaft around the stricken man.

I ran round to the beach to get a better view. By the time I got there, one of the team of Waimea lifeguards, Hall Dannon, was in the water, whirling an arm over his head, signalling for a helicopter. The lifeguard in the tower radioed through, but the helicopter was in action on the other side of the island. It would be at least twenty minutes.

Other surfers clustered round the tower, hungry for information.

'What happened?'

'He took off on a big one and ate it.'

'Looks like a neck injury.'

'No, it's a gut injury.'

'Could be a broken leg.'

'Titus, I can't believe it, the guy's built like Superman.'

A powerful rip current swept the party of surfing samaritans towards the bone-crushing rocks of Coffin Corner at the west end of the Bay, where what was left of Ken Bradshaw's board was being pounded to pieces. The tower gave an ominous loudhailer warning. 'There's a big set coming. Repeat – a big set of waves is approaching you fast. The helicopter and ambulance are on their way.' The surfers scrambled, vanishing into a trough. They reappeared sliding over the lip of the last wave.

One of the group struggled into shore.

'What's happened to the helicopter? Titus is freaking out.' He explained that Kinimaka had been crushed by the lip, compacted on his board, 'squashed – like an insect splattered on the wall'. The impact had ripped his right leg out of its socket. As the next couple of waves passed over him, his ankle leash continued yanking on the injured limb. His leg had turned blue and ballooned up to double its size. He was haemorrhaging, suffering from cramps and hypothermia, and going into shock.

Darrick Doerner said, 'You can die from that. You go into trauma and that's it. Can't you get him in?'

'No chance. He's begging us not to move him. We can't risk the shorebreak.' Waimea's shorebreak has a habit of slamming you onto the beach, ripping you apart, and then sucking you back out to do it all over again. You need all your power and skill to manoeuvre your way through it. An injured man wouldn't make it.

Lifeguard Kenny Rust sprinted out on his long white rescue board with an oxygen tank. Through my binoculars, I could see Australian Robbie Page treading water and propping up Kinimaka's head. Michael Willis and his brother Milton were massaging his body, trying to keep him warm. Barton Lynch peeled off his wetsuit top and tenderly placed it around his shoulders.

The helicopter clattered round the point. It hovered over the churning sea and winched down a rescue cage. Darrick Doerner and Louis Ferreira, a friend of Kinimaka's, gingerly steered their fragile charge aboard and climbed in with him. The helicopter banked and swung over the beach, gently lowering its cargo onto the sand.

Titus was writhing in agony. Police barked at gawping sunbathers to keep back. Photographers jockeyed for position around the cage. Ken Bradshaw helped to stretcher Kinimaka into the waiting ambulance where he was shot full of pain-killing drugs before the helicopter freighted his limp body into Honolulu for an emergency operation.

Bodo had arrived to supervise the rescue. 'When the lip of a wave like that hits you, it's like a tree falling on you', he said. 'Titus was strong. But the ocean is stronger. It never gets tired. It's relentless.'

Michael Willis brushed away compliments and praised the others who had joined in the rescue. 'Every one of those guys was a hero. That was true brotherhood. If I ever got into trouble, they would be the people I would want around me.' It was Michael who had shaped Titus's board. 'Titus is the main man. He's the heaviest guy at the heaviest spot – on the heaviest wave. That was the meanest, baddest, most awesome, beautiful wave.'

A bronzed girl in a bikini said, 'I feel sick. I can't stand the sight of blood. To know a guy is in that much pain – I feel sick.'

Surfers hung around and compared their battle wounds and reminisced over buddies who didn't come back. Ken Bradshaw said he'd seen three people die right in front of where we were standing.

'Were they any good?' I asked.

'They thought they were good', he said grimly. Then his mood lightened. 'It's funny, you know when the surf's best? Christmas Day, Easter, Thanksgiving. Valentine's Day, too. Whenever you should be with your family or your girlfriend. It's bad luck surfing on a day like this.'

Someone else thought it was karma: Titus was too 'amped' in the water, too greedy for waves.

Don Mayo, a Californian, said it could happen to anyone any time. He told me about a friend who had died at Honolua Bay on Maui a month before and another who had broken his leg the previous week. Then he gazed out at the break and said, 'Maybe this is a good day for trying out my nine-footer.'

One by one, surfers paddled back out to the line-up, ready

to run the gauntlet again. This time the gods had seen their prey snatched away from them. But there would be other victims. Would-be martyrs were queuing up to join their ancestors in the surfers' Valhalla.

45

IT WAS the day after Christmas. I laughed at Callahan for missing Waimea. He said he'd been too tied up with his family and girlfriend.

'Jane got me a great present – a turtle-neck sweater. Looks like the kind of thing you'd wear in England. I don't know why she got it for me. Crazy.'

'What did you get her?'

'Sweater.'

What had brought Callahan out to Sunset was the start of the Billabong. The waves were a clean six to eight, the wind was offshore, and Randy Rarick was impatient to get started.

A pattern had emerged in the Triple Crown contests. Dave Macaulay, the 'Invisible Man', went out in his first heat again, leaving Derek Ho as runner-up in the ASP world title stakes. Randy Rarick was dismissive. 'If you can't cut it in Hawaii, you don't count. Real men surf Hawaii well.' Exceptionally on the North Shore, man-on-man duels were standard in the Billabong. But again the locals dominated; Mike Latronic got the highest score of the day and thrashed Damien Hardman. Mike's progress through the heats at least took Dolle's mind off *The Boyfriends* and kept her off my back for a while. Barton Lynch ended dismally at the contest where he sealed the world title in 1988, going out early to Brock Little. Richie Collins bombed out too: the Lord was putting him through another trial.

The Billabong was a moveable feast: it could be held almost

anywhere on the North Shore. But Randy had tried Waimea in other years and more or less rejected it. There was just too much fear. 'Anyhow, Waimea doesn't lend itself to the ASP format. It's essentially a big-wave arena — whoever gets the biggest wave wins. It's not for manoeuvres. Better would be Pipeline, spitting tubes all day, or clean, classic Sunset, eight to ten. Either of those would be perfect for the final.' In the end, the Billabong finished where it had started.

The following days were uncontestworthy: patchy five to six. The end of the holding period for the Billabong was 4 January. The ASP was running out of time. Everyone was hoping for an eleventh-hour miracle like the year before. On 3 January, Sunset was six to eight: the surf was not all-time, not epic, not even classic. But there was no other swell scheduled, so Randy called the contest on again.

Paul Holmes, the English editor of *Surfer*, who had gone to Newquay Grammar School with Roger Mansfield, said, 'It isn't a miracle, but a kind of redemption.'

Sarge said, 'It's a panic measure. Still, maybe they've got a right to panic with only one day left.'

Betty said, 'This would have been perfect for the women.'

There was one foregone conclusion: Pottz had already sewn up the world title. Nothing could change that. And there was one dead cert: Gary Elkerton, with a first at Pipeline and a second at the Hard Rock already under his belt, was a natural for the Triple Crown. But every one of the surfers in the water wanted to win the Billabong's $50,000 first prize. Elkerton could only reach the quarters before being put out by the blitzing Mike Latronic. Dolle was worrying about what to do with the $50,000. Pottz crashed out in round three to Australian Cheyne Horan.

Randy said, 'No one remembers who won in Brazil. Everyone remembers who won in Hawaii. Pottz has still got to win here.' It was an Hawaicentric view of the world that beguiled non-Hawaiians too.

Cheyne Horan had been runner-up for the world title four times at the end of the seventies, usually to Mark Richards (known for his idiosyncratic stance as 'the wounded gull').

He began experimenting with board design in his search for the elusive edge that would take him right to the top. For a season or two he tried the twin-fin, which had a brief vogue before the tri-fin took over. Then he developed the revolutionary 'star-fin,' adapted from the 'winged keel' of the 1983 America's Cup yacht. He won a certificate from the Australian Hall of Fame for technical innovation, but not much else. 'It was like an anchor round his leg', Callahan said. 'It was insane, but he wouldn't give it up.' The eighties saw him slide progressively down the rankings. At the end of 1988, he was 22 in the world; his best Hawaiian finish had been 13th.

But this winter he had already taken third at the Pipeline Masters. A win at the Billabong would not only make him considerably richer, but restore him to the privileged ranks of the Top 16. Second place would leave him at 17. But in the gruelling world of pro surfing, they say once you're down you never come back. He hadn't won a contest since 1984. Some called him 'the Heartbreak Kid'.

Horan was a popular figure. At twenty-nine he was accorded the kind of respect you can usually only expect if you have a white beard. Horan only had white, white hair. He was everything a true surfer should be. He looked as if he came from a planet closer to the sun. He was not just radical in the water, but a committed subversive out of it: unorthodox, environmentally aware, macrobiotic, an adept of yoga and Eastern philosophies. He had made a stand on apartheid. Betty was in love with his steely blue eyes.

Horan came up against Mike Latronic in the semis. I asked Ted what his strategy would be. 'Go for the second wave in the set', he said, squinting at the break like a biologist inspecting a slide under the microscope. 'It varies from day to day, but today it's the best one.' Just then a two-wave set came through. Latronic took off on the first one: it petered out. Horan took the second: it was big, long, and tubey. 'I should be out there', said Ted. The peak was jumping around like a snappy terrier. Sunset was Latronic's home break, but Horan was always mysteriously in the right place at the right time.

Throughout every round he had out-manoeuvred, out-tubed, and out-powered all opposition. Now he finally put paid to Dolle's hopes and dreams by out-pointing her son. She would have to go back to the arms of *The Boyfriends*.

The final was an all-Australian affair between Horan and Ross Clarke-Jones. Going for his first wave, Clarke-Jones fell and smashed his board. His caddie brought him a replacement, but after that he was never in contention. I identified with Ross Clarke-Jones: in that final he surfed like me, he was always either too far back or too far forwards, missing the take-off or going over the falls.

Cheyne Horan didn't put a foot wrong. He was pulling off vertical snaps and off-the-lips and catching tubes like it was rush hour on the London Underground. 'That guy is just going off!' blurted the Tannoy.

'I've been fighting my arse off for years to get back in the Top 16', Horan said in his victory speech. 'Now I have and it's going to be a bloody long while before they get me out again.' He not only won the Billabong, but took second place in the Triple Crown. 'I'm feeling rejuvenated, recycled, and ready for the title. When you're in the Top 16 there's only one thing to aim for. I can't say much more, I think my surfing did the talking for me.' Later I heard him talking on the phone to Australia in the press trailer. 'I'm stoked. I'm totally stoked. Man, I'm stoked.'

46

I HEARD a lot of theories about why the big-wave riders were doing what they were doing: it was sex, it was drugs, it was religion, it was Russian roulette. The most articulate philosopher, almost the patron saint, of surfing is Ricky Grigg, one of the trail-blazing pioneers of Waimea Bay. He'd been described to me as combining the body of Charles Atlas with the mind of Socrates. At fifty, he is a professor of oceanography at the University of Hawaii and still regularly rides the Bay. He said it was like being both an economist and a stockbroker: when you'd figured out the logic of the system, you wanted to play it for all you could get.

On the balcony of his spacious house overlooking Sunset, Grigg introduced me to his girlfriend and his daughters – all more or less of an age. Grigg didn't look so much older, as wiser. He was as well preserved as the relativistic spaceman who travels a short while at the speed of light and returns to earth to find all his contemporaries in the grave and his children grown-up.

We had one thing in common: he had once spent a sabbatical year at Cambridge. 'Great place', he remembers. 'The surf was a little flat, though.' He was joking, but he was right: it was hard to fantasize about tidal waves sweeping up the Cam and engulfing the colleges.

All surfers look at the world through turquoise-tinted spectacles. They judge a place according to the size of its waves. Like a strict political credo, this outlook gives coherence to their world-view. Nations are not split into democrat and despot, capitalist and communist, but into surfing and non-surfing. I had read a letter from a Californian surfer in the correspondence column of *Surfing*. Briefly passing through Germany on a world tour, he went to visit the Berlin Wall. Sighting an East German border guard in a tower, he yelled out to him: 'You're bummed: you will never know what surfing is.'

Ricky Grigg was a modest man who didn't include himself among the handful of people who had surfed a thirty-foot wave. He estimated at around twenty the number of serious big-wave riders, men whose whole *raison d'être* was big waves. There were three names I had heard associated with the early days of big-wave riding: Grigg, Peter Cole and Greg Noll. Grigg told me that Peter Cole was a supreme waterman. He was in the Olympic swimming team. He could hold his breath for a couple of minutes underwater and swim thirty miles without blinking. One of the primary requirements then was sheer power and endurance, what Grigg called 'a high strength-to-weight ratio'. Although Grigg himself could 'swim the channels', from island to island, he was never in the same league as Cole.

But just as important was 'sea-sense', a knowledge of the ocean. 'What stops most guys is the fear factor; but what causes fear is ignorance.' When I went out in the water I had only the haziest idea of what was happening. 'When we go out we know how deep the water is, what way the current's moving, how fast it's moving, we know whether the surf's going up or coming down, we've looked at the weather charts, we know what the wind will do, and the tide. We're equipped to deal with the variables.'

The imagery of big-game hunting and bullfighting was common in talking about big-wave riding. The boards were 'elephant guns' and 'rhino chasers', their riders 'matadors' of the surf. So it didn't surprise me that Grigg should draw on Hemingway for an analogy. But the comparison wasn't framed in terms of existential *Angst* and heroism and toughness. 'The thing about the big-game hunter was that he knew the animal: when a rhino was bearing down on him at thirty miles an hour, he knew what his gun would do, he knew what the animal would do. He wasn't out there on a fluke.' And so it was with big-wave riders. They had stamina, durability, stoicism, but above all, they had knowledge.

'Is that the definition of a "waterman"?' I asked.

'There are watermen who don't have what it takes to ride big waves. You need a bit of reckless abandon thrown in for good measure. Like Titus the other day: he was really hot, he was doing things he'd never done before at Waimea, and he got over-confident, he pushed it too far, and the wave just cracked him.'

Grigg recalled friends who had overstepped the line. José Angel was another of the early band of big-wave explorers. He enjoyed danger the way other men enjoy a pipe and slippers: he surfed, he dived, he flew to unwind. 'He was all guts and he didn't care.' He knew that 250 feet was the limit for sustained work in the ocean. After that, nitrogen narcosis was a virtual certainty. But when he hit 250 feet and the reef he was trawling for black coral went deeper, Angel just kept on going – all the way down to 340 feet. That was rather like Ken Bradshaw going out at Waimea when the waves were past the bath-house. To some men, prohibition is tantamount to provocation. The difference was, Angel died. 'The ocean has no mercy when it comes to exceeding what a human being can endure. It's like falling off a fishing boat in the Antarctic: you've got nine minutes and that's it. At Waimea, if a twenty-five-foot wave unloads on you, it's going to break you. If a horn goes in, you're going to be gored. There's no way round it.'

I liked the idea of the intellectual surfer, the scholar of the waves, who had done his homework on the sea before paddling out to do battle with it. But Ricky said that although you needed a lot of knowledge, you didn't necessarily think that much on the wave. 'There comes a point where you're completely committed and nothing and no one can pluck you out of that situation, where you're not so much a god as an animal. You're all instinct. You don't feel human any more. You're under this mountainous curl of green water with the light coming through it and your body is reacting like an enormous chemical machine. You feel young and strong and powerful.' The big-wave rider was perfect understanding transformed into pure being. His mind was his body and his body was his mind. For the duration of the ride, his person coalesced with the Truth.

Ken Bradshaw had said that riding a big wave was like living out your whole life in miniature. The ride seemed to condense the seven ages of man into less than half a minute. The take-off was equivalent to birth, the elevator drop was the wild rush of childhood, the bottom turn was adolescent bravado, the swooping ascent into the tube, the lover's embrace, from which you emerged through various mid-life crises onto the quieter slopes of late maturity, while the whitewater tail-end of the wave was like white-bearded old age.

'You'd have to include death in it, too', Grigg said. One of the attractions for him lay in satisfying his curiosity about death without actually dying. He wanted to know what it felt like when the horns of the bull missed him by an inch. 'I like to flirt with death, to run just as close as I possibly can to becoming history. It's like turning round in an alley and seeing this guy who wants to kill you and you're up against a wall. All the organs squirt. And the next day, I feel reassured that I'm here for a little while longer. It's completely revitalizing.'

Grigg's allegory of rebirth put me in mind of Orpheus or Aeneas descending into the underworld, briefly experiencing what it must be like to be dead, and then re-ascending into the light of day. I was under no illusions about how difficult the last part was:

> . . . easy is the descent to Avernus:
> night and day the door of gloomy Diss stands open;
> but to recall thy steps and pass out to the upper air,
> this is the task, this is the toil.

It was only when Grigg spoke of the *alley* and *the guy who wants to kill you* and *the horns of the bull* that I realized that the wave was a labyrinth, a marine equivalent of the subterranean system of rooms and passages that was easy to get into, almost impossible to get out of, and inhabited by a monster. In the deepest darkness of the tube you would encounter the Minotaur, and either slay him or be devoured.

Grigg liked my theories about surfing. But he thought I'd neglected the concept of faith. He invoked the story of Abraham leading his son Isaac up the mountain, binding him to the altar, making ready to light the fire and plunge in the knife, before God releases him from his terrible contract, and father and son are reprieved. 'The difference is, you're offering yourself as a sacrifice and it's yourself you get back again – or not.'

The big waves of Waimea Bay were a mountain and an underworld rolled into one, Olympus and Hades. The perfect ride embodied a paradox, whereby you were on top of the summit and submerged at the same time, underwater and still breathing air, inside a wave and bone dry. Big-wave riding was like diving more than 250 feet for black coral without oxygen. It was life and it was death. The big-wave rider was a god and he was an animal. He was Apollo and Dionysus. He was Theseus, he was Lazarus.

The North Shore as a whole reflected that duality: it was only twelve violent miles, but it was also the biggest impact zone in the world; it was a temple and a torture chamber, a madhouse and a monastery; it was thunderbolts and earthquakes, alpha and omega, Shangri-La and Room 101: a place where your dreams and your nightmares came true. When you paddled out at Sunset, you didn't know if you were about to spend a night with Marilyn Monroe or go ten rounds in the ring with Mike Tyson.

Ricky showed me a book by Greg Noll, probably the first man to surf Waimea in the winter of '57, who had been known as *Da Bull* for his size and his aggressive, no-holds-barred technique. It was called *Life over the Edge*. 'But the greatest stories you'll never hear', he said. 'The best of the big-wavers don't talk about it, they just do it.'

A tall, loping man, a little older than Grigg, wandered into the garden with a board under his arm. 'That's Peter Cole', Ricky said and introduced us. 'He'll tell you all about big-wave riding. Peter, come and talk.' But Cole, visibly distressed at the prospect of idle conversation, backed off and took cover in the shade of a cluster of palm trees.

Cole was a living reminder of a passage Liese had quoted from the *Tao Te Ching*:

> He who knows does not speak;
> He who speaks does not know.

His silence was a reproach.

47

*T*HERE *WAS* a New Year tradition on the North Shore that Michael Willis was always first man out at Sunset. It was his good luck charm. Many had tried to take this honour from him, and paddled out secretly in the darkness, but when the sun came up it was invariably Michael who rose with it to catch the first wave. And so it was on the first day of the new decade.

'I like to build up some momentum for the year to come', he explained. 'I've been too kicked-back these last few years. I must have rock fever.' 'Rock fever' induced a state of lethargy and apathy among its sufferers, summed up in the refrain, *It ain't no big thing*. 'But all that's going to change. Who was last shall now be first.'

Michael was full of resolutions. Betty had mentioned to him that Alan Gibby, a television company producer, was looking for someone to replace Mark Foo as on-the-beach interviewer for the Eddie Aikau. Foo felt he couldn't compete and interview at the same time. Betty had done similar work in the past, but this time Gibby wanted a man.

'Why shouldn't it be me?' said Michael. 'I have the knowledge, I have the experience, I know the guys and I know the Bay like the palm of my hand.' He wanted the job to finance his dream of the biodegradable surfboard.

Like Alec Cooke, Michael had not been invited to compete in the Eddie. 'Why? Because I don't have big money and a big name to go with it, that's why.' He thought the Eddie should be thrown open to all-comers. 'How many do they think are going to go out in twenty-plus Waimea? Half the people they've invited shouldn't even be out there.' He thought Ace Cool had as much right as anyone to win the Eddie. 'If Ace gets the biggest wave, give him the money.'

Now Michael saw his exclusion from the contest as an opportunity to establish himself as a surfing commentator. All he had to do was present his CV to Alan Gibby. But since he didn't own a pen or a pencil or a sheet of paper he was stymied. Would I help? Perhaps I would have helped him anyway, but it occurred to me that to lend Michael a hand might encourage him to get down to work on that Phazer with my name on it.

MICHAEL WILLIS

Born: 23 August 1956
Height: 5' 10"
Weight: 165 lbs

Shaper, designer, surfer since 1968. Based on the North Shore since 1974.

My qualifications for the job of interviewer in the Quiksilver Eddie Aikau can be summarized as follows: I have a long history of surfing Waimea Bay and building surfboards specifically for that break. I know what it's like to surf a 25-foot wave. And having participated in several rescues at Waimea, I know what it's like to get hurt at the Bay. I know the power of the Bay. I also have an intimate knowledge of everyone who will be competing in the Eddie Aikau: I surf with them and I shape for them. I have a thorough understanding of the physics of the Bay: its reefs, its bottom contours, its currents, and rhythm.

Having worked on television and radio interviews, and produced articles on the subject of surfing, I can confidently state that I have developed the skills to convey the grandeur, the drama, the danger and the beauty of Waimea Bay to a wide audience.

I expressed doubts about the 'articles on surfing'. He said he had 'collaborated' with a writer. Since he had also been 'technical adviser' to the crew making *North Shore* he could even claim some film experience. I attached a letter of recommendation. Michael had an idea my credentials — rookie newshound? truant lecturer in French? chief haole? — might add weight to his application. When I listened to Michael, I often thought he was so far out he'd seen Pluto. He may have been 'grounded', but he wasn't the most down-to-earth of potential commentators. I wrote that he was 'articulate', 'sympathetic', and 'wise'.

With the Billabong over, people returned compulsively to the unresolved question of the Eddie Aikau. But there was at least one person on the North Shore with something else on her mind. Dolle Latronic had made some progress with *The Boyfriends*. The obsessive, almost encyclopedic nature of Dolle's project put me in mind of Jules Verne and his determination to carry out a comprehensive survey of the world's surface and heavens. The trouble was it was like trying to write the *Voyages extraordinaires* while still on a rocket to the moon: she was too busy doing the research to do the writing.

But now she wanted to interest a publisher in her book. I refused point-blank to have anything to do with writing her résumé for her. Cathy and Shelaine had said that if God should come to the North Shore He would choose me as his spokesman. So far He hadn't, but just about everyone else on the North Shore had. I was in danger of becoming a public scribe. I felt like Cyrano de Bergerac being solicited to compose love letters on behalf of tongue-tied suitors. 'But, Andy,' Dolle whined, 'you said you'd help me.' She hung around the house and tormented me with the doleful look of a spaniel who hasn't been walked for a week. Finally I gave in. But I was in a mean mood and wrote an assessment which was part panegyric, part moral indictment.

THE BOYFRIENDS

The Boyfriends belongs broadly in the category of poetic autobiography. But it is unusual in this genre in being devoted exclusively to the evolution of personal relationships. This priority gives the book its distinctive shape and themes.

The author is uninhibited both in her attachment to a series of men – often of a rather outlandish nature – and in the portrayal of her liaisons with them. The characters in the book are diverse: variously weird, crazy, criminal, domineering, submissive, cruel, callous, sensitive, subtle. It seems as if the entire spectrum of male attitudes is on display. And at the centre of their sometimes atrocious activities is always the narrator, who seems to tolerate everything in the name of love.

What gives the book its bitter-sweet flavour is the manner in which a lifetime's drama is related. The style is pithy, immediate, subjective, a sequence of almost pure sense-data, uncompromised by explanation or justification. The reader is left free to make his or her own judgements. The sharp, streetwise, slangy language, sliced up in pacey but unobtrusive versification, succeeds in conveying the flavour of lived experience, with all its tantalizing ambiguities.

I placed this statement in a sealed envelope which I hoped Dolle would not open before I left.

My skills as a front man and PR specialist led to further commissions. Michael was always thinking about the future, about 'proleptic man' and the way surfing was going. 'Surfing,' he said as we were driving back from a surf movie in his beaten-up North Shore jalopy, 'can be a monkey on your back, or it can be an angel lifting you up to heaven.' He thought it was becoming 'a rich kids' game' and looked back nostalgically to a pre-commercial, more soulful, golden age.

'You know, Andy, we were all equal once. The birds were equal, the fish were equal, and we were equal with all of them. And the first time anyone managed to get unequal with anybody was through pure evil. Through exploitation and domination. And it's still evil.'

The ASP contests only confirmed his point. 'They're just a stunt. But surfing is . . . surfing. It'll always be that.' He sounded like Humphrey Bogart telling Ingrid Bergman they'd always have Paris. Since you needed money simply to enter, it wasn't even a fair fight. 'They're turning the whole thing into a horse-market', he complained. 'Potter shouldn't be called World Champion: he's just the ASP champion. He only has to surf against thirty other guys the whole year. That's not a contest. There's contests take place out there every hour of the day. And do you know the name of that fifty-three-year-old guy who just caught the biggest wave of his life? No, of course you don't. Why should you? But that's the real contest. Between man and wave. Not between men.'

Michael had decided his destiny was to lead a moral crusade

against competitive surfing. He wanted to write a universal declaration of soul surfer rights. This time I felt certain that the Phazer would be mine. Michael dictated, and I played Las Cases to his Napoleon, recording and occasionally rectifying what he said.

MANIFESTO OF THE SURFING MASSES

Once upon a time, pro surfing was a tiny seed that needed care and cultivation to come to fruition. It was such a delicate plant that any harsh wind threatened to snuff it out. We protected and nourished it. Then it grew. And kept on growing, beanstalking upwards and outwards, until finally, like a mean and hungry triffid, it has gone on the rampage, wreaking havoc and terrorizing innocent citizens of the surf. I believe the time has come for some radical rethinking which would put an end to this menace.

The ASP has become a bullying, dictatorial élite, concerned only with lining its pockets at everyone else's expense. Consider the example of the North Shore this winter. The ASP bandwagon rolled into our peaceful town and, like a bunch of heavies in a bad western, proceeded to take the place over, shooting up anyone who got in their way.

Throughout the entire month of December the ASP circus sat on the best surf spots and ruthlessly excluded anyone not a member of the chosen few. A reign of terror ensued, which only came to an end in January with the completion of the Billabong Pro. But like a nuclear bomb going off, the whole incident has left a kind of fallout hanging over the North Shore. The ocean is lethally irradiated with bad vibes.

No one can take seriously any longer the claim that pro events are having a beneficial effect on surfing as a whole. All they produce is a huge publicity bubble. Surfers will continue to surf with or without the ASP. Meanwhile we are being swindled, having the best waves in the world stolen from under us.

The water should be open to everyone all the time, not just to those with money and power. There are thousands of surfers in the world. The number of pros is insignificant by comparison. But the influence of the ASP mafia is disproportionately huge.

The current situation is a kind of sacrilege. Jesus kicked the money merchants out of the Temple. On the North Shore it's the ordinary pilgrims and worshippers who are being banished from surfing's greatest shrine.

Surfers should be demanding equality for all, and liberty in the water. But fraternity goes along with those values, too. Just as the pro surfing politburo should be more tolerant towards recreational surfers – who will always be the true soul of surfing – so too we should be tolerant towards pro surfing.

Let the contests continue – but not at our expense. The only obvious course for pro surfing to follow is to build more wave pools. Let the ASP invest their money in some proper facilities. It's a fraud to hold contests in uneven conditions where chance plays such a strong factor. Let every competitor have the same wave as every other and then you will have a fair contest. Do tennis players play on different sized courts? Spectators will pay to go and watch the action. And, meanwhile, the North Shore will not be taken over by squatters.

Surfers of the world arise and unite! We must struggle to free ourselves of the terrible tyranny of the ASP.

'They'll probably blackball me for saying this', Michael said when he read the finished document. He seemed to hesitate for a moment. 'But, hell, I'm blackballed already.' He submitted the manifesto as an opinion piece to *Surfer*. As far as I know, they never published it.

I sensed that some of the wind had been taken out of Michael's New Year sails. 'I can't force anything', he said. 'I can only hold the door open so long. Then my arm gets tired and it shuts on me again.'

48

*B*ETTY HAD given away the Corona. Ted had burned the Excalibur. Bullshit Alan's offer had blown away like smoke. My Willis Brothers Phazer had still not materialized. I was boardless and knew in my heart that I could not boast I had got the North Shore wired. My time was running out and I feared I would be going home defeated. Then another board entered my life.

Louis had been married to Debbie Beecham at some stage in the past. Now they were good friends. He had come over to visit her from California and was crammed into Yvon's room too. About the first thing he said to me was: 'Andy, you don't happen to have any socks, do you?'

It was like the time a friend at school with a reputation as a snappy dresser approached me and asked if he could borrow my suit. I had a standard grey two-piece, of the kind that mothers buy their sons. I was flattered that this man of fashion should turn to me. It wasn't till later that I learned he was going to a funeral and didn't have anything dull and sober enough to wear.

I loaned Louis a pair of long Argyle socks, purple with green and yellow flashes from Blazers in Cambridge. He had never seen anything like them before. My footgear was a constant source of wonderment to the shoeless, sockless inhabitants of the North Shore. Louis was so impressed with the socks that he asked to borrow them again. 'They caused a sensation at the party', he said.

I was glad to help out: I had a plentiful supply of socks. But there was something faintly depressing about being known as the Man with the Socks. If only someone had asked to borrow my 100% Mambos or the shirt with toucans and cockatoos I had picked up at Wild Clothing.

Louis had a beautiful board. It was a remake of a classic sixties malibu: nine feet long, broad in the hip, but light, with a rounded nose and three fins, in deep blue with orange stripes and a crimson rim. It bore the signature of Quigly, a West Coast shaper who had been prominent in the revival of the longboard in the eighties.

I lusted after that Quigly. Thus it was that when Louis wondered if there was anything he could do for me in return for the socks, I mentioned I was currently without a board.

'You want to borrow my Quigly?' he said. It was more a plea than a question. Unscrambled, his message read: 'Please don't take my Quigly! It's the love of my life.'

I was implacable. 'If you can spare it for a few hours', I said.

'Have you surfed much on the North Shore?' he inquired.

'Sure', I said, truthfully. 'Jocko's, Freddie's, Haleiwa, Lani's, Backyards. All over.' I passed over the details of what had taken place.

'Oh well, I guess that's all right, then.' He sounded reassured.

The following morning I steered the Quigly into the car like a kidnap victim and headed for Haleiwa. Bodo and Damon were waiting for me.

'That's a fine board you have there', said Bodo.

'A Quigly', I boasted.

'Wow!' gasped Damon. 'They're like gold dust in California.'

I had a good feeling about that board. It felt right as I gave it a solid basting of wax and uncurled the leash, and it felt right as I paddled it out: well-balanced, smooth through the water, responsive. Bodo called it a 'modern tanker': it was a subtle compromise between a gondola and a toothpick, combining the virtues of robustness and sensitivity, stability and speed.

I followed Bodo and Damon out through the channel. The Quigly sliced through the oncoming waves like a knife through butter, so by the time we hit the line-up I was still in good shape. There was a right-hander and further over towards the harbour a left. We opted for the left, which was less crowded. Bodo and Damon drove straight at the peak.

But I didn't want to push my luck and followed my usual cautious procedure of testing out the unoccupied shoulder.

I lined myself up with an easy-going four- to five-footer as it ambled into shore, despised by the hunters further out who were stalking bigger game. I got into gear and rammed the Quigly ahead of the swell. Then I felt the wave hook itself under the rear and start to jack it up. I cranked out another couple of strokes and leapt to my feet.

It was almost too easy. It was like riding a bicycle successfully for the first time: you can't understand why you had so much difficulty before, just as before it was impossible to understand how the deed could ever be done. My feet were planted in the textbook position: my left foot half way up the board, sideways on but angled towards the nose, my right foot slanted across the board at the tail. Surprised to find myself still upright I flung out my arms and crouched, modelling myself on the famous picture of Eddie Aikau. The Quigly planed down the face and, almost without my exerting any effort, began to curve into a leisurely bottom turn. Behind me and to the right, the wave was bursting apart; over my left shoulder was an unbroken section. I leaned over, slid my weight onto my right foot, and the Quigly carved a voluptuous line along the crystal blue wall, like Michelangelo shaping his Madonna. I had no idea how long I'd been standing up. Chronometrically, it would be insignificant; but I have a mental clock permanently arrested with its hands on that morning and that wave. 'No one times how long the ride is', Mark Foo had said to me. 'It's so intense, the duration doesn't matter. A second is a long time on the wave.'

The breaking wave was like Jean Cocteau's *Le Sang d'un poète*, which opens on a shot of a factory chimney stack as it starts to collapse and finishes as it hits the ground: everything happens in that split-second of demolition. There is a story by Jorge Luis Borges, *The Secret Miracle*, which is a mirror-image of that film. Jaromir Hladik is about to be executed by firing squad, and the sergeant has already delivered the order to fire, when God brings the physical universe to a halt, granting Hladik a reprieve of a year in order to finish, in his head, a poetic drama entitled *The Vindication of Eternity*. The last line is completed punctually, the year expires, a rain-drop that has remained immobile on Hladik's face for twelve months slides down his cheek, the rifles fire their volley and he slumps dead on the ground at the appointed hour. The wave, similarly, was in a time-zone all of its own: it was set to the time that ticked by in your brain and pulsed through your body, to Bergson's *duration*, not exterior, clock-measured time.

I was whooping with incoherent joy as I raced back to the line-up. Liese was right, I thought: you just have to wait: everything furthers. I knew I would remember this day for ever. I latched on to another wave and rode it till it curled up and died. Each wave was already a trophy in my memory. The Quigly was a Venus de Milo among boards: I was head over heels in love with it. How much more pleasure was it possible to experience?

Bodo caught me paddling back out again, looking for my third ride. One more practice run, I reckoned, and I would be ready to join the big boys on the higher hurdles of the main peak.

'Come on over here', he yelled. 'I'll find you a wave.'

It was a siren voice I couldn't resist: it was the Lieutenant of Lifeguards drumming up business.

'Now listen', said Bodo, 'there's just one thing you've got to know about this left-hander. And once you know it, it's simple. You see that booee out there?' I had heard 'buoy' pronounced 'booee' enough times to know what to look for. I spotted the grey truncated bell-tower bobbing about a quarter of a mile away.

'When you see that booee disappear, you know a set is coming. It gives about twenty seconds' warning. Just keep your eye on that booee and you'll be all right.'

I staked out a zone for myself. Bodo was about ten yards away on my inside. I sat up on my Quigly and gazed out to sea. It looked tranquil, dormant, seamless, so blue it was almost colourless, indistinguishable from the azure above. Surfing is like an empty sky intermittently streaked with lightning: it's watching and waiting shot through with flashes of ecstasy and terror. The sea was a landscape without landmarks, an inscrutable mask. It was strange to think there was nothing between me and Alaska. On my right, America; on my left, Asia. Straight ahead, the North Pole. I felt as if I was balanced on the fulcrum of the world, an axis around which North and South, East and West endlessly swung.

I don't know how long it took me to recall that to see nothing was to know everything, that absolute zero of perception was a red flag of danger. But I know that I reacted late. The buoy had vanished, buried beneath an oncoming set. I wondered if I could distantly hear the tolling of a bell. I span the Quigly round, proned myself against it, and struck out madly.

Out of the corner of my eye I glimpsed Bodo powering forwards. But I couldn't rely on his wisdom to guide me: it doesn't matter who you go out with, you still have to make it back on your own. When you surf the North Shore, you surf alone.

I felt the sea boil up behind me and prepared to leap to my feet. I asked Bodo afterwards if he'd seen what happened. He said, 'You just didn't stand up, Andy.' The lip tipped me through 90 degrees till I was perpendicular to the surface, like a spent rocket falling to earth, plunging down gravitic currents. Instead of swinging my feet under me, I was diving forwards, down with the exploding wave, down with the white curtain, down with my board, down until I kissed the Quigly and we tumbled around underwater, entwined in a hectic embrace.

49

AT 11.30 this morning I turned to Betinna and said, "Andy is going to get hurt today".'
I might have guessed that Liese would have some premoni-

tion of my accident. But Betty too had the gift of prescience. She was driving by with Rick and Debbie and Louis but persuaded them to park on the beach at Haleiwa with the prophetic words, 'Let's watch Andy go over the falls.' She felt a pang of remorse afterwards that she might have caused what she predicted.

'I knew that Quigly wasn't the board for you. You need a Phazer', said Michael.

I was just about the only person on the entire North Shore who didn't have advance knowledge of the events of that day.

'It is as well,' said Liese, 'otherwise you would have learned nothing.'

We were discussing my continuing education as we drove into Honolulu for the ASP banquet. I was wearing a hired tuxedo and Bodo's shoes. I had borrowed Bodo's wife as well. The annual awards ceremony was being held at the Royal Hawaiian Hotel, a plush, pink-pillared palace on the shores of Waikiki. It was the most beautiful building on Oahu, an opulent temple dedicated to the gods of leisure and wealth. The ASP used to hand over its congratulatory cups and medallions on the beach. Now surfers had exchanged their baggies and tee-shirts for DJs and bow ties, and rubbed shoulders with vacationing company executives, stole the limelight from Hollywood starlets, took over the tables of politicians, lawyers, and the idle rich. Surfing was in danger of becoming a success, a pretext for doing deals and making contracts.

I had hitherto passed almost incognito among the pros. But now I was a marked man.

'That's a wonderful scar you've got there', said Shaun Tomson, former world champion from South Africa. 'How did you get it?'

Everyone stopped for a second look. I had a twin tier of twenty stitches jutting out of my forehead like barbed wire. They were my passport to recognition among the surfing fraternity. It didn't matter how many articles I wrote about surfing, how many interviews I conducted, it was only by mingling my blood with theirs in the great transfusion bottle of the sea that I had at last been initiated into the brotherhood.

When I had finally managed to extricate myself from the stranglehold of the Quigly, I wanted to paddle straight back out again. But Bodo insisted I pay a visit to Dr Badener, strategically placed a few hundred yards from the beach. He had a steady stream of patients served up by the surf.

Dr Badener inspected the hole in my head, then looked me up and down, frisking me with his eyes. I was still in my boardshorts, dripping salt water and blood all over his floor. 'Do you have your wallet on you?' he said. He hated to ask that kind of question, but he had been stung once too often by injured Australians who blew town as soon as they were mended. He was willing and ready to stitch me up but he wanted to see the colour of my money first. It would cost me $280.

I asked Betty if I really needed the stitches. She contemplated the gaping wound over my eye and said, 'Well, you can't go back in the water with your brains hanging out.'

The stitching was painless, but the horrific stories about other surfing injuries were agony. I was lucky: I had escaped without ruptured intestines, amputated limbs or severed testicles. 'Yeah, he had to paddle in carrying one of them in his hand. If he got wiped out again, it was all over for him.'

It was $280 well spent. I had always wanted a scar and now I had a souvenir of the North Shore engraved on my forehead. 'What does the other guy look like?' cracked Barton Lynch. I had earned a reputation as a bruiser. I walked tall that night at the Royal Hawaiian.

Wendy Botha, the women's champion, wept with emotion: it was like watching the coronation of Miss World. Pottz still hadn't shaved properly or combed his hair. He was wearing a black bolo on a black shirt and a sawn-off velvet jacket over black jeans. He had finished a record 3,000 points ahead of the runner-up, Derek Ho. Triumphantly hoisting the silver surfboard trophy over his head he said, 'This title means more to me than living.' He limited himself to one acknowledgement: 'Peter made me believe in my dreams.'

Martin Potter was the guest of honour at the banquet. The leading surfers could be fined $100 for not attending. Ted Deerhurst had to pay $100 to get in. 'It was worth it, this is the night of the year. If I don't get drunk, stoked, and hosed tonight it won't be for want of trying.' He was wearing a sky blue silk bow tie and a wing collar.

Liese was a trained physiognomist, adept in the art of telling the mind's construction in the face. She volunteered an assessment of Pottz: 'He has an aptitude for danger.' I asked her to take a look at Ted. She surveyed him from afar, like Captain Cook taking sightings of some exotic and uncharted isle. 'He has a great heart', she concluded.

Martin Potter was number one in the world. Ted Deerhurst was 235. He had slipped from 189 last year. That was bad enough in itself, but what irritated him most was that another British surfer, who had made it through a couple of qualifying rounds in only one event, the Hot Tuna at Newquay, now appeared a couple of notches above the name of Deerhurst in the rankings. 'I ask you, is that justice?' I nodded compassionately. There were three hundred surfers on the ASP ladder and what I couldn't figure out was how anyone could be *below* Ted. I didn't ask him, though. I didn't think the timing was right.

'I've had a terrible Tour', he admitted over a brimming glass of *Mai Tai*. 'My worst ever. But I'll be back again next year. Realistically, I don't think I've got much of a shot at the title. But I still have a goal: I want to get the Most Improved Surfer of the Year award.' Ted figured that he only had to jump from his current lowly position into the top one hundred to achieve the fastest rise in the history of professional surfing.

'You know, I threw away the self-esteem book', he confided. 'There's nothing wrong with my ego.' Ted had developed a new theory to explain his temporary failure to win anything. 'I'm too repressed. I've been living like a monk. All I need is a really hot chick giving me non-stop sex for the entire pro Tour.'

'That's his best strategy yet.' Callahan for once was sympathetic. 'Maybe his results won't improve, but at least he'd have something to look forward to after bombing out.'

Martin Potter had earned over a million dollars in winnings and endorsements in 1989. Ted Deerhurst was going back to a job as a waiter to finance his next contest. The first event of the new year was the O'Neill/Pepsi Cold Water Classic held at Steamer Lane in Santa Cruz, California. 'I'll be virtually on my home ground then, that must give me an edge.' He laughed. 'I guess I don't know how to quit. I enjoy it too much. I'm just a surf junkie.'

I bade farewell to Ted to go and talk with Martin Potter. Ted wanted me to forget work for a while and relax. 'I'm a journalist', I said.

'No, you're not', he said. 'You're a man with twenty stitches over his eye. You're a surfer. Go wild tonight.'

Liese and I drove back along the Kam Highway and I pulled over as we went by Haleiwa harbour. 'I want to check if you can still see the blood', I said. We got out of the car and sat on the harbour wall with our legs dangling over the side. The full moon shone through the silhouetted palm trees and turned the gentle waves into silver fish dancing on the surface of the water. I looked down at Bodo's shiny black shoes and the shoes looked back up at me. Among so many other disciplines at her school of Chinese medicine, Liese had studied palmistry. I asked her to consult my palm. My love line was healthy: I would probably have many children. And what about my life line? She brought my hand closer and traced out my destiny with her finger. 'Look', she said. She read it like a map but all I could see was a maze. 'The primary line bifurcates here, then it gets tangled up in all these other secondary lines.' I checked my palm: it looked like a shattered mirror.

'Sounds as though if I want those children I'd better not hang about.'

I was no palmist but I took her hand in my hands and studied it. Even in the moonlight it had lines as clearly defined as a painting by Mondrian. 'What do you see?' she said.

'A wonderful hand', I said and kissed it. She leaned back and laughed. Her eyes turned heavenwards and her shadowy golden hair fell off her shoulders and down into the darkness. Then she straightened herself and looked into my eyes.

'Women are like waves', she said. 'You cannot have them all.'

50

*I*T WAS my last day on the North Shore. It was five to eight feet. I had missed the Eddie.

'This moon is the biggest we've had for ten years', said Michael. 'There's a giant swell on the way. I heard it from an astrologer.'

We were in his surf shop in Haleiwa. 'Look at that weather chart', Milton interjected. 'Is there a sign of a big swell anywhere within two thousand miles? No, of course there isn't.'

Michael smiled tolerantly. 'Milt, I've been speaking to a couple of psychics too, and they told me the same thing. It'll hit within a fortnight. The Eddie is coming, believe me.'

'Damn it,' I said, 'I knew it would happen as soon as I flew out.'

Michael wanted me to stay. 'Forget Europe. Do they have the Eddie?'

I had caught a couple of good waves at Haleiwa. I had twenty stitches bristling like a misplaced moustache on my forehead. I felt I was ready for Sunset. Callahan was pessimistic about my chances.

'The outside waves are all taken and the inside waves are lethal. If you're lucky you'll only get your leg ripped out like Titus.'

Ken Bradshaw had told me that the old Hawaiian name for Sunset was Paumalu. 'Know what it means? *To be taken by surprise.*' Ken agreed to go out with me, but somehow I kept missing him. Michael said, 'I'll take you out. It's your manifest destiny.'

He hadn't shaped me a board after all. But he loaned me one. 'This is a great board,' he said, 'it won't let you down.' It was a slim nine-footer, the shape of a javelin, crimson with wavy blue lines smeared diagonally across it.

We clambered down the rocks in front of Betty's house, where the sea had smashed down the wall and the wooden stairway, and walked along the beach together towards Sunset. It was late afternoon. 'See that peak out there, that's Sunset Point. It's a right-hander. That's where we're heading. Look, there's Peter Cole.'

In the distance I saw a small figure describing an arc under the looping shadow of a wave. 'How do you know it's Peter Cole?'

'Look at that straight-backed style of his. No one else surfs like that. He's riding a single-fin.'

As we plunged into the channel, the sun was going down. The colour of the sky shifted gears through blue to orange, to green and lilac. The water felt cold. 'That's a good north coming through. All the way from Alaska. And look at that moon.' The moon was already glimmering palely overhead. 'Look at the size of it! A big swell is coming, I can feel it, can't you?'

I could. From the beach I'd estimated the waves at five to six feet. After the half-mile paddle out, they'd shot up to the size of the Empire State. I remembered something big-wave legend Buzzy Trent had said: *waves are not measured in feet and inches, they are measured in increments of fear.* 'See that,' Michael said, 'double overhead barrels.' He said it the way most people would say 'double chocolate chip cookies' – he was all but licking his lips. 'That's the equivalent for you of twenty-foot plus for Titus. In fact, it's more of a challenge. You'll be all right. That's Titus's board you're riding.' The red board turned white-hot between my legs. I felt like jumping ship, only I didn't have a life-raft.

Captain Cook's last day in Hawaii, 14 February 1779, was his last day of all. Many Hawaiians had ceased to believe in the divinity of the white men with cloth for skins and long tails and triangular heads, who smoked like volcanoes. Gods did not lie with women; gods did not bleed when scratched. The gods came from Kahiki and did not have speech like the twittering of the *o'o* bird. Palea was one of those who no longer believed. He had been struck down with a club by one of the strangers. Palea and his men stole a boat from Lono's ship. It was a test of divinity: the god was a bringer of gifts: he would not miss a single boat. But Lono and his men decided to hold the great chief Kalani'opu'u hostage until the boat was returned. Kalani'opu'u agreed to go with Lono. But when, on the beach, he learned that his friend Kalimu had been shot, he refused to go on, fearing the same fate.

Captain Cook fired his musket and killed one man. When the natives held back, he turned towards the water. Behind him, a thousand and more irate Hawaiians; in front of him, Kealakekua Bay. The boat which had brought him to shore was just a short swim away. But Captain Cook could not swim. His whole purpose in life had been to dominate the seven seas, to rule the waves, not to play among them: to extend the mastery of dry land over the liquid element. He hated getting wet. He signalled to the boat to come in. When he hesitated at the water's edge one of the chiefs clubbed him over the head and another stabbed him between his shoulders with an iron dagger. They knew now that he was only a man and not a god. The haole fell face forwards into the water among the lava rock and was set upon and slaughtered. Cook died because he was not a waterman. He could not be Lono because Lono could swim. Of his men, only those who could swim escaped.

Kalani'opu'u offered Captain Cook's body in sacrifice to the true god with a prayer to grant life to himself and his dominion. The bones were restored to the strangers on the ship, but some were saved by the priests, placed in a basket covered with the sacred red feathers, and worshipped.

The strangers sailed away, but they would be back in greater numbers. It was as if the Hawaiians had wrought premature vengeance for the repressions and destruction that would follow. Now the ancient sport of surfing flourished anew in its birthplace, watermen were abroad once more, and Hawaii had spread its influence among all nations. Many Englishmen who were watermen too came here now: Pottz and even Ted had stolen waves. Captain Cook wouldn't lie down and die: in one form or another – as reason, as religion, as writing – he was always liable to return. Perhaps it was time for another sacrifice.

'Here comes one,' yelled Michael, 'it's yours!' I took one look at that solid slab of destiny with my epitaph written all over it and high-tailed it for the horizon. I clawed my way up the face of the wave, up to the sky, up to the light. I thought I was over the lip when it kissed the nose of my board and flipped me head over heels. Suddenly I was surfing Sunset upside down.

It was virtually dark by the time I made it back to the line-up. A medium-size maneater was lying in wait for me. Too tired even to get out of the way, I turned around and prayed. The wave licked me up with its tongue and spat me down the face. Somehow my feet found the deck. I tried to straighten out and aim for the beach but Titus's board had other ideas.

The wave opened its yawning cavern of a mouth. The lip pitched out and loomed over me. I was inside the belly of the beast. For an instant, as if through the lens of an immense telescope, I had a glimpse of heaven and hell, of pleasure and pain; I saw my birth and my death, I saw Liese and Bodo, I saw Eden Burberry, I saw the ghosts of Eddie Aikau and Duke Kahanamoku, I saw Kaena Point and Kahuku Point, Jocko's and Haleiwa, Alaska and Japan, I saw the whole of the North Shore. I saw myself, reflected and multiplied in an infinite hall of mirrors. Then the wave closed over my head and the light of the world went out.

Epilogue

The 1990 Quiksilver in Memory of Eddie Aikau took place on Sunday, 21 January. Exactly a fortnight after I left Hawaii, the biggest swell for a decade hit the North Shore. Most of the pro surfers had left too. Pottz had gone, Elkerton had gone, Ted had gone.

Rumours of the return of *El niño* had sent everyone into a frenzy of anticipation. George Downing had been consulting the buoys that were his sentinels, stationed across the breadth of the Pacific. The word was out that he was taking twenty-three-foot readings. During the night of Saturday to Sunday, Betty was dogging his footsteps. At 4.20 a.m., after digesting the latest printouts, he said, 'All right, let's do it.'

According to Betty's letter, this is the way their conversation went.

> I said, 'Excuse me, Mr Downing, does that mean we're having the Quiksilver in Memory of Eddie Aikau today?' He said, 'Yes.' I said, 'It's for sure?' He said, 'Yes.' I said, 'Is that a definite yes?' He said, 'Yes, call the crew!'

She added: 'Man my heart was going with the thought of those booee readings.' But when George Downing made his decision to end three years of waiting, everyone was a little nervous. The swell was still small. No one was sure if they could really rely on those far-flung booees. At 8 a.m. the waves were only a marginal fifteen feet and it looked like another false alarm. Soothsayers were predicting that the twenty-foot minimum would not be met. But George Downing stuck by his readings and insisted the contest was on. By the time the first heat hit the water at 11 a.m. under a grey sky, the sets were a solid and consistent twenty to twenty-two feet, groomed by the offshore southerly blowing out of the valley. The swell reached its peak between noon and 3 p.m., pushing the waves up to twenty-five to thirty.

By this stage, traffic on the Kam Highway was backed up in both directions from Sunset to Haleiwa. Two thousand spectators lined the beach and the point or gazed down at the thundering Bay from the *heiau*. Photographers were bad-mouthing the skies and the occasional squalls of rain that gusted into their lenses. Callahan hadn't really believed it would happen. He had a hangover and a raging head-cold and only shot three rolls all day. He wasn't ready.

Alan Gibby had given the job of interviewing the contestants to Betty. This was what she wrote to me:

Mark Foo set an example, he ate shit so bad that when the other competitors saw him they slacked off and moved over to the shoulder. Mark came in with his board in three pieces. Fins ripped off. Bradshaw lost his board, he was afraid to take a ride with the patrol, thought it was illegal. Finally he did, it was life or death, legal had nothing in common with Waimea at 25 plus.

Louis Ferreira almost died. When I interviewed him his face looked like it had white sunblock on it, pale pale. I was making a joke about it and he stopped me, said 'No, I almost died, I really don't want to go back out but I have to.' I tell you, I've never seen anyone with lost colour like that. I heard about it from Brian Keaulana. He said, 'I saw his hand surface after one wave, but before he could come up the next wave hit him.' Can you imagine? And you thought Haleiwa was hectic!

Brock Little got an unreal tube. Richard Schmidt, perfect ride, 10s across the board. One huge wave he 'sideslipped on, I was airborne, fins caught and I made it.' That wave was 30 feet solid, he got third. He's such a nice guy. He was so peaceful with his efforts, I'd like to interview him again.

Darrick Doerner, what an amp dog! I've never seen

anyone so adrenalined out. He came out of the water just wanting to scream into the camera, wild, happy. Unreal the energies. Michael Ho was the quiet one, fourth, he just flows with it, the man of wisdom. Got a barrel bigger than Brock's. Brock's was 18–20, Ho's 20–25.

So Keone Downing I never noticed, he's camera shy, never came near it. He was consistent I heard. I really never saw him ride much. Just solid, consistent waves I heard. Kerry Terukina I saw go down hard. Hardcore kid.

Cheyne Horan I'm secretly in love with. What a philosopher! He said, 'I learned as much here as in 30 years of surfing.' Blue eyes gleaming. I also interviewed my long-standing hero, Reno Abellira. And you know I can't remember a word he said. I was asking him questions and he just blanked me out. I remember thinking, yeah, he's been a big-wave surfer for so long, respected, forgotten in a way, sadness inside, he's strung out, I know, on what, I'm not sure.

I tell you, the view from the heiau was unreal, beautiful, the best Waimea I have seen in 12 years. I watched the waves come up the day before at Sunset, I recorded each set, wishing I could go out again some day. For me Waimea was sad in a way, I felt left out, because I hadn't made my personal statement there lately. Even if I only ride 18–20 it's still me and my level. So I felt strange interviewing the guys. But it was an honour for sure, my fate. Thanks Alan Gibby! Thanks Lord!

In a postscript, she added:

Listen, just to let you know, Titus was there, no crutches, he'll be back.

Keone Downing, thirty-six, the son of George Downing, riding a 9 ft 4 in single-fin shaped by his father, took the $55,000 first prize. He dedicated the day to 'Pops' Aikau, Eddie's father. Brock Little was second. Eddie's brother Clyde took fifth, with Darrick Doerner sixth. Ross Clarke-Jones was seventh. Johnny Boy Gomes was tenth, James Jones eleventh, Mark Foo fourteenth, and Ken Bradshaw was down with the tail-enders at thirty.

Michael had said the real star of the North Shore was the ocean. The waves were, I heard, 'all-time', 'epic', 'Hall of Fame', 'worth waiting three years or a lifetime for'. I cursed the evil luck that had caused me to miss the event of the century by a few miserable days. But I knew that it had to be that way. I still had to earn the right to see thirty-foot Waimea.

Ace Cool was ready for 21 January. He wasn't in the Eddie, but at 11 a.m. he roared out of Haleiwa harbour in the twenty-foot 125-horsepower US Navy Zodiac boat captained by Ivan Trent, son of Buzzy, with a video photographer on board. Ace was armed with a twelve-foot gun, a twenty-five-foot leash, and oxygen tanks.

From sketchy reports, this is what I pieced together:

Within twenty minutes, the boat reached Outside Log Cabins. Trent tried to line the craft up with the peak, but the howling offshore wind made the sets as unpredictable as fruit machines. Ace and Trent paddled away from the boat and into the shifty line-up. A colossal set way outside caught them all out of position. The boat and the two men in the water sprinted out, making it over the first wave, the boat catching a few feet of air. They cruised over the second only to discover that the ultimate wave was lurking right behind it, and already cresting. The Zodiac wheeled round in a hurried 180 and raced for the shoulder, leaving the two men in the firing line.

The Zodiac climbed over the wall, but the surfers were hammered. Trent's leg-rope snapped and his board was split in two. He found the pieces later on Ke Iki beach. Ace held on and made it back out to the line-up. He had been preparing for this day for five years, and he wasn't going to let one measly forty-footer get in his way. The spotter on Pupukea Hill, seeing the ocean revert to a state of primeval chaos, radioed through and called for the crew to abort the mission. Just then, a set came through: Ace tore after it, but it slid uselessly under him. He reluctantly agreed to return to the boat and the Zodiac beat a retreat back to harbour.

Afterwards, Ace reckoned that he could have caught the

forty-footer if only he'd had a bigger gun. He commissioned Michael Willis to build him a thirteen-foot single-fin pin-tail. It would be not so much a rhino chaser as an *olo*: like one of the ancient Hawaiian boards made from the wili wili tree, the biggest board to catch the biggest wave.

Bodo was promoted from lieutenant to captain. That meant he had to shift his base of operations from Haleiwa to Honolulu. He had to wear shoes and a shirt and spend whole weeks in the office without even getting wet. Occasionally he would return to the North Shore on business. There were several deaths during the rest of that winter. Waimea claimed a German tourist. Exactly a month after the Eddie Aikau, a professional surfer from California, Barry Wilson, in training for the Big Island Pro Am contest, paddled out in six-foot Rocky Point. The rip dragged him into the impact zone at Gas Chambers, a wave flung him underwater, and his leg-rope wrapped itself around a coral head. He struggled in vain to release it. Another surfer eventually freed him, but not in time to save his life.

When I read the obituary in *Groundswell* I couldn't help recalling something Liese had said to me as we drove to the airport. 'Why do you come to the North Shore? Nothing happens here. Nothing except big waves and dead bodies.'

I never rode Waimea, real or unreal, never personally tangled with a twenty-footer. No one on the North Shore would have expected me to: I just wasn't ready. But, back in England, a headline writer thought otherwise. I wrote an article for *The Independent on Sunday* on the events of Christmas Day and my big-wave idols. Over the dramatic water-shot of a man on a board in a tube, I read:

DIGGING HIS TOES INTO A SMASHED-UP CHAMPION'S BOARD,
ANDY MARTIN RIDES THE BREAKERS IN HAWAII'S WAIMEA BAY.

Glossary and Selected Bibliography

GLOSSARY

THIS IS not intended as an exhaustive lexicon of **surfspeak**, only as a convenient guide to some of the terms used in this book.

aerial   a manoeuvre in which the board briefly flies free of the wave; a Martin Potter trademark

ASP   Association of Surfing Professionals

blank   fibre-glass block from which a surfboard is carved

bodyboard   a shorter board ridden lying down

bottom turn   the first crucial turn of the ride, banking at the foot of the face

bowl   concave section of the wave, liable to close out

close-out   a wave that breaks all at once, without peeling, across an entire section

curl   the pout of the **lip**, creating a hollow wave face

drop in (on)   bad manners: stealing someone else's wave

elephant gun or **rhino chaser**   the biggest board for the biggest wave: more a javelin than a gun, long, narrow, and pointed

face   the surfable, unbroken (or **green**) part of the wave

floater   an **off-the-lip** combined with a re-entry across the whitewater

glassy   smooth, glistening look of the unruffled wave in ideal conditions

gnarly   challenging – and proportionately satisfying – conditions; commonly, **big and gnarly**

goofy   a surfer who stands on the board with his right foot forward

haole   Hawaiian for white man, literally 'breathless' or 'ignorant'

he'enalu   Hawaiian for surfing (literally: wave-sliding), hence **hui o'he'enalu**: surf-club

icecream head   the hypothermic effect of being dunked in cold winter water

impact zone   where the waves break the hardest: to be avoided if possible

insane   a compliment, applauding the most **radical** moves or, sometimes, the waves themselves

leash or **ankle rope**   (actually semi-elastic urethane) attaches board to surfer's leg; despised by old-timers

left-hander   a wave that breaks from right to left from the perspective of the surfer

line-up   the waiting zone just beyond the break where surfers queue for waves; roughly equivalent to **out-the-back** or **outside**

lip   the pitching crest of a hollow or semi-hollow wave

malibu   long board with a rounded nose, originating in California in the 1950s but currently undergoing a renaissance

mele   Hawaiian surf-chant

natural   surfer who stands with his left foot forward

off-the-lip   tricky manoeuvre, also known as a **ricochet**, involving bouncing the board hard against the top of the breaking wave and reversing horizontal direction

olo   traditional Hawaiian longboard, reserved for chiefs

outside   beyond the break; but see **sneaker set**: the outside can become **inside**

peak   highest part of the wave, the first to **feather** (begin to break)

quiver   collective term for a set of boards, of different lengths and shapes, to suit a variety of waves

radical or **rad**   describes far-fetched but controlled manoeuvres

rail   edge of the board

right-hander   a wave that breaks from left to right from the perspective of the surfer

rip   (1) n.: a dangerous current flowing out to sea; (2) v.: to **shred** the wave, i.e. pull off daredevil manoeuvres

rocker   the amount of curvature in the longitudinal bottom contour of the board

roundhouse or **roundhouse cutback**   reversing the board horizontally on the wave in a wide radius arc, usually turning back towards the **curl**

set   a family of serious waves

shaper   a board builder: perhaps the most important person in your life

shoulder   still part of the wave, but only just, far away from the **peak**, **curl**, and **lip**

sneaker set   the occasional bigger set that breaks outside the normal line-up, liable to 'clean up' unwary surfers

soul surfer   someone who refuses to have anything to do with competitive surfing

stoked   elated, ecstatic, hence **stoke** (noun), excitement

stringer   strip of wood that runs down the length of the board; the larger boards may have two or three of them

swallow tail   a board with steps cut into the rails and a chunk hewn from the stern to produce an avian effect

tanker   longer, broader surfboard, nine foot and over, useful in big waves, hence **mini-tanker**: around eight foot

thruster   minimal modern surfboard with three fins

tsunami   tidal wave generated by underwater subsidences

tube   also known as **barrel**: a cylindrical wave you can disappear into, the surfer's dream

wall   steep unbroken wave face, extending to the **shoulder**

wipeout also known as **being taken out to lunch**, **eating it**, **getting hammered** etc.: coming to grief on your board

SELECTED BIBLIOGRAPHY

The following have been particularly helpful in the preparation of this book:

Lorrin Andrews, *A Dictionary of the Hawaiian Language*, Lahaina, Maui, 1865.

Tom Blake, *Hawaiian Surfboard*, Honolulu, 1935.

—— *Hawaiian Surfriding*, Flagstaff, Arizona, 1961.

John Conway, *Surfing*, London, 1988.

James Cook, *The Journals*, ed. J. C. Beaglehole, 4 vols. (especially vols. 3 and 4), Cambridge, 1967–74.

Ben Finney, 'Surfboarding in Oceania: Its Pre-European Distribution', *Wiener Völkerkundliche Mitteilungen*, Vienna, 1959, pp. 23–36.

Ben R. Finney and James D. Houston, *Surfing: the Sport of Hawaiian Kings*, Tokyo, 1966.

Abraham Fornander, *An Account of the Polynesian Race, Its Origin and Migrations*, Tokyo, 1969.

Ricky Grigg and Ron Church, *Surfer in Hawaii*, Dana Point, California, 1963.

C. G. Jung, *Collected Works*, ed. Herbert Read, Michael Fordham, and Gerhard Adler, trans. R. F. C. Hull, 20 vols., London, 1950–79; especially *Introduction to the Religious and Psychological Problems of Alchemy* (vol. 12) and *Symbols of Transformation: An Analysis of the Prelude to a Case of Schizophrenia* (vol. 5).

Duke Kahanamoku (with Joe Brennan), *World of Surfing*, New York, 1968.

Samuel Manaiakalami Kamakau, *Ruling Chiefs of Hawaii*, Honolulu, 1961.

Drew Kampion, *The Book of Waves: Form and Beauty on the Ocean*, Santa Barbara, 1989.

Jack London, *The Cruise of the Snark*, New York, 1911.

Brian J. and Margaret Lowdon, eds., *Competitive Surfing: A Dedicated Approach*, Torquay, Victoria, 1988.

Leonard Lueras, *Surfing: the Ultimate Pleasure*, New York, 1984.

Greg Noll, *Da Bull: Life Over the Edge*, Bozeman, MT, 1989.

Dieter Schori, *Das Floss in Ozeanien*, Völkerkundliche Beitrage zur Ozeanistik, Bd. 1, Gottingen, 1959.

Mark Twain, *Roughing It*, Berkeley, 1972.

Nat Young, *The History of Surfing*, Palm Beach, NSW, 1983.

A Selected List of Titles Available from Minerva

While every effort is made to keep prices low, it is sometimes necessary to increase prices at short notice. Mandarin Paperbacks reserves the right to show new retail prices on covers which may differ from those previously advertised in the text or elsewhere.

The prices shown below were correct at the time of going to press.

Fiction

☐ 7493 9026 3	**I Pass Like Night**	Jonathan Ames	£3.99	BX
☐ 7493 9006 9	**The Tidewater Tales**	John Bath	£4.99	BX
☐ 7493 9004 2	**A Casual Brutality**	Neil Blessondath	£4.50	BX
☐ 7493 9028 2	**Interior**	Justin Cartwright	£3.99	BC
☐ 7493 9002 6	**No Telephone to Heaven**	Michelle Cliff	£3.99	BX
☐ 7493 9028 X	**Not Not While the Giro**	James Kelman	£4.50	BX
☐ 7493 9011 5	**Parable of the Blind**	Gert Hofmann	£3.99	BC
☐ 7493 9010 7	**The Inventor**	Jakov Lind	£3.99	BC
☐ 7493 9003 4	**Fall of the Imam**	Nawal El Saadewi	£3.99	BC

Non-Fiction

☐ 7493 9012 3	**Days in the Life**	Jonathon Green	£4.99	BC
☐ 7493 9019 0	**In Search of J D Salinger**	Ian Hamilton	£4.99	BX
☐ 7493 9023 9	**Stealing from a Deep Place**	Brian Hall	£3.99	BX
☐ 7493 9005 0	**The Orton Diaries**	John Lahr	£5.99	BC
☐ 7493 9014 X	**Nora**	Brenda Maddox	£6.99	BC

All these books are available at your bookshop or newsagent, or can be ordered direct from the publisher. Just tick the titles you want and fill in the form below. Available in:
BX: British Commonwealth excluding Canada
BC: British Commonwealth including Canada

Mandarin Paperbacks, Cash Sales Department, PO Box 11, Falmouth, Cornwall TR10 9EN.

Please send cheque or postal order, no currency, for purchase price quoted and allow the following for postage and packing:

UK	80p for the first book, 20p for each additional book ordered to a maximum charge of £2.00.
BFPO	80p for the first book, 20p for each additional book.
Overseas including Eire	£1.50 for the first book, £1.00 for the second and 30p for each additional book thereafter.

NAME (Block letters) ....

ADDRESS ....

....

....